Beating Low Cost Competition

ADRIAN RYANS

Beating
Low Cost
Competition

HOW PREMIUM BRANDS CAN RESPOND TO
CUT-PRICE RIVALS

A John Wiley & Sons, Ltd., Publication

Copyright © 2009   John Wiley & Sons Ltd, The Atrium, Southern Gate, Chichester,
West Sussex PO19 8SQ, England
Telephone (+44) 1243 779777

Email (for orders and customer service enquiries): cs-books@wiley.co.uk
Visit our Home Page on www.wiley.com

Other Wiley Editorial Offices

John Wiley & Sons Inc., 111 River Street, Hoboken, NJ 07030, USA

Jossey-Bass, 989 Market Street, San Francisco, CA 94103-1741, USA

Wiley-VCH Verlag GmbH, Boschstr. 12, D-69469 Weinheim, Germany

John Wiley & Sons Australia Ltd, 42 McDougall Street, Milton, Queensland 4064, Australia

John Wiley & Sons (Asia) Pte Ltd, 2 Clementi Loop #02-01, Jin Xing Distripark, Singapore 129809

John Wiley & Sons Canada Ltd, 6045 Freemont Blvd. Mississauga, Ontario, L5R 4J3 Canada

Wiley also publishes its books in a variety of electronic formats. Some content that appears in print may not be available in electronic books.

Library of Congress Cataloging-in-Publication Data

Ryans, Adrian B., 1945–
    Beating low cost competition : how premium brands can respond to cut-price rivals / Adrian Ryans.
        p. cm.
    Includes bibliographical references and index.
    ISBN 978-0-470-74297-6 (cloth : alk. paper) 1. Product management. 2. Price cutting. 3. Brand choice. 4. Brand name products. 5. Marketing. I. Title.
    HF5415.15.R93   2008
    658.8′27—dc22

                                                                                            2008053896

British Library Cataloguing in Publication Data

A catalogue record for this book is available from the British Library

ISBN 978-0-470-74297-6 (HB)

Typeset in 11/15pt Times by SNP Best-set Typesetter Ltd, Hong Kong
Printed and bound in Great Britain by TJ International Ltd, Padstow, Cornwall, UK

Contents

Preface

In many industries, the drumbeat of low cost competition is intensifying. Many industry leaders from developed countries in Europe, North America and Asia are facing a growing challenge from low cost rivals. Regional airlines, such as Ryanair, Southwest Airlines and Air Asia, are challenging traditional airlines around the world. In grocery retailing, giants, such as Tesco and Carrefour, are facing fast-growing hard discounters like Aldi and Lidl. In the wind energy market, first world companies like Vestas, GE and Gamesa are being challenged by Suzlon from India, and Goldwind and Sinovel from China. Indian and Chinese car manufacturers are starting to move out of their home markets and could soon be seriously challenging the global leaders in selected segments. From wedding dresses to heavy construction equipment, no industry seems immune.

Low cost competition has seemingly been around forever, but now it seems to emerge in new industries and new product categories much more rapidly than it has in the past. The quality of the products and services from new low cost rivals soon seems to reach levels that are "good enough" for significant segments of the overall market.

Traditional companies are often uncertain about how best to respond to the challenge: should they introduce their own low cost offerings under their existing brand or a new brand? Alternatively, should they retreat into the high end of the market and concentrate on continuing to develop industry leading products and services that are "superior" to those of their low cost rivals? Or, should they focus more on building tight partnerships with selected customers, who want to work closely with a supplier that will tailor his "offering" to meet their needs? Or, should they do some combination of these three options? Tough, very tough, choices.

There are no easy answers. However, by focusing on four areas, executives will be able to make better choices. First, it is important to understand the forces influencing many industries that are accelerating product life cycles and speeding up the commoditization of many products and services. In some cases, traditional companies can leverage some of the same forces to strengthen their competitive position.

Second, it is important to develop a deep understanding of the firm's low cost rivals and how they play their games. There are often some commonalities across industries, but usually there are unique elements. Part of this assessment process involves assessing how the strategies of some of the low cost rivals might evolve over time and whether they might be able to seriously challenge the traditional competitors in their core markets.

Third, building on the assessment of the low cost rivals, management should make an early and carefully thought out decision whether to confront the low cost rivals in the "good enough" market segment. If the decision is positive then a number of key implementation issues must be addressed.

And finally, whether they decide to enter the price value segment of the market or not, the traditional companies will usually have to strengthen their position in their traditional, premium segments of the market.

Throughout the book, the importance of making the appropriate decisions in a timely manner is emphasized. Often companies put off making the tough decisions about how best to respond to their low cost rivals until it is very late in the game – sometimes too late.

Acknowledgments

It is impossible to acknowledge all the people who influenced my thinking and shaped my ideas on understanding and meeting the challenge of low cost competition. Some of the thinking goes back a couple of decades and some of the concepts and tools even further. But one person whose ideas have had a huge influence on my thinking is George Day, who has been a mentor, colleague and friend for most of my career. I have rarely had a conversation about strategy or marketing with George without taking away a few useful ideas that I have subsequently used in my teaching and writing. His footprints are all over this book. I have tried to make appropriate acknowledgments in the book, but I am sure many more of George's contributions are not formally recognized.

Over the years, I have had the opportunity to work with numerous companies and executives while writing cases, teaching or consulting. They have let me try out some of my ideas and through their questions and challenges have contributed to my thinking on many of the topics covered in this book. Among the companies I owe a particular debt to are GE, National Semiconductor, TD Bank, Saurer (now part of Oerlikon), ING Direct, Tektronix, Fluke (now part of Danaher), ASML, Nortel Networks, Keithley Instruments, Varian, EMC, LSI Logic, Holcim, Medtronic, Georg Fischer, Vestas and Caterpillar. Executives who have been particularly influential include Henry Fischer, the former CEO of Saurer, Arkadi Kuhlmann of ING Direct, Dick Levy of Varian, Keith Grey of TD Bank, Dave Churchill of Agilent, and Mike White of National Semiconductor.

I have also benefited particularly from discussions, both in and out of the classroom, with participants in the Low Cost Competition executive program at IMD in 2007 and 2008. They helped me refine my thinking on many issues and contributed several very interesting examples. I also benefited from email questions and challenges sent in by viewers of several IMD webcasts on low cost competition.

Several faculty at IMD have influenced my thinking, particularly Kamran Kashani, Peter Killing, Martin Koschat and Robert Hooijberg, who were my faculty colleagues on the Low Cost Competition program. I have also benefited from the support of Stephanie Sequeira, who did some of the background research on several of the cases discussed in the book and Atul Pahwa who did a masterful job of writing the Ryanair case. I am very appreciative of the efforts of two IMD editors: Anita Hussey did a thorough editing of an early draft of the book and Michelle Perrinjaquet, who worked on many of the figures in the book and turned them into a publishable form, as well as reading the proofs.

Peter Killing, Terry Deutscher and Jim Ryans read early drafts and provided extensive feedback. Peter, ever the master teacher, gave me some very useful ideas about how to position the book and better engage the reader. Terry, my first and longest-standing academic colleague and friend, made many helpful suggestions and additions. Jim, my son, who has a wide-ranging knowledge of many companies and industries, suggested both conceptual improvements and new examples that helped bring some of the ideas and concepts to life. The book was greatly strengthened by their contributions.

I certainly owe a big debt of gratitude to Peter Lorange, who was the president of IMD when I began working on this book. Peter encouraged me to develop materials in the area of low cost competition and was very supportive of this project.

This book is dedicated to my wife Bev Lennox, who provided both emotional and editorial support during the writing of the book. She was an interested and challenging listener to many of my ideas and she gave me some frank and useful feedback. She also put her professional editorial skills to work and did a thorough and complete edit of the final draft. In the process, she made significant improvements.

CHAPTER 1

The growing challenge from low cost competitors

Every year at the International Motor Show in Geneva, automotive companies like BMW, Audi, Lamborghini, General Motors, Toyota and many others present their new cars. In 2007, executives from these companies saw a potential new competitor presenting its cars at the show for the first time. The new competitor was a Chinese company called Brilliance. Its initial sales goals for Europe were modest – 150 000 cars over five years but it also planned to enter the US market in a few years. Few Europeans or North Americans had heard of the company or the brand. The company's pricing in Europe looked quite attractive – the price for one of its models being almost 40% less than that of a 5-series BMW with similar specifications.

Many automotive executives might have been tempted to dismiss this threat. Brilliance had just opened its first significant production facility in 2002 with an annual capacity of about 100 000 units; clearly, it lacked the decades of experience of its major Western and Japanese competitors. Complacency might also have been encouraged by a lukewarm review in a UK automotive magazine when the first Brilliance car was launched in Europe. This low cost competitor, however, probably represented a much bigger threat than these indicators would suggest. Brilliance was BMW's joint venture partner in China producing 3- and 5-series cars, initially from knockdown kits; they later utilized more and more locally produced parts. This experience undoubtedly helped Brilliance learn about high-quality manufacturing and quality control. It had also entered into a technology transfer agreement with Toyota. For the cars it manufactured and sold under its own brand, the company used the design services of Italian designers such as Giugiaro, who has designed cars for Ferrari.[1] One of its engines was manufactured by a joint venture with Mitsubishi, a Japanese company with decades of experience in the automotive industry. Johnson Controls – a world-class player in car interiors – manufactured the car seats. And, the cars' air bags and safety systems were developed in cooperation with TRW, a North American-based company with extensive automotive experience. With this kind of support and a very low cost structure, given its base in China, Brilliance could become a world-class manufacturer and a formidable low cost rival for European, North American, Japanese and Korean manufacturers.

However, there were some initial setbacks. Brilliance's largest sedan, the BS6, disastrously failed a crash test in Germany in June 2007. Brilliance, with the help of a leading European engineering company, rapidly redesigned the car body and it performed acceptably on a second European crash test in late 2007. Perhaps more worryingly, the Brilliance BS6 was targeted at a market segment that was declining in sales in Europe. In addition, the car lacked a diesel engine option and a station wagon model, both of which were important selling points in this segment.[2]

Even if Brilliance does not achieve its initial objectives, the executives at the European, American, Japanese and Korean automotive companies can be sure that more than one of the dozens of low cost players that are developing automobiles in China and India will be a serious challenge to the industry titans. Perhaps one of these companies will be Tata, an Indian company with formidable engineering skills. Tata launched its 100 000 rupee (US $2500) Tata Nano in India in January 2008, with plans to start selling variants of it in other countries in the future. Perhaps another will be Chery, a Chinese manufacturer that had some early successes in peripheral markets, such as Russia and Eastern Europe.

Similar developments are occurring in industry after industry in many parts of the world. And these low cost or value competitors that offer "good enough" products and services at low prices represent a large and growing challenge for executives and managers in a variety of traditional companies – those companies that tend to compete more on the basis of the performance, quality, fashion or style leadership, or on the basis of the close and intimate relationships they have built with their customers. The emergence and growth of these low cost competitors suggest that there is a tremendous appetite for low cost products and services that are good enough – something traditional companies in many industries have often been slow to recognize and to capitalize on.

In this chapter, we will begin by looking at some examples of low cost competitors in a variety of industries. While many low cost competitors are based in developed countries, an increasing number can be found in developing countries like China, India and Brazil. We will argue that it is these competitors in developing nations that represent a particular threat to Western, Japanese and Korean companies in many industries. Yet, companies that compete in the very high end of their markets sometimes feel insulated from the threat this type of competitor poses. We will discuss how low cost competitors can threaten the profitability – and even the survival – of traditional companies while at the same time actually creating new opportunities for the high-end players by opening up markets. Some executives believe the myth that the products and services provided by low cost competitors are inferior and will therefore never appeal to their customers. As we will see, this complacent and even arrogant attitude often does not coincide with the perception of many customers who see the low cost offerings as meeting their needs, although perhaps only in certain applications or for certain uses.

The threat from low cost competitors is real, and it creates a very depressing picture for some executives about the future of their companies. In many industries, however, the traditional companies are fighting back, quite successfully in some cases. Some have found effective ways to stay ahead of their low cost competitors – at least for now. The final section of this chapter features a flowchart to help the reader think through the challenge that low cost competition presents, as well as deciding how to respond to that challenge. This flowchart provides a useful introduction to the organization of the rest of the book.

THE CHALLENGE IS REAL AND IT IS HERE TO STAY

When McKinsey surveyed almost 3500 executives around the world in 2006, 85% of the respondents described the business environment in which their companies operated as "much more competitive" (40%) or "more competitive" (45%) than it was five years previously. "More low cost competitors" was singled out as being the most important factor contributing to this increased competitiveness by 23% of the respondents. In several industries, such as consumer products, heavy industry and telecommunications, it was identified as the single most important factor (see Figure 1.1).[3]

What single factor contributes most to the increasing competitive intensity in your industry today?

	Industry of respondent's company							
	Business services	Consumer	Banking, finance	Healthcare	Heavy industry	IT	Telecom	Other
Improved capabilities of competitors (e.g. better knowledge or better talent)	27	21	27	18	25	30	18	20
More low-cost competitors	25	25	11	18	36	24	27	14
More competitors	18	13	15	10	9	11	9	18
Growing size of competitors	7	13	14	10	8	10	9	8
Growing number of innovative market entrants	10	9	9	9	3	10	17	10
Regulatory changes (e.g. market or industry deregulation, trade agreements)	4	4	12	22	8	3	17	10
Rising consumer awareness and activism	3	5	5	9	3	4	1	14
Growing number of attractive, accessible markets	3	4	5	1	6	5	2	2

% of respondents who describe the business environment of their companies as "more" or "much more" competitive than five years ago (n = 2963)

FIGURE 1.1 McKinsey survey of business executives indicated that low cost competition was increasing competitive intensity in many industries
Source: McKinsey Quarterly Global Survey of Business Executives, March 2006.

Retailing

Wal-Mart, the second largest company in the world in terms of revenue, is a low cost retailer that dominates many retail product categories in the US, Canada and Mexico, with a smaller presence in a number of other countries. However, for almost a decade, Wal-Mart struggled to establish a strong position in Germany and finally withdrew in 2006. One of the reasons for its failure in Germany was the entrenched position of the so-called German "hard discounters". The major players Aldi (actually two separate companies Aldi Sud and Aldi Nord) and Lidl, and some minor players, had captured over 40% of the retail grocery market in Germany. These hard discounters, and other similar low cost competitors, had significant and growing shares of the retail grocery market in almost every European country. Across the whole of Western Europe, their market share in 2004 was 18% and they were growing much faster than the more traditional retail formats in many markets, including those outside of Europe.[4] Hard discounters are not only a threat to other grocery retailers in their markets but they have become a thorn in the side of fast-moving consumer goods (FMCG) manufacturers such as P&G, Nestlé and Unilever. The hard discounters carry almost no, or a limited range of, branded products. Their own private label products account for most of the inventory in their stores. Given the high market share of hard discounters in several countries, many FMCG manufacturers have lost a significant degree of exposure to their potential consumers. Even worse, in some respects, has been the response that these hard discounters have provoked in the other retail customers of FMCG companies. Many of these other customers have introduced a range (sometimes more than one range) of their own private label products in an attempt to be more competitive with the hard discounters. This has resulted in the FMCG companies facing a private label challenge from a majority of their customers.

In many clothing categories, the low cost retail chains such as Zara and H&M are competing effectively with traditional, higher end manufacturers of fashion clothing like Liz Claiborne. These low cost competitors have been expanding rapidly and many are reporting very good financial results. To compete more effectively with the well-known and more expensive fashion brands promoted by Liz Claiborne and others, the low cost retail chains are increasingly introducing exclusive lines endorsed by such celebrities as Madonna and Kylie Minogue.

In all these segments of the retail market, executives and managers at the traditional retailers must figure out how to respond effectively to this low cost competitive threat. It is also a major issue for the branded manufacturers like

Nestlé, P&G and Nike that supply traditional retailers and, in some cases, their low cost competitors.

Airlines

The first major low cost airline, Southwest Airlines, was launched in 1971. Two key elements of Southwest's operating model were the use of only one type of aircraft (the Boeing 737), which simplified many aspects of its operations, and the use of a "point-to-point" system rather than the "hub-and-spoke" system favored by many major airlines. Southwest also preferred secondary airports that often had lower charges and less congestion, which allowed planes to be turned around more quickly. Since that time, Southwest's concept has spawned numerous airlines that have copied key elements of its business model. Today there are over 50 low cost carriers in Europe including such giants as Ryanair and easyJet, several in India and many others in major aviation markets worldwide. In Europe, where the low cost airlines have been particularly successful, well over 100 million passengers per year fly with them, accounting for about 30% of all scheduled intra-European traffic.[5]

The leaders among the low cost airlines are some of the most profitable airlines in the world, and they have created significant shareholder value. Southwest has been the most consistently profitable of all the large US airlines, and by at least one measure – net margin – Ryanair has been in several recent years the most profitable major airline in the world.

Executives at some of the traditional carriers have now been struggling for more than a quarter of a century to find an effective way to deal with this threat. Some approaches have been more successful than others, but the low cost carriers keep growing and expanding into new market segments, thereby increasing the pressure on the traditional players.

Banking

Modern direct banking first appeared in Europe in the late 1980s. In the UK, Midland Bank launched its 24-hour, seven-days-a-week telephone banking service (with its toll-free phone number 0800 24 24 24) in 1989. In the late 1990s, the Internet became an additional channel and, ultimately, the main channel for customers to access their direct bank's services. ING Groep, the large Dutch bancassurance group, has been most successful in capitalizing on the interest of many consumers in a bank that offered high interest rates on savings and low interest rates on mortgages and loans. From a successful pilot of ING DIRECT in Canada in 1997, the bank rapidly expanded its direct banking service into a number of other countries. By 2008, the bank had operations in nine countries in Europe, North America and Australasia. In many developed banking markets, such as the US, Canada and several countries in Western Europe, there are now a number of direct banks in operation.

Direct banks have had a significant impact on the industry's competitive dynamics in several markets. Traditional "bricks and mortar" banks, such as Citibank and HSBC in the US, have been forced to open their own direct banking services with competitive offerings to prevent further erosion of their customer bases. For ING, its aggressive entry into direct banking resulted in about €700 million of before tax profit in 2006. One investment bank valued the ING DIRECT bank component of ING Groep at €10 billion in 2007[6] – not bad for a business less than ten years old!

Fast-moving consumer goods

In a wide variety of consumer product categories, the traditional branded manu-facturers are facing serious low cost competition. As mentioned in the discussion above about retailers, the hard discounters put a heavy emphasis on their private label products. Often, these private label grocery products are of high quality; in many cases, the companies that have the number three-, number four- or number five-ranked brand in a market produce them. These manufacturers have come under increasing pressure as many traditional retailers have decided to allocate their limited shelf space to the number one and number two brands and perhaps their own private label brand or brands. Many of the producers that have lost their position on traditional retailer shelves are mid-sized manufacturers in desperate need of orders to keep their manufacturing plants operating at high levels of capac-ity utilization. This makes them very receptive to the hard discounters who promise very high and predictable volumes on a very small number of stock-keeping units (SKUs). Some industry observers estimate that Aldi sells about 150 times the volume per SKU that Wal-Mart does giving it, and the other hard discounters, tremendous purchasing power. The quality of these products is often excellent. In independent product testing, they often match or even outperform the brands of the leading FMCG companies. While the hard discounters demand high quality and very low prices, they are usually relatively inexpensive to serve because they buy centrally on long-term contracts, need little support, want delivery in

truckloads and are not interested in promotional activities. Many of the hard discounters are also loyal to manufacturers that live up to their commitments.

Consumer electronics

In Switzerland, the market leader in units for fixed line telephone handsets sold
to consumers in 2007 was not Swisscom (the leading Swiss telecommunications
company), Panasonic, Siemens or Sony but a small Swiss company called Telgo
– operating under the brand name of Switel. Telgo was launched in 2001, and
it soon became a leading supplier in Switzerland of both fixed line handsets and
a variety of other related consumer telecommunications products; it also began
expanding into other European markets. The company takes advantage of new
technology and has been quick to enter new emerging product categories such
as Voice over Internet Protocol (VoIP) telephone handsets. It is a low cost competitor and, according to its CEO, it is perceived as the market leader in its home
market in terms of "value for money". [7] It has strong relationships with a number
of major retailers, and the Switel product is often their "value" line in the product
categories in which Switel competes. While its sales and product line have
expanded quite rapidly, Switel has been able to accomplish this with only
about a dozen employees. Most of the development and all of the manufacturing
is outsourced to partners in Asia. We will discuss in Chapter 2 how the appearance of focused companies that specialize in innovation, product design and
infrastructure activities, such as manufacturing and logistics, has allowed small
companies like Switel to focus on building relationships with customers. Sometimes these small players have grown into significant forces in the markets in
which they compete. The extensive outsourcing has allowed Switel to grow very
rapidly, and in the product categories in which it operates, it is a significant
competitor for large global companies such as Philips, Panasonic, Sony and
Samsung.

   In North America some of these same leading consumer electronics companies are being challenged with regard to LCD flat-panel TVs by another competitor Vizio. In early 2004 Vizio was a six-person company with sales of less
than $20 million per year. By the last quarter of 2007 Vizio had annual sales of
almost $2 billion and had captured 12.4% of the US LCD TV market, just behind
Sony's 12.5% and Samsung's 14.2% market shares. Again, Vizio managed to do
this by working very closely with a focused manufacturing partner in Asia, who
had also bought an equity stake in the company.[8]

Business-to-business products and services

The threat posed by low cost competition is at least as strong in many business-to-business product and service categories as it is in business-to-consumer categories.

One industry being threatened in a number of product categories is the chemical business. Not surprisingly, for many of the commodity chemical products the low cost challenge is coming out of the Middle East and other regions with access to very low cost energy and feedstock. But the challenge is also strong, and growing, in specialty chemicals and pharmaceuticals, which have traditionally been dominated by European and North American manufacturers as well as those from the most developed Asian economies. These companies have invested heavily in research and development to create unique, patented products. In some cases, considerable process expertise is required to produce these products efficiently and to meet the demanding quality standards of their customers. However, some of these companies are now finding themselves challenged, often by companies based in China and India. In some cases, the companies have been surprised at how quickly their Asian competitors have been able to catch up to them. In one case, a European specialty chemical company had a major product for which the patent had expired. One of its leading European competitors tried to copy the product but failed to develop something that fully matched its offering. A few months later, an Asian competitor was successful in copying the product and was meeting the demanding quality standards of key customers. And it was selling the product at half the price of the original European player. The challenge for executives in the chemical and pharmaceutical industries is to come up with effective responses as some of these low cost competitors strive to offer products that provide more and more value to their customers.

IT services is another area where low cost competitors have been making major inroads, for example Indian companies such as Tata Consultancy Services, Wipro Technologies and Infosys Technologies. Initially, they capitalized on the low cost and wide availability of well-educated, English-speaking workers in India. Their first big opportunity was rewriting legacy software to cope with the new millennium. A lot of the software written in the mid- to late-20th century had not anticipated calendar dates after 1999 and much of this software needed to be repaired, rewritten and tested. This was a major challenge for many companies, and was very labor intensive and not very exciting work for software developers. The Indian companies were willing and able to undertake the work and many performed well at the assigned tasks. Having established credibility with their Western customers, they were soon given assignments that were more challenging.

As their labor costs have risen, and as they have developed even closer relationships with customers in other parts of the world, these companies are expanding rapidly outside of India and are increasingly providing services that are more advanced. The growth rates for Indian IT service companies in the last few years have been very high, bringing them into increasing competition with the major global IT services companies such as IBM Global Services, HP and Accenture, both in India and around the world. As they continue to build up their local presence in global markets, they pose an increasing challenge for the global leaders.

Open source programs like Linux and MySQL are another increasingly important low cost threat to such leading software companies as Microsoft and Oracle. Initially these kinds of open source software were little more than a nuisance to the mainstream software vendors. However, the threat grew as both start-ups like Red Hat and large traditional companies like IBM and Sun threw their support behind some of the open source software. Some of the largest young corporations like Facebook and MySpace were reported to use no traditional commercial software in their information technology infrastructures.[9] By 2008, IBM was also working actively with a number of partners to make it very easy for corporations to deploy "Microsoft-free" PCs in their organizations.[10]

The examples above are only the tip of the iceberg. Low cost competitors occupy a large and growing part of many industries. Some of these companies are very profitable, and they have created tremendous shareholder value. It seems that almost no industry is safe from low cost competitors. Even the large commercial aircraft market is threatened by low cost competition. In mid-2007, Jim McNerney, the CEO of Boeing, said that he expected a third player to emerge to challenge Boeing and Airbus and he suggested that the challenger would probably be Chinese.[11] As McNerney pointed out, China has developed a formidable supply chain to support the Chinese automobile industry – something nobody thought possible in the late-1990s. If China made similar progress in the aviation manufacturing industry, it certainly would not need the almost 30 years it took Airbus to challenge Boeing for leadership in that business.

IN MANY INDUSTRIES THE MAJOR THREAT IS COMING FROM ASIA

Boeing is not the only company that is watching carefully what is happening in Asian countries such as China and India. As suggested in some of the previous examples, the threat is either a direct Asian threat, such as specialty chemicals or IT services, or is an indirect threat, such as those low cost products marketed under the brand names of Switel and Vizio – produced, and in many cases designed, in Asia.

These Asian challengers, particularly the ones based in China and India, represent a very serious threat, in part because they are based in countries with huge domestic markets for numerous products and services. For example, some 45–50% of the world's cement is currently sold in China. China is also the largest market in the world for telecommunications equipment and mobile phones; it is the number two market in the world for aircraft. In 2006, it accounted for 25% of the elevators and 50% of the escalators installed in the world. India is also rapidly moving up the global rankings for many products and services. It is, for example, the largest market in the world for tractors.

If players in developed countries wait until some of the domestic companies in China and India emerge onto the world stage, they could face competitors with unbeatable economies of scale. Additionally, the competition among the local Asian players in some of these industries is fierce; there are sometimes dozens of players competing furiously for market leadership. In China, the large number of players in some industries is the result of different provinces, or other government entities, encouraging and then protecting local companies to create jobs and economic growth. In 2007, many local Chinese entrepreneurs and companies sensed there was a good opportunity in the wind turbine market. Wind power generation was rapidly becoming a major market in China as the Chinese government set ambitious goals for renewable energy. The number of local competitors went from about a dozen to more than 50 in less than a year. Goldwind, one of the local Chinese players that had produced almost no wind turbines prior to 2004, was the market leader in China with a 35% market share by 2007. This was no mean feat in the world's second largest wind turbine market where most of the world's leading global players, including Vestas, GE Wind, Gamesa and Suzlon, were also competing.

Japan and Korea provided protection for many of their industries in the early stages of their development. This meant that their companies did not have to compete head-to-head with leading multinationals in the home market before they were well established. This has been much less the case in China and some of the other more recent emerging economies. Their companies have often had to battle not only with many other domestic competitors but also with leading multinationals right from the start. This intense competition has sometimes resulted in deep, highly innovative and very flexible infrastructures that have driven costs down rapidly and improved quality. One good example of this has been the motorcycle industry in China that is centered around the city of Chongquing.[12] China has over 100 companies that assemble motorcycles. The privately owned assemblers rely on a network of companies that provide components and subassemblies. These suppliers take collective responsibility for the detailed design of these components and subsystems to meet the broad design parameters set by the motorcycle assemblers and brand owners. They are free to innovate to achieve the design targets and they do. The result has been a dramatic fall in costs, much of which has been passed on to their customers in the form of lower prices. By 2006, China was producing 18 million motorcycles per year, accounting for 50% of the world production, and over 60% of this production was exported. In some markets, such as South Vietnam, Japanese motorcycle manufacturers have lost most of their market share to the much cheaper Chinese bikes.

Many Western companies, sometimes belatedly, have recognized the opportunity afforded by the large and rapidly growing Asian domestic markets for many products and services, particularly in China and India. In many cases, they have established a manufacturing presence in Asia to try to tap into this growth opportunity, as well as the lower costs. At first glance, some of these manufacturing operations are quite successful with rapidly growing sales as additional capacity is being added. However, on closer examination the results are not always as positive as they first seem. For some companies, almost all the output is being exported back to their home markets, or to other export markets around the world, but very little is actually being sold in China or India. Thus, while the companies are taking advantage of the low cost manufacturing opportunities in Asia, they have not always been able to capture significant market share in local markets. So, if part of the objective of establishing a presence in China or India was to contain the local players by challenging them on their home turf, they have failed. When Chinese or Indian competitors appear on the world stage, some are doing it from a relatively secure base in their home market. The Western companies, on the other hand, are missing out on the learning opportunities that would have been available if they had gone head-to-head in the Chinese and Indian domestic markets against the local players.

When we hear companies bragging about their success in Asia, we should always look carefully at their claims. Yes, it is very useful to build a successful manufacturing presence in Asia, but it is often strategically much more important to build a fully-fledged business there with a significant market share in the region's major domestic markets.

MANY CUSTOMERS PREFER GOOD ENOUGH PRODUCTS AND SERVICES

Think about it. It is not always just about price. It is often more about the total value proposition. Many customers choose to buy good enough products from value competitors because they are cost-conscious and/or because their needs are fully met by the value player's solution. In some cases, these customers even think that the value competitor offers more value at lower cost.

Aldi and Lidl, for example, offer their customers an attractive value proposition. For some manufacturer-branded products, their prices are sometimes higher than the hypermarkets'. However, the everyday low prices of their private label products are often significantly lower than prices in other grocery stores. For many hard discounter customers, a very important aspect of the value proposition is the combination of store proximity and very limited choice, both of which provide shopper convenience. Some 80% of German households live within 20 minutes of a hard discounter. Hard discounters carry a very limited number of SKUs, often around 1000 versus up to 25000 in a traditional supermarket and many more in a hypermarket. This limited range means that the customer does not have to choose between the 10 to 20 brands, product variants and sizes found in many traditional supermarkets or hypermarkets. This simplifies and speeds up decision-making.[13] As mentioned earlier, the quality of their products is satisfactory and, in some cases, compares favorably to leading branded products. For many customers, this combination of low prices, high quality, convenience and simplicity is a winning value proposition. This applies to both low-income consumers who rely on reduced prices and higher-income consumers who see themselves as smart shoppers. In

Germany many consumers think it is "cool" to find bargains at stores like Aldi and Lidl – and even have a saying for it, "Geiz ist geil" (stinginess is smart).

Similarly, many customers find the "service" of a direct bank totally acceptable – they do not want or value personalized service or a relationship with a bank. These customers would rather earn high interest on their savings and pay low interest rates on their loans. They may also prefer to do their transactions via the Internet at their convenience. They do not see much value in waiting in lines for teller service and having to endure what might be indifferent service, at best. In banking, as in many other industries, technology is advancing quickly and making self-service faster, more convenient and more effective. Some customers of low cost airlines, such as Ryanair, find that the smaller and less crowded airports that the carrier uses result in greater convenience, better punctuality and shorter, more predictable travel times.

LOW COST COMPETITION IS NOT ALL BAD NEWS

The emergence of low cost competition is certainly not all bad news for traditional companies. It often signals that there is a significant segment of the market not satisfied with the traditional offerings; in other words, there is a need for good enough products and services at low prices. As we will discuss later in the book, this segment may seem to be quite small initially. However, it often grows exponentially as both the demand side of the business develops and the supply side infrastructure grows to support the low cost players.

Smart executives and managers in traditional companies recognize the opportunity early and may decide to move quickly to stake a claim on the new emerging market and capture a first-mover advantage. As we discussed earlier in this chapter, ING Groep saw the direct banking opportunity before many other large financial services companies (but still several years after it had first emerged) and moved to capitalize on it in many of the major countries around the world.

After stumbling at first in the low-end segment of the Chinese mobile phone market, Nokia bounced back with handsets designed for those customers. And perhaps more importantly, they developed a distribution system that allowed the company to penetrate markets deeply in the third- and fourth-tier cities and the rural areas. Based partly on its successes in China and India, Nokia is believed to have about a 50% share of the world's "below €50" mobile segment.

In some industries, customers first enter a market by buying good enough products and services at low prices, often from low cost players. However, as their needs evolve over time, customers may buy from a supplier that offers a more advanced product with better performance or service. In some cases, this may be from a traditional company that does not compete in the good enough segment of the market. However, in other cases, if they have been satisfied with the low cost competitor's product, and if the low cost competitor provides products and services that meet the more advanced needs of customers, they may continue to buy from the low cost player. Thus, a traditional player without a low-end offering may find it difficult to access these customers as they "move up" in the market.

Many FMCG companies are recognizing the opportunities with consumers who are further down the income "pyramid" than those whom they have traditionally served. These consumers not only represent an "upgrade" opportunity over time but can also represent an attractive market in their own right. While they lack the individual purchasing power of their higher-income, traditional consumers, collectively they represent a significant market opportunity. Additionally, these consumers often shop in traditional "mom and pop" retail channels that have much less buying power than retailers in the "organized" segment of the market, which gives manufacturers more power and control in the relationship. Several leading FMCG companies are now aggressively "tiering down" to pursue this consumer group in the developing world for both the immediate market opportunity they represent as well as the longer term "upgrade" potential. Nestlé, for example, has a major thrust to provide "Popularly Positioned Products" to consumers in the developing world. Many of its products have been specially formulated to offer these consumers nutritionally balanced products, in small package sizes and at affordable prices. Nestlé hopes that these consumers will recognize the value that is being offered and that they will become loyal purchasers of Nestlé products. This will give Nestlé an advantage if and when these consumers start buying higher-end products in the product categories in which the company competes.

The same kind of dynamic exists in many business-to-business markets where new companies often enter a business by producing very basic or commodity products. For example, a Chinese entrepreneur might see an opportunity to enter the yarn manufacturing business. Initially, he twists cotton fiber to make coarse or medium-grade yarn. This is the easiest segment for him to enter and a basic twisting machine from a low cost local Chinese manufacturer might be totally adequate for this purpose. These basic machines are simple enough that a local mechanic might be able to make some replacement parts for them as well as do the servicing. Because there are few barriers to entry, however, many other entrepreneurs have the same idea and the business becomes very competitive with low margins. As the entrepreneur becomes skilled and gains more experience in the business, he sees that if he were to twist fine or very fine cotton or wool, the margins might be much better since the barriers to entry are higher. To do this, however, he needs to buy more sophisticated twisting machines. He may also have to buy replacement parts from, and perhaps even get more sophisticated servicing done by, the machine manufacturer. These machines might only be available from European and Japanese suppliers (at least initially until a few of the local Chinese players can begin to match their offerings). The entrepreneur then becomes a customer for the traditional textile machinery manufacturers, focusing more on quality, performance and industry-leading technology.

UNDERSTANDING AND RESPONDING TO THE CHALLENGE OF LOW COST COMPETITION

Beating Low Cost Competition is designed to help executives and managers in traditional companies better understand low cost competitors and their strategies. Traditional companies can only hope to compete effectively with their competitors by having a deep understanding of them. This will help them to develop strategies for their business that will not only allow them to counter the threats from low cost competitors but also, in some cases, take advantage of the opportunities in some of the more cost-conscious segments of their markets.

In Chapter 2, we will introduce a simple conceptual framework that allows these executives to place their own strategy and those of their competitors, including their low cost competitors, within a common context. We will also explore some of the major reasons that low cost competition has become such a major challenge for companies in a variety of industries. The chapter discusses the three core value propositions – performance, price and relational value – that companies use to appeal to their customers. We will argue that many product categories, if not whole industries, are moving more quickly than ever before from the introductory phase, through the growth phase and to maturity. This leads to relatively rapid commoditization of the core product or service and results in players emphasizing price value emerging more quickly and more vigorously than we have seen previously. We will discuss some of the reasons why there seem to be more low cost competitors than ever before and why they are appearing more quickly. As we shall see, fundamental changes in the business environment in many industries have contributed to this. The growth of price value players has been actively encouraged in some industries, by both the suppliers and customers of traditional companies. Additionally, in many consumer product categories, the consumers themselves have become much more receptive to good enough products and services at low prices.

Figure 1.2 shows the overall flow of the book and the major questions that are addressed in Chapters 3 to 7. These are the questions that company management teams or business unit teams facing the threat of low cost competition should be asking themselves.

In Chapter 3, we will deepen our understanding of how some low cost competitors from a variety of different industries play their game. We will see that while these companies compete in quite different industries, they often share a number of common characteristics. Many of these companies have been quite innovative in their own ways. In some cases, traditional companies can learn valuable lessons from how these low cost competitors operate and how they manage their businesses.

In Chapter 4, we look at the fundamental challenge facing many traditional companies that are, or soon will be, threatened by low cost competitors: Should we tackle the low cost competitor in his market segments, or should we try to avoid a direct confrontation by focusing on other segments? In this chapter, we will explore why many companies fail to address this tough question in a timely manner. An important element in this analysis is developing an understanding about how the strategies of the low cost competitors may evolve over time. In only a few years, what may initially be a remote or minor threat can sometimes evolve into a direct and powerful threat to the core of a company's business. It is essential that company management think through the likely long-term evolution of the strategies implemented by their low cost competitors. Many executives in traditional companies fail to take into account the creative strategies that low cost competitors can adopt to attack their core business.

In Chapter 5, we take a close look at the issues facing a company that is seriously considering challenging the low cost competitors in the price value segment of the market. We will examine, in detail, the major arguments for and against confronting the challengers in their market space. We will also argue that

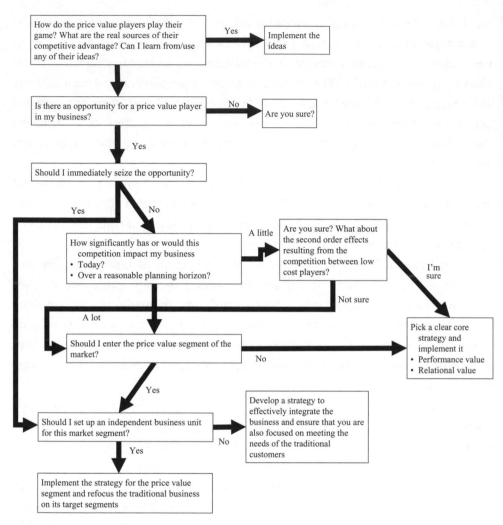

FIGURE 1.2   Responding to an actual or potential low cost challenge – thinking through the key issues

if the decision to move against the low cost competitors is positive, it is much better to move quickly and pre-emptively before the low cost competitors are established in the market. After discussing these issues, we will turn to some of the major decisions regarding implementing a competitive low cost strategy. These decisions include the degree of independence that the two parts of the business should maintain, major tactical decisions such as "make versus buy", branding and "go to market", and other considerations like sales and distribution infrastructure.

In Chapter 6, we show that whether or not a company decides to confront the low cost players in their segment of the market directly, some tough choices have to be made about how to strengthen its position in the other market segments. Some companies try to contain the low cost competitor in the "low end" of the market or even exploit the price value segment in markets that are remote (e.g., geographically remote) from where its traditional business competes. Other companies decide to focus on either performance value or relational value. In Chapter 6, we will look at some companies that have adopted these various approaches and examine some of the strategic and tactical decisions they have taken. We will also review how well they seem to be working.

In Chapter 7, we will step back and look at the issues facing the leadership of companies or business units that are being challenged by low cost competitors, or will be in the near future. Implementing an effective response is often an exercise of major organizational change and one that may take years to be successful. It almost always requires significant cultural change throughout the organization. And whatever direction the company takes, a flawless execution will be absolutely essential if it is to succeed.

Finally, in Chapter 8, we will look to the future and discuss some of the major issues a company's management team should be addressing as we head towards an even more challenging world where low cost competition will play an ever bigger role.

CHAPTER 2

Why the threat from low cost competition is intensifying

One of the reasons that low cost competition is such a headache for executives in traditional companies today is that these competitors seem to emerge more quickly, and much more energetically, than they did a decade or two ago. In some industries, it seems that almost as soon as a new product category is developed, the first low cost or value competitor enters the market. DVD players were first launched in Japan in late 1996, in the US in 1997 and in Europe in 1998. In little more than five years, there were literally hundreds of different brands of DVD players available, most of them marketed by low cost players who were competing almost solely on price. The low cost airline market in Europe began to emerge in 1992 when the European Union (EU) deregulated the airline industry; this allowed an airline based in one EU country to operate between other EU countries. Ryanair was the first low cost carrier to take real advantage of the opportunities the agreement created. In 1995, easyJet entered the business, and by 2005, there were over 50 discount airlines operating in Europe. In some other types of markets, where the barriers to entry are lower, the response time is measured in months rather than years.

In this chapter, we will explore some of the reasons why the barriers to entry for low cost competitors have been reduced and how this has led to an explosion, in many industries, in the number of value competitors. As we will see, some of the forces that encourage and support low cost competitors can also be exploited by traditional players – helping them to be more competitive against their low cost challengers.

We will begin this chapter with a discussion of the basic types of value propositions and how the emphasis on the different value propositions, in a given product or service category, tends to evolve over time. With the accelerating tempo of technology and business, new markets and new product categories within existing markets seem to move to maturity much more quickly than in the past. This means that markets can quickly become fertile breeding grounds for low cost competitors.

One of the major factors enabling the growth of value competitors in many industries has been the emergence of new specialized business models that are replacing the traditional corporation. Additionally, in some industries these specialized companies can provide core building blocks that facilitate new entrants in putting together complete solutions for their customers. And in some industries "network orchestrators" have emerged that put together a custom supply chain for their clients, providing the clients with products that meet their customers' needs. All the client has to do is identify and build relationships with the potential customers for the products.

The phenomenon, however, is not only supply-based. It is also demand-based. In some cases, companies actively encourage new low cost players to enter the market to both become new low cost sources for products or services and to put pricing pressure on their existing suppliers. Also, the growth of low cost or value competitors would not be possible if there were not greater customer acceptance for the products and services they provide. There is growing evidence in many consumer markets that the products and services of value players are becoming more widely accepted – and not just by the lower income and more price-sensitive customers in the market. In some cases, other players in the value chain have helped build the credibility of these new entrants so that more customers will be willing to buy their products and services.

VALUE PROPOSITIONS HAVE THREE CORE ELEMENTS

Customers buy a product or service because they believe that it will meet their needs better than any other offering on the market. Suppliers of products and services try to craft value propositions that will resonate with their target customers, as well as provide them with convincing reasons to believe that their product or service is better than competitive offerings on the key factor or factors about which the customer is concerned.[14] Many business observers have recognized over the years that there are three fundamental types of value propositions – performance

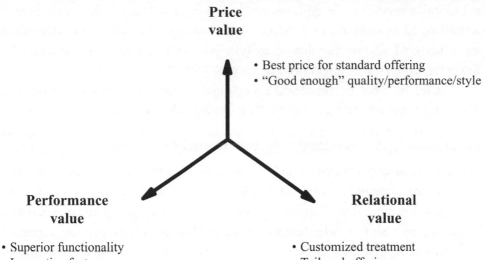

Price value

- Best price for standard offering
- "Good enough" quality/performance/style

Performance value

- Superior functionality
- Innovative features
- Exceptional quality
- Fashion/style leadership

Relational value

- Customized treatment
- Tailored offerings
- Complete and integrated solutions
- Convenient/rapid response
- Mutual trust

FIGURE 2.1 Value propositions have three core elements

value, price value and relational value – but businesses usually stress one (see Figure 2.1).[15]

Performance value

Companies that emphasize and provide real performance value, such as Apple Computer, offer their customers some combination of superior functionality, innovative features, an exceptional user experience, excellent quality and style or fashion leadership. In recent years, Apple has successfully launched a number of industry leading products and services such as iMac, iPod, iTunes and iPhone. Not all of its products and services were winners, but enough have been successful to establish a strong reputation for performance leadership. Even its retail stores reinforce its image for fashion and style leadership.[16] Another company that has typically emphasized performance leadership has been BMW, which claimed for over 25 years (in English-speaking countries) that it made the "ultimate driving machine."[17] Toyota on the other hand, with products such as the Prius hybrid vehicle, is often viewed as the performance leader in environmentally friendly cars. In the financial services market, many observers believe that the Bloomberg subscription service is the performance leader in its industry. With its distinctive terminals, Bloomberg provides access to almost any financial information and a lot of personal information that an analyst, investor or the professional staff of a financial services firm might need or want.[18]

Clearly, what is considered exceptional performance will vary from one product or service category to another. It may also vary from one customer segment to another; it may even vary over the life cycle of the category. In the introductory stage, performance value might simply be that the product actually delivers the basic functionality, and is reasonably reliable, when competitive offerings are struggling to provide even this basic level of performance. But over time, basic performance often improves rapidly and the basis for performance value leadership may shift to other aspects of the product or service that are important to certain groups of customers. For example, when Apple introduced the Macintosh it seized the lead over its personal computer (PC) competitors by dramatically improving the ease of use of its personal computers, as well as having a form factor that many customers found attractive.

At any point in time, different customer segments may have different priorities among the various dimensions of performance value. In the early and mid-1990s, for example, industrial grade projectors were used in a variety of end-use applications, including boardrooms and control rooms in many companies, educational institutions, entertainment venues and simulators for training pilots and others. In the educational/training segment, many customers paid particular attention to ease of use, since many different, often technically unsophisticated, instructors might have to use a projector. Ease of use was much less critical in simulation applications since the organizations doing the training had technicians supporting the simulators. Outstanding picture quality was most critical in this application because the environment had to be so realistic that the pilot would believe he was flying a real plane, not just a simulator, and act and react accordingly. As this example illustrates, different companies can have the performance-leading products in different sub-segments of a market by focusing on delivering different bundles of benefits.

Price value

Price value is very much focused on providing good enough solutions and offering these standard products and services at a very attractive price. This is the core value proposition of the low cost competitors, such as Aldi, Lidl, Wal-Mart, Ryanair,

Southwest Airlines, ING DIRECT and many of the contract manufacturers that assemble and make many of the hard and soft goods that we buy today.

Relational value

Relational value tends to be particularly important in situations where some customers have complex and diverse needs and see value in being able to purchase an integrated solution from one supplier. Here, the company tries to provide its customers with customized treatment, tailored offerings and very complete solutions – if that is what the customer wants. In some cases, this means being very quick to respond to client needs. Often the customer and the supplier become quite dependent on one another and the relationship often involves a great deal of mutual trust since it may be very difficult to spell out all the nuances of the relationship in contractual terms.

Companies as diverse as private banks, high-end retailers, Dell (in the corporate market for information technology), GE Healthcare, Cisco and IBM Global Services all try to build high relational value. Clearly, the absolute level of relational value will be very different for a private bank than it would be for a high-end retailer like Nordstrom. But relative to others in its industry, Nordstrom, a high-end US department store chain, clearly differentiates itself from its competitors in the eyes of many consumers by its willingness to be very responsive and attentive to its customers, particularly its "best" customers.

One core value proposition is usually emphasized

Certainly most customers want as much performance, price and relational value as they can possibly get when they buy a product or service. However, they usually have to make compromises; in a competitive industry, one offering is very unlikely to be the best on all three core value dimensions at the same time. For a certain product or service, at a particular point in time, customers fall broadly into segments that are aligned with one of the three core value propositions. Within these broad segments, as we discussed earlier, there may very well be sub-segments. Different industry players may be more or less successful in meeting the different needs of these sub-segments.

Most of the companies operating in a market attempt to lead in one of these three core value propositions and be at an acceptable level on the other two from the perspective of their target customers. For example, a company that chooses to emphasize relational value will try to lead in that aspect but will also have products and services that are reasonably close to the market leader, or leaders, in the performance value dimensions, again to satisfy its target customers. In some cases, the company may even source best-in-class products from competitors if it does not have the appropriate product or service in its own portfolio. Additionally, its price should bear a reasonable relationship to that of the price value leader, particularly in situations where its products or services are not highly differentiated and where customers can readily compare both the prices and value delivered. A flag carrier, for example, that emphasizes the relational value it provides for its first-class and business-class travelers might try to be reasonably competitive on economy fares on routes where it competes directly with a low cost carrier. For the economy passenger, the flag carrier's service level may not be highly differentiated from that of a low cost carrier on the same route, so it doesn't want to create the impression that its prices are outrageous. However, on routes where it only faces competition from similar flag carriers, such as routes between Europe and Asia, it may be less constrained in its pricing. However, a private bank providing sophisticated and personalized service to its clients may be able to charge substantially higher fees than the private banking unit of a mass-market bank, if customers perceive a significant difference between the two players. Clearly, companies tend to have more pricing latitude relative to the price value leader when important elements of the value proposition are based on style, brand image and other more emotional elements. In some cases, as we will see later in the book, companies may try to offer different core value propositions to different segments – these different offers may well come from different business units.

What is acceptable today, of course, may be totally inadequate tomorrow. Companies are faced with the constant challenge of updating and recalibrating their offerings to keep pace with the changing market requirements. So, in most industries, whatever core value proposition a company or business unit has adopted, it will need to continue to improve on all three values over time. Acceptable performance, acceptable relational value and acceptable price (at least in real terms, prices usually fall over time) are all likely to improve.[19]

The relative size of the different value segments may evolve over time

Product and service categories go through a life cycle of introduction, growth, maturity and decline. During the early stages of a new product or service category, the biggest segment of customers is often concerned about performance value. Why? Because customers look for good performance and it is generally not very good in the early development of new products or services. In the early days of mobile phones or notebook computers, for example, the products left a lot to be desired. They were large and bulky, their performance was often poor, battery life was short, they were aesthetically unattractive and the user interfaces were often clumsy. As a result, it was no surprise that many users, or potential users, were focused on performance value. Many of these customers waited eagerly for new generations of the product because they knew there would be meaningful improvements in product performance on a least some of the key product attributes. Different vendors might have been seen to be leading on different performance aspects. In the early days of personal computers, many businesses bought computers from several different suppliers. People who worked in graphics and design may have preferred Apple computers while road warriors might have purchased Toshiba laptops due to their perceived ruggedness. The standard issue for most employees was most probably IBM, Compaq or Hewlett Packard.

There are undoubtedly always other customer segments that are more focused on price value, or relational value, but these segments are usually relatively small in the early stages of the product life cycle.

During a new product category's early days, performance often improves quite quickly. As the category matures, however, meaningful performance improvements are harder to achieve – the cost of developing these meaningful improvements often rises, sometimes exponentially. This is shown in Figure 2.2 where the performance improvement achieved between t_5 and t_6 is much less than the improvement achieved between t_1 and t_2. On the other hand, there may still be significant opportunities for meaningful reductions in price (increases in price value) and improvements in relational value in these later years.

As the product or service category matures, a couple of things start to happen from a customer perspective. Product or service performance often reaches a level that is increasingly good enough for many potential customers and further improvements are not highly valued by these customers. Their attention may then switch to one of the other core value propositions. Some customers become much more focused on price value – selecting good enough products that are attractively priced. Other customers may be much more focused on being "taken care of" by a company that offers high relational value. They may still want a relatively high performance value product or service but are willing to trade off some

Introduction ⟶ Growth ⟶ Maturity

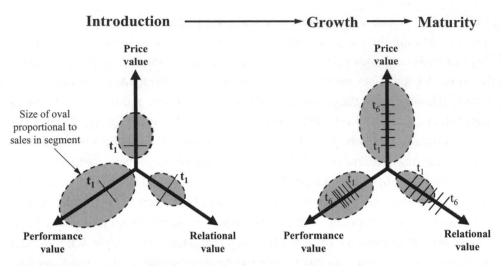

FIGURE 2.2 Markets develop and evolve over time
Source: Based partly on private communications with Professor George S. Day, Wharton School, University of Pennsylvania.

performance value for greater relational value. Using the personal computer example again, a company might conclude that performance was similar across the leading brands and decide to work closely with only one vendor. As an example, Dell might be selected as the company's supplier due to a perception of having reasonable offerings for all employee groups and providing services that allow the company to manage its personal computers more cost effectively.

When Toyota first introduced its Lexus brand in the North American market, some of its customers were willing to trade off the performance that they might have received from a leading European automobile manufacturer for the very good performance, excellent product quality and the high relational value that Toyota provided through its dealer network. The level of service provided by Lexus dealers was perceived by many customers to be superior to that provided by the dealers of the high-end German automobile manufacturers.

As the market matures, we usually see relative growth in the price value and relational value segments and a relative decline in the performance value segment or segments. The relative size of the three core segments obviously varies dramatically from market to market and with the stage of market maturity. And in some markets the nature of the product or service, as well as customer needs, means that there may never be a large relational value segment.

There are significant discontinuities in some product categories brought about by changes in the business environment such as major technology advances and/or regulatory change. For example, the core technology in television for most of its history was cathode ray tubes. For many years, Sony was perceived as the performance leader with its Trinitron variant of the cathode ray tube technology. Other companies were eventually perceived as matching Sony's picture quality; the performance differences between the major players and the performance improvements from year to year were not perceptible to most consumers. But with the emergence of new projection technologies in the television market in the 1990s, like LCD and plasma, the game started over. In both of these new technologies, there were new leaders and perceptible differences in performance between competitors. This resulted in an increase in the number of customers focusing on performance value and the television product category began to move through a new life cycle.

Product category life cycles are getting shorter

In recent years, many industries have seen dramatic decreases in the length of time between the introduction of a product category's first item and the time when that product category reaches maturity. For example, it took almost ten years for cumulative global sales of VCRs to reach 20 million units, whereas DVD players and DVD recorders reached the same level of sales in less than five years and less than four years, respectively (see Figure 2.3). The chief technology officer at P&G estimated that between 1992 and 2002 the life cycle of consumer goods in America had been cut in half.[20] Typically, price value players now enter the market sooner than they did in the past. It is not clear whether this is a cause or a result of compressing product life cycles. Clearly, price value competitors, who by their nature focus on cost and price reductions to gain competitive advantage, make the products more affordable, accelerating market growth. On the other hand, once a market has matured to some degree from a performance point of view and is attractive in size, low cost competitors will see the market opportunity as a desirable one.

One of the factors helping to accelerate the entry of value players is the dramatic lowering of entry barriers in many industries. A major factor contributing to this development has been the movement away from the traditional "integrated" corporation towards three more focused business models.

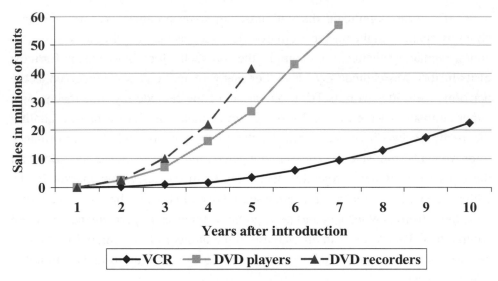

FIGURE 2.3 Product life cycles seem to be shortening
Source: Based on a slide in a presentation by Rudy Provoost, "Changing Industry Dynamics", Philips Analyst Day, 5 November 2003.

THE TRADITIONAL INTEGRATED BUSINESS MODEL IS DISINTEGRATING

For years, many companies have outsourced ancillary activities that were clearly non-core to their business or too small to justify hiring the necessary specialized resources. Food services, such as employee cafeterias or restaurants, and specialized legal work are two common examples of work that was outsourced. During the 1990s, an increasing number of companies began to outsource more business processes such as information technology management and human resources administration.[21] As more and more business processes are standardized, it becomes easier for companies to outsource them. With standardization, costs and benefits become much more visible to companies leading to the commoditization of their processes and then lower prices.

The modularization of many products is another trend that has contributed to the growth of both outsourcing and the number of low cost competitors. An early example of this was the personal computer based on the Microsoft operating system and Intel microprocessors. These two companies, as well as manufacturers like IBM, helped drive the development of standards for the PC. By establishing a set of standards, and standard interfaces, a variety of specialized companies could develop modules for the PC such as disk drives, key boards, graphic cards, etc. Different companies were able to focus on different parts of the PC and develop improved solutions independently, allowing rapid improvements in overall performance. This allowed many unsophisticated companies, and individuals, to assemble advanced PCs by buying the modules from a variety of different suppliers and putting them together to meet the user's desired specifications. Others were doing all the difficult engineering work. This modularization has spread to a number of product categories in many industries. Companies like Intel (in their case for microprocessors) have actively encouraged modularization – it stimulates fierce competition at several levels of the value chain helping to commoditize the end products, lower their prices and stimulate demand. Because Intel has almost a monopoly position in PC microprocessors (its market share has generally been higher than 75–80%), it has achieved very attractive profits. As a result of the modularization, and the resulting ease of market entry for assemblers, the number of potential outsource partners available in the affected industries has increased significantly.

Dramatic improvements in communications technology, particularly the Internet, and supply chain infrastructure over the past 10 to 20 years are two other major factors that have helped support the move to greater outsourcing. This better communications capability has enabled companies to improve the value propositions they offer their customers. By leveraging relationships with strategic partners, often scattered around the world, companies can potentially offer superior levels of price, performance and relational value than were possible a few years ago.

In order to capitalize fully on these new opportunities, some companies have decided to adopt one of three focused business models: an innovation and commercialization model, an infrastructure model or a customer relationship model.[22] By organizing an entire company, or a business unit, around one of these core business models and outsourcing many of the activities associated with the other two models to best-in-class partners, a company may be able to develop a much more attractive value proposition for its customers. Even within the chosen focus area, some of the non-core activities can be outsourced to other best-in-class partners allowing the company to be even more focused. In many industries, this has allowed focused players – often new entrants – to gain a competitive advantage over their more traditional horizontally integrated competitors. Cisco,

Ryanair, TSMC, Quanta, Qualcomm and ARM Holdings are among the companies that have transformed their industries by focusing primarily on one of the three models and relying on best-in-class partners for the other two. Several have fundamentally changed their industries, often irrevocably.

Three core processes underpin any business

All companies have three core processes or groups of activities: innovation and commercialization activities, infrastructure activities and customer relationship activities.[23] The first group of activities is focused on the creation and development of commercially viable, innovative new products and services and bringing them to the market in a timely manner. The second group, infrastructure activities, involves managing the manufacturing facilities, supply chains, logistics systems and information networks that are critical if a company is to deliver the solutions it has promised its customers. In the case of a service business, such as a mobile telecommunications services provider, the infrastructure activities include the network of base stations or transmitters scattered around a country together with the network that connects all the transmitters and the IT infrastructure that routes calls and manages the network. The final group, customer relationship activities, involves identifying and capturing customers, building relationships with them, and designing and providing compelling "solutions" that meet their needs.

Each of the three core sets of activities, or processes, has a fundamentally different economic driver and thus, the focus of a management team responsible for each of these core sets of activities is different (see Figure 2.4). Innovation and product commercialization processes that allow a company to develop and commercialize truly differentiated products and services require creative individuals and teams who not only bring the products or services to market in a timely manner but also hit the appropriate market window. The more revolutionary the innovations are, the more dependent the company is on attracting the most talented, creative individuals and getting them to put extraordinary efforts into the project. Companies that focus on innovation and commercialization generally put a lot of effort into creating a very attractive work environment that will appeal to these types of individuals. Some, like Google in its early days, "coddle" their employees with an extensive array of services including gourmet meals, on-site laundries and dry-cleaning, extensive sports and game facilities, etc. In many industries, relatively small, highly focused organizations are often the most effective at accomplishing truly revolutionary product innovations. Many small

	Customer relationships	Infrastructure	Innovation
Key success factors	Scope	Scale	Time to market and timing
Management focus	Customers	Costs	People

FIGURE 2.4 Key success factor and area of management focus for each of the emerging business models
Source: Based on John Hagel III and Marc Singer (1999) "Unbundling the Corporation", *Harvard Business Review*, March–April, pp. 133–41.

biotechnology firms are typical of this type of company and account for an increased proportion of the pharmaceutical industry's new product development activity.

ARM Holdings in the UK, which designs and licenses the microprocessor cores used in such products as mobile phones, iPods and digital cameras, is another example of this type of company in the microprocessor industry. Essentially, ARM is in the business of developing and selling intellectual property. It earns an average royalty of about 11 cents for each microprocessor based on its design that is used by a customer (and there could be several in one mobile phone). But when you earn that royalty on well over two billion microprocessors per year, it becomes a very significant revenue source, about $200 million! Add to that the company's revenue from selling licenses for its intellectual property – the result was a $400 million business in 2008. Qualcomm, which owns many of the key patents underlying advanced mobile communications products such as mobile phones, is also largely an innovation-focused company with revenues of almost $2.8 billion in license fees and royalties from its intellectual property business unit in 2007.

Acquiring and building the relationship with a new customer is often a very expensive proposition. Therefore, executives managing the customer relationship activities typically want to sell as broad a range of products and services to a customer as possible, whether that is a retailer selling to individual consumers or a company selling products and services to business-to-business customers. By selling a large number of items, a company is more likely to get a good return on the relationship building investments – be it in advertising, personal selling or other promotional activities. Dell Computer, for example, has focused increasingly on customer relationship activities; once it has built a customer relationship, it doesn't just want to sell laptop computers.[24] The company would also like to supply desktop computers, servers, printers, networking gear and various services including support. In this way, the largely fixed costs of relationship development and management activities can be amortized over a much larger volume of sales. Additionally, this more extensive relationship with a customer is likely to be "stickier", making it more difficult and less likely for the customer to switch to another supplier. Selling a broader range of products and services to the customer, however, can sometimes result in a loss of focus in both the innovation and infrastructure activities. This is because the company spreads its limited research and development and manufacturing resources over a broader range of products and services.

By contrast, leverage in infrastructure processes usually comes from doing repetitive activities in high volume and fully utilizing the infrastructure that has already been developed to deliver the products or services to the customers at low cost. For example, in the early 1990s, the three largest Canadian banks recognized that they could benefit from a specialist infrastructure supplier doing all of their transaction processing activities, such as check processing and statement preparation. Collectively, the banks set up a company called Symcor to do these activities for them and a variety of other customers in financial services, retailing and other industries with similar transaction processing requirements. Successful infrastructure-focused businesses such as Symcor, TSMC (a leading Taiwanese company providing semiconductor manufacturing services to companies that lack their own fabs or manufacturing facilities), Flextronics (a leading EMS – electronics manufacturing services – company that manages supply chains and assembles computer and storage, telecommunications, industrial electronics and many consumer products) and UPS (a provider of logistics solutions) place heavy emphasis on cost control and the high utilization of the company's expensive assets.

Giving balanced attention to all three core processes can lead to conflict

When a company is trying to do all three of these core processes in one "integrated" organization there are often significant conflicts between the needs of the various departments focusing on each of the key activities. How can one company simultaneously concentrate on its costs, customers and its own employees without facing major conflicts? Can a company simultaneously drive out every cost element of its manufacturing and logistics operations while still offering, for example, free massages or serving "free" gourmet food in its cafeteria – incentives which may help attract the best engineers and software developers in the business?[25]

In the past, when the costs of interacting with outside suppliers and partners were high, most organizations chose to manage these conflicts internally, even if it led to sub-optimal performance in some, or all, of the individual activities. Some companies tried to reduce this conflict by putting the three core activity types into separate business units and adapting policies and procedures to meet the needs of the various businesses. Some compromises had to be made because all of the business units were still part of one company.

In a world where communications and information technology are converging, logistics systems have improved dramatically and business processes are increasingly standardized, many companies have recognized that there is no reason for all the key processes to be housed in one company. Now it is much easier to couple processes and work effectively with partners all over the world. A web of best-in-class players – each focused on one of the core processes and closely linked together – can compete very effectively with a more traditional, integrated company trying to do everything internally.

As a result, a customer relationship company might partner with a number of specialized sub-system and manufacturing partners, logistics suppliers and others to ensure that its infrastructure activities are performed to world-class standards. Since these suppliers are probably also simultaneously working with many other companies, perhaps even some of the company's competitors, they learn from working with diverse customers on a variety of challenging assignments. In this way, they often improve more rapidly than a captive operation only serving one company; this benefits all the companies to which they provide products or services. Maximizing the benefits from working with a number of highly specialized and competent suppliers, and giving them the flexibility to innovate and add value in their specialized areas, requires new management capabilities on the part of the customer relationship company. It also necessitates a certain flexibility that some companies have difficulty mastering. While the challenge is high, the potential payoff may well be worthwhile.

The same challenge faces the customer relationship company if it also decides to outsource some of its innovation and commercialization activities. To develop winning new products, it will need to become skilled at marrying a deep understanding of its customer needs with promising technology and innovation from partners who could be scattered all over the world.

In some businesses, there may still be value in having all core business processes in one organization to ensure effective coordination between the processes. Arguably, a business, such as Intel's core microprocessor business, benefits from having the innovative and infrastructure businesses in the same company due to the high interdependencies in the two sets of the core activities – both at the leading edge of technology. GE also remains quite integrated in several of its businesses, such as jet engines, partly to prevent the leaking of intellectual property and trade secrets to competitors through suppliers and partners. But the number of businesses in this situation is declining as technology advances, processes are standardized and coordination mechanisms improve.

Thus, what we are seeing in many industries are companies focusing on one of these core processes, resulting in three more focused business models: innovation, infrastructure and customer relationship businesses (see Figure 2.5). No matter which core process the business focuses on, the company must still

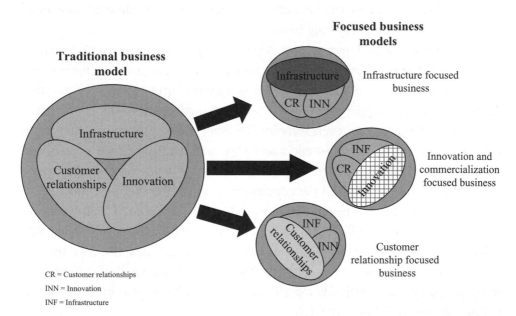

FIGURE 2.5   From a traditional business model to a more focused business model
Source: Based on John Hagel III and Marc Singer (1999) "Unbundling the Corporation", *Harvard Business Review*, March–April, pp. 133–41.

have all three of them. One core process, however, is clearly dominant; the other two are designed to support the dominant one.

For example, EMS companies, such as Hon Hai Precision Industry Company (the world's largest contract manufacturer of electronic products, which also makes many of the components and sub-systems it uses) and Celestica, are primarily infrastructure businesses but they also need both customer relationship and innovation processes. Their customer relationship activities, however, are limited since they are focused on developing and maintaining relationships with a relatively small number of original equipment manufacturers (OEMs) like Apple, IBM, Dell, Philips, Hewlett Packard (HP) and Nintendo, rather than the millions of customers who actually use the products they make. Hon Hai and Celestica's own innovation activities are limited in scope; they are focused heavily on trying to improve the efficiency and effectiveness of their manufacturing, operations and supply chains. A company like Hon Hai develops a great deal of intellectual property around the various manufacturing processes it uses and it actively patents this intellectual property. The product innovation and development activity, however, usually remains the responsibility of the OEM or its innovation partner or partners. In some cases, in order to differentiate their offerings for OEMs, EMS companies will offer design services to those clients. Typically these "innovation" type activities do not generate "revolutionary" new products but rather help the OEMs create evolutionary, commercially viable new products – often developed by assembling modules available from a number of different suppliers who have either developed the intellectual property themselves, or licensed it from innovation companies. This is common in many electronic product categories such as personal computers and mobile phones. Sometimes this product development activity is done by an in-house design team, within the EMS company. In other cases, they might sub-contract the design to an independent design house.

A specialized innovation company, like one of the thousands of small biotechnology companies scattered around the world, will also need some infrastructure and customer relationship activities to support its efforts. Clearly, in this case, infrastructure consists of the laboratories and research equipment the company needs to support its mission. Its customer relationship activities may be oriented towards building relationships with strategic partners, such as pharmaceutical companies, that will be critically important if the firm is to be successful in developing an innovative new product. If a small biotechnology company develops a breakthrough product, it often lacks the infrastructure for conducting large-scale clinical trials and the marketing and sales organization required to commercialize the product successfully on a global basis. At that point, its options are to license the product to a large strategic partner with the necessary capabilities, or to agree to be acquired by one of those companies.

Similarly, a customer relationship business also requires some innovation and infrastructure activities to support its core set of customer relationship activities. A company like Dell has a very sophisticated, largely Internet-based, infrastructure to support its marketing, sales and service activities. This infrastructure allows many of its customers to buy products and services from Dell and even service their own computers, or have their computers serviced, without any direct personal contact with Dell personnel. A significant amount of Dell's resources is spent on innovation to support its customer relationship building activities and trying to stay ahead of its competitors in terms of performance and cost.

Companies are leveraging the specialized players

In many industries, the growth of specialized innovation and infrastructure players has made it much easier for new value players to enter markets. It is now relatively easy for these value competitors, by working with a number of best-in-class specialized players, to offer good enough quality at very attractive prices. In Chapter 1, we cited the examples of a small Swiss company, Telgo, and the larger US company Vizio that have been able to capture significant market shares in different consumer electronics product categories from leading global companies, like Sony, Philips, Siemens and Panasonic, by leveraging design houses and EMS companies in Asia.

In a very different industry, Ryanair was able to offer very attractive prices and grow its business at over 25% per year for several years by leveraging a host of specialized players. Most of its ticketing, ground handling and baggage handling are outsourced to specialized players at each of the numerous airports the carrier utilizes. If the company had to provide its own services at airports where it has very few flights per day, it would be saddled with some very high fixed costs for both staff and equipment. By leveraging specialized infrastructure suppliers Ryanair replaces high fixed costs with relatively low variable costs. Similarly, the company's Internet booking system, food, beverage, and most of its aircraft and engine maintenance and the ancillary services it sells are outsourced to specialized third parties. Thus, Ryanair can focus its efforts on controlling and reducing its costs, growing its customer base and working with the various stakeholders that can influence the growth of the business. While the airline clearly puts a lot of emphasis on trying to drive business costs down by working with suppliers, it needs to understand its customers so that it doesn't totally alienate them by too many cost-cutting efforts. Over time, Ryanair has steadily stripped away elements of the "total experience" passengers expected from an airline. Increasingly, its fare has only covered the basic transportation of a passenger from A to B. If a customer wants any more than that, such as checking a bag, priority boarding, using a credit card or having a beverage, then the customer must pay extra. The company must know enough about its customers' needs to be able to identify additional products or services it can sell to the people visiting its website or flying on its planes. In a sense, Ryanair is a customer relationship focused company, albeit an unusual one.

It is not only value players that are leveraging the specialized players. Many companies that emphasize relational value also take advantage of the same, or similar, networks of suppliers so they can concentrate their efforts on their customers. Cisco – the global market leader in supplying networking equipment and network management for the Internet – is a large and focused company that has been able to achieve global market leadership in its industry. The company provides its customers with industry leading, or close to industry leading, products and services.

For many years most of Cisco's manufacturing and logistics activities have been outsourced to specialized partners, although it monitors quality very carefully. While Cisco did much of the evolutionary development of its product line internally, much of its revolutionary new product development was "outsourced" to start-up companies. In some cases, Cisco served as a venture capital investor in companies working on promising new networking and telecommunications technologies that might be a fit with its current portfolio of products or growth strategy. In some cases, Cisco even encouraged its own employees that had interesting new product ideas to go off and try to develop their ideas. If a start-up was successful in developing products that promised to be commercially successful, Cisco often acquired the company and integrated it into its own organization. Acquisitions have often taken place at about the time the company is launching its first product or service. It has found that at this stage most start-ups have not yet developed a strong culture of their own and can be more readily integrated.

By operating in this manner, Cisco's top management, particularly CEO John Chambers, could focus more time on building and maintaining relationships with key or potential customers. This strategy of focusing on customer relationships, as well as largely outsourcing its infrastructure and innovation activities, has played a major role in making Cisco one of the largest technology companies in the world with 2007 revenues of almost $35 billion.[26]

Distributors represent another increasingly powerful force within many industries. At one point, many distributors were relatively small players who distributed passively the products of the manufacturers they worked with. Currently, some of these distributors are multi-billion dollar multinationals due to the rapid consolidation of distributors in many businesses. Some of these companies are now taking advantage of their growing power and privileged positions within their distribution channels. They are starting to source some of their own good enough products from specialized low cost infrastructure players, allowing them to compete with their branded suppliers. This has become a significant low cost challenge for the traditional branded manufacturers in many industry segments.

The practice of focusing primarily on customer relationships is not just a phenomenon of first-world companies. Bharti Airtel was the largest mobile operator in India by 2007. There is not a lot of fundamental innovation done by mobile phone operators. Most of that is done by the handset manufacturers and their suppliers, as well as by the companies that provide the network infrastructure of base stations, switches and associated software such as Ericsson and Nokia-Siemens. The infrastructure of a mobile operator is critical to its success since it determines, to a significant degree, the quality of telephone service that a customer experiences. Bharti Airtel decided to outsource the design, installation and operation of its network infrastructure to Ericsson and Nokia-Siemens Networks.[27] Those companies look after certain geographical areas for Bharti and are totally responsible for the network. Bharti pays the two companies on the basis of the traffic that they carry on the network and the quality of the service they deliver to Bharti's customers. Bharti has also outsourced the bulk of its information technology services, including customer billing, management of customer accounts and the operation of the Bharti intranet to IBM. Nortel plays a similar role with respect to customer contact centers, including providing a sophisticated voice response solution allowing Bharti customers to complete routine transactions over the phone.

Bharti's founder, Sunil Mittal, believes that without outsourcing many of its infrastructure activities to best-in-class suppliers it would not have been able to grow at anything like the rate it has in recent years. Bharti only needs to focus on developing attractive value propositions to attract new customers and keep its existing customers happy – its partners do the rest. In fiscal 2008, Bharti added 25 million subscribers to its existing base of 37 million. And, although India's mobile phone rates are probably the lowest in the world at $0.02 per minute, the company managed to grow this rapidly in a highly profitable way. In fiscal 2008, Bharti had a net profit of $1.7 billion on revenues of $6.8 billion.[28]

Tata Consultancy Services, one of the world's leading business software services companies based in India, has developed a "global innovation ecosystem" involving academic partners, start-ups, large independent software firms and some of its customers. This ecosystem has helped it to move rapidly from being a low cost provider of basic services to a company able to challenge IBM Global Services and Accenture for very advanced projects.[29]

Companies with focused business models are playing a much bigger role in many industries

As the examples above suggest, companies with focused business models have become significant players in many industries.

Nowadays, in many countries, there are often several mobile telephone players. Generally, three or four are traditional integrated companies with their own network infrastructures, an innovation and commercialization function that develops new service offerings and a significant marketing and sales organization focused on attracting and retaining customers. Like the more traditional companies, Bharti Airtel has a dedicated network infrastructure but one that is built and managed by a strategic partner or partners. The other operators in a country are likely to be virtual mobile network operators (VMNOs). These VMNOs buy time and service wholesale from one of the traditional players with its own network infrastructure such as Vodaphone, Sprint or T-Mobile. These traditional companies may also provide some, or even all, of the other non-network infrastructure, such as customer billing, required to support the operator.

The VMNO may be a telecommunications company that does not want to invest in building its own mobile infrastructure (such as Virgin Mobile or Tele2 in many European countries), a retailer (such as Tesco or Aldi), an entertainment company (Disney briefly had a VMNO in the US), a cable company that wants to offer telephone services, etc. The VMNOs are often targeted to very specific market segments such as a lifestyle segment or a particular language group (e.g., the Turkish community in Germany). There are hundreds of VMNOs operating around the world. Some have struggled to make money but others have prospered.

Virgin Mobile in the UK, which has some four million customers, was sold for more than $1 billion in 2007 – not bad for a company with very few hard assets!

Similarly, there have been a number of focused players in the financial services industry for a number of years. For example, GE through its GE Money business offered private label credit card services to customers. These types of services allowed companies with a strong brand to offer financial service products to their customers. Retailers, and others companies with a strong brand and a willing customer base, were able to offer their customers credit cards, bank accounts, loans, mortgages and various types of insurance products. Tesco is one retailer that offers its UK customers a fairly comprehensive suite of banking and insurance products. Credit cards, in particular, have been popular with many businesses and organizations including airlines and affinity groups such as alumni of universities.

As discussed earlier in the book many, if not most, consumer product markets have a host of specialized players making it very easy for companies with customer relationships to offer a variety of products to their customers. Consumer electronics of all sorts, clothing and sporting goods are just some of the many product categories available. Even in consumer durables – as the Brilliance automotive example in Chapter 1 suggests – some product categories are opening up in the same sort of ways. Almost all the services and major subsystems for cars are available from a variety of suppliers – companies like Magna Steyr in Austria, for example, are available to do final assembly on a contractual basis. In recent years, Magna Steyr has assembled cars for Mercedes-Benz, BMW, Volkswagen, Audi, Jeep, Chrysler and Saab. It also provides a variety of other services to automobile companies. It is possible in the near future that we will see a significant car company emerge that focuses solely on the customer relationship side of the business, outsourcing the innovation and commercialization, and infrastructure activities to third parties.

The pharmaceutical industry is another segment where specialized, focused players have appeared both in the innovation and commercialization, and infrastructure areas. As mentioned earlier, an increasing amount of the breakthrough innovation activity for pharmaceuticals is being shouldered by hundreds of small biotechnology companies. There are any number of specialized firms that will do things like manage the clinical trials; there are also a growing number of players with strong skills in manufacturing pharmaceutical products. The market for these services is expanding quite rapidly and an increasing amount of this activity is being done in Asia, particularly in China and India.

Some large pharmaceutical companies are moving more and more in the direction of outsourcing their manufacturing activities. At least one of the largest players has made it clear that it intends to outsource its manufacturing activities completely. As David Smith, the executive vice-president of operations of Astra-Zeneca said, "Manufacturing for AstraZeneca is not a core activity. AstraZeneca is about innovation and brand-building. There are lots of people and organizations that can manufacture better than we can."[30] On the innovation front, an important element of the strategies of AstraZeneca, Novartis and many other major pharmaceutical companies was to use partnerships, alliances and acquisitions to strengthen their product portfolios.[31] So clearly, the customer relationship activity, including brand building, was the one area that wasn't being "outsourced" to a significant degree.

In the semiconductor industry, many of the companies are "fabless", that is they do not have their own manufacturing plants. For a variety of reasons, including the huge cost and the difficulty of keeping up with the latest manufacturing practices, many semiconductor companies have decided to totally outsource all manufacturing. This has benefited the specialized large contract manufacturers, such as TSMC, UMC and Chartered. Again, many of these contract manufacturers are based in Asia.

We see the emergence of companies that focus on one, or a portion of one, of the core sets of activities in industry after industry. Moving forward, this trend is likely to continue, making it much easier for low cost competitors to access the resources and capabilities they need to compete with traditional companies.

Many more companies are opening their business models

As with the AstraZeneca case, many companies have not yet fully adopted a focused business model, such as a customer relationship model. They are nevertheless taking advantage of the emergence of specialized players. Many companies find themselves challenged by the rising cost of new product development on the one hand and by shortening windows of opportunity on the other – timeframes in which they can exploit the new products before their competitors introduce "copycat" products or services. One way they are cutting new product development costs is by leveraging external development, for example, by licensing technology or innovative products from innovation focused companies. At the same time, some of these companies are also trying to get a better return on their internal R&D activities by licensing some of the intellectual property they have developed. In other cases, they might sell the intellectual property outright or spin off a company to independently exploit the intellectual property. Over time, these more open business models are impacting an increasing number of industries.

P&G is a good example of a large traditional company that has moved in this direction. CEO A.G. Laffley, who has led the company through a very significant turnaround since about 2000, set the objective of having about 50% of P&G's innovations coming from external sources.[32] In a program called "connect and develop", P&G is committed to identifying useful innovative ideas, both inside and outside the company, and connecting these ideas together to develop innovative new products.

The "outsourcing" of innovation activities to specialized players all over the world is accelerating. It is also enhanced by the growth of Internet-based organizations, facilitating the ability of companies to access, or contract for, specialized R&D that they may need, while at the same time making it is easier for the suppliers of intellectual property to contact potential customers.

One of the more successful of these organizations is Innocentive.[33] Originally founded by Eli Lilly, Innocentive was later set up as an independent organization. Companies that may have a technical problem that they either can't solve or don't have the resources to solve in a timely manner are able to post their challenge on the Innocentive website. These "seekers" also indicate the "reward", or amount of money, they are willing to pay if an individual or organization can develop a solution to their challenge. Wide varieties of "solvers", over 160 000 by 2009, have access to the challenge. These "solvers" may be faculty or students at a university, contract research organizations or retired scientists or engineers and could be located anywhere in the world. If one of these "solvers" is able to find a satisfactory solution to the challenge, they then receive the reward. In essence, this theoretically allows a company to tap into the brainpower of thousands of people all over the world with a range of skills and experience that are unlikely to be matched by any one company's R&D organization. A number of other similar types of organizations are focusing on other application areas. Some, such as yet2.com, also make it much easier for a company to access "surplus" intellectual property that companies have developed and are willing to license or sell. These networks can be accessed and used by low cost competitors, as well as traditional companies. Not surprisingly, P&G has become a significant user of several of these services as it has tried to meet its target of obtaining 50% of its innovation from external sources.

Boeing also handed over control of some important elements of the Boeing 787 development to suppliers, both to take advantage of their particular areas of expertise and to try to reduce the overall time to market and cost.[34]

In all of these cases, the users of these networks benefit from working with suppliers who are working simultaneously with many other companies and who are also facing challenging issues. The suppliers learn from these many assignments and can progress more rapidly down their learning curves than could most in-house suppliers in an integrated company, that likely face a more limited set of challenges.

But there are significant risks in relying more on strategic partners

The move to a more specialized business model, with greater reliance on strategic partners, is not without its risks. Boeing suffered delays on the 787 project when some suppliers were not able to deliver their work on time.[35] Clearly, given the role these strategic partners play in the success of a company, the risk is often significantly greater than it would be if one were dealing with the typical supplier of a component, sub-system or service. If the partner fails in a major way, this can have serious repercussions on the company's brand and reputation. Mattel, the world's largest toy company, suffered significant financial losses and damage to its brand image when some of its Chinese manufacturing partners' sub-suppliers substituted cheaper, and unauthorized, lead-based paints for the paints specified in the contracts.[36] While most companies have extensive quality control systems in place to catch these kinds of problems, it is impossible to control everything. Ultimately, it depends on a high degree of trust between the company and its partners.

In addition, there is a risk of having intellectual property or trade secret information leak to competitors through their strategic suppliers. A company can try to protect itself by obtaining patents and employing non-disclosure agreements and non-compete clauses. But there are enough examples of products being copied or even counterfeited, particularly in China, to indicate that these legal safeguards clearly are not enough in all instances. Again, mutual trust is critical.

In the extreme, if a company decides to commit to a focused business model it is, in a sense, "putting all its eggs in one basket". It is betting that it can be, or become, extremely good at managing customer relationships, for example, and developing strong working relationships with what are sometimes dozens of the right business partners in order that it can take on all-comers in its industry.

In some cases, traditional companies see committing to a new business model as the biggest risk. They fear not being able to implement the change successfully or executing it as well as the traditional model with which they have grown up. And it is true that many of the most successful examples of companies that have adopted one of the specialized business models are those that entered the business with this type of model either initially or early in their development, before a more traditional culture and systems had become entrenched.

Despite the risks in some industries, there may be no choice. A network of best-in-class specialized players might perform much better than any of the traditional players. The traditional players may have to change to remain competitive.

Total solution coordinators are helping some companies leverage these networks

The growth of companies providing one-stop solutions for customers that are seeking to introduce products is a trend that has made it much easier for new players to enter markets. A leading company of this kind is Li & Fung, based in Hong Kong.[37] Li & Fung is a "network orchestrator" that will provide its clients with an end-to-end solution including product design, raw material sourcing, production planning, factory sourcing, manufacturing control, quality control, export documentation and shipping. It provides this service for such products as clothing, footwear, toys, sporting goods and handicrafts. Li & Fung owns no factories itself but instead orchestrates a network of design houses and suppliers to provide its customers with solutions. It has relationships with about 10 000 suppliers of products and services, in almost 40 countries, which enables it to provide the complete solutions that its customers are seeking. Many of Li & Fung's customers are retailers looking for private label products; companies such as Tesco, The Limited, Abercrombie and Fitch, and Avon Products.[38] For each customer, Li & Fung selects and creates a custom supply chain designed to deliver the right product at the right price and at the agreed time based on the customers' exact specifications. The whole network is linked together by a sophisticated IT and logistics system.

Li & Fung and other similar "total solutions" companies, such as the original design manufacturers (ODMs) in the electronics industry often based in Greater China, make it very easy for new players to enter a given market. They can look after the entire sourcing issue for a principal – in North America, Europe or any-where else in the world – so that the company can focus its efforts on developing channels and customers in its market. If the company lacks a well-known brand name that can support premium prices, then it is likely to compete in its market as a low cost or value player.

GROWING SUPPORT FOR LOW COST COMPETITORS

Other players in the value chain are encouraging the growth of low cost competitor companies. In numerous business-to-business markets, including retailers dealing with their suppliers, we see businesses actively encouraging new suppliers to enter the market and supporting their entry in various ways. Consumers in many business-to-consumer markets are increasingly willing to purchase products and services provided by low cost players, particularly if these products are sold by a trusted retailer.

Low cost entrants sometimes have powerful supporters

One important factor influencing the growth of low cost competitors has been the efforts of many companies to bring in new low cost players to improve their bar-gaining power relative to their traditional customers or suppliers. This would potentially result in these companies capturing more of the profitability in their value chains.

Unilever, Proctor & Gamble and some pharmaceutical companies, for example, are believed to have played a role in encouraging Indian and Chinese companies to enter certain specialty chemical markets to provide price competition to Western specialty chemical companies. Many of these specialty chemicals used in personal care, household product and pharmaceutical categories were originally patent protected. As a result, the Western specialty chemical companies could often initially charge their customers relatively high prices. When the chemical ingredients came off patent, some personal care and other product manufacturers encouraged Asian manufacturers to enter the market by committing to buy some of their output. This gave them access to lower cost suppliers and put pressure on the Western specialty chemical companies to lower their prices.

As mentioned in Chapter 1, almost 50% of the world's cement is sold (and manufactured) in China. Not surprisingly, a number of domestic suppliers of cement equipment and plants have emerged in China to meet the massive demand for new cement plants. These companies can build plants in China for a fraction of the price that their Western competitors can. These Chinese suppliers are now competing for contracts to build plants outside of China. While the prices the Chinese companies charge outside of China are considerably higher than the prices within China, they have still been able to undercut Western suppliers by about 30–40%. CBMI, the leading Chinese manufacturer, offered all types of cement manufacturing equipment and had the capability to build "turnkey" cement plants anywhere in the world. It has worked with most of the leading cement companies, including Holcim, Lafarge, Heidelberg and Italcementi, in either China or elsewhere. Since these leading companies were very concerned about the quality of the equipment and the quality of the construction of the cement plants, they often closely supervised both the manufacturing of the equipment and the erection of the plants. In some cases, they hired ex-employees, including retirees, from leading Western cement equipment companies to monitor CBMI's work. The feedback CBMI received from these highly experienced engineers helped accelerate its learning process and helped it to rapidly close the gaps between it and its Western competitors.

For decades, a common route for offshore low cost competitors to break into a developed country market has been through major retailers. Japanese television manufacturers first broke into the North American market by selling private label televisions to mass merchants like Sears. Sears educated its suppliers about the needs and tastes of North American consumers so that they could design products that would sell well in its stores. Today that process is much more sophisticated. Companies like Wal-Mart and Tesco have sourcing operations based in China that work closely with potential suppliers, ensuring that they will develop products that will meet both the needs of their customers around the world and their own sourcing standards. With the retail sector's increasing concentration around the world, new players, including low cost players, can quickly gain access to a major part of the global market by working with a few big retailers. Twenty years ago, this was much more difficult since retail markets were more fragmented and some smaller retailers could only be reached through more complex distribution systems.

In some cases, if the end-use market is price elastic, a supplier can expand the overall demand for its products by encouraging and helping new value players who will compete on price, thereby increasing both its sales and profitability. Intel, as mentioned earlier in the chapter, has done this very effectively in the PC and server microprocessor markets. The company has taken a number of steps to make it very easy for new low cost competitors to enter the market – by supporting standardization and modularization of the PC product, and by designing, and in some cases building, the motherboards for PCs, it has eliminated all the difficult engineering for a new entrant. Through the Intel Inside campaign the company sought to convince customers that the most important thing about a PC was the brand of the microprocessor, not the brand of the manufacturer. As long as an unknown value competitor could place an Intel sticker on the PC, it would gain some degree of market acceptance.

In the case of the more complex servers, where the risk to the buyer of the product not interfacing properly with other hardware and software is bigger, Intel went one step further; they certified that their "packages" of server components, sold to small assemblers, would work with the hardware and software from other companies. This allowed these small Intel customers, who may be relatively unknown new entrants, to compete more effectively with HP, IBM and Dell, thus diluting the power of these big customers.[39]

Customers are increasingly willing to buy from low cost players

The increasing presence of value players in many markets, and the intense competition between these value players, has clearly driven prices to unprecedented low levels. These extremely low prices have clearly stimulated demand for many products and services. One study of low fare airline passengers suggested that about 60% of the passengers on those carriers would not have flown if there had not been a low fare airline available.[40] Of this 60%, 70% would not have traveled at all (the others would have traveled by car or rail).

It also appears that wealthy customers in many countries seem to be increasingly willing to buy inexpensive products and services, across many product categories, that meet their needs. There no longer seems to be a stigma attached to buying value products or services or shopping at value retailers, even among the wealthy. For example, in a recent study of shoppers in Germany over 90% of the respondents agreed with the statement, "Buying in discounters is as well accepted socially as buying elsewhere." Many individual customers seem willing to buy both inexpensive and expensive products in the same general product category, depending upon their psychographic characteristics, the use occasion, the application, etc. One day on a business trip, they might fly Cathay Pacific's or Lufthansa's business class, and on the next day fly Ryanair or Southwest Airlines to go on vacation. Similarly, some people may shop for fashionable low cost clothing at Zara or H&M but purchase accessories from Coach or Gucci. Many of these people see themselves as "smart" shoppers.

CHALLENGE QUESTIONS

Which companies in your market are the performance leaders? Which are the price leaders? Which are the relational value leaders?

Which core value did your company emphasize ten years ago (or when it was founded)? Has it changed? What is it today?

In your markets is there significant change occurring in the relative size of the segments that focus on each of the three core values? Which segments are growing and which ones are declining? What are the implications for your business? Should you be emphasizing a different core value in five years from now?

Is there any evidence in your market that more focused innovation, infrastructure and customer relationship companies have emerged or are emerging? If it has not happened yet, do you expect it to happen soon?

Are the traditionally structured companies in your industry under pressure from these new players; if not, do you expect them to come under pressure in the next few years?

Are there examples of low cost competitors that are leveraging focused players?

Are there any total solution, or network orchestrators like Li & Fung that can help companies like yours put together supply chains that will deliver competitive products?

Are there seeker-solver or similar networks such as Innocentive or yet2.com that already serve or partially serve your industry? Could you leverage them?

CHAPTER 3

Understanding how low cost competitors play the game

Low cost competitors are posing a serious threat to traditional companies in many industries, as several of the examples outlined so far in the book have demonstrated. So, how can executives and managers in traditional companies develop effective strategies to compete with them? First, they must gain a deeper understanding of how they operate and how they play the game. Even if they choose not to compete head on with the low cost players, traditional companies can learn from them and develop improved ways of running their own businesses more effectively and efficiently.

In this chapter, we will develop a better understanding of how the successful low cost competitors operate. We will begin by taking a close look at two well-known successful low cost competitors, Ryanair and ING DIRECT. These companies will be used as a foundation for developing some of the common themes that not only characterize their achievements but also the success of low cost players in a variety of industries, both in business-to-business and business-to-consumer markets. We will then turn to the lessons that traditional companies can learn from these and other low cost competitors.

RYANAIR

Performance has been outstanding

In an industry known for its generally dismal financial performance, Ryanair has been a standout performer for about 15 years. The International Air Traffic Association estimated that the global airline industry lost over $40 billion in the five-year period of 2001–2005.[41] Ryanair was consistently profitable during this period, and in many recent years it has been the world's most profitable major airline in terms of operating profit margin. For example, in 2006 its operating profit margin was 21% – two to three times as high as Emirates (11%), Southwest Airlines (10%), Singapore Airlines (9%), easyJet (7%), British Airways (7%) and Lufthansa (7%).[42]

Founded in 1985, Ryanair initially challenged the Aer Lingus and British Airways (BA) duopoly on the London–Dublin route.[43] Over its first five years, it lost about £20 million. Since the original business model was clearly not working, Tony Ryan, the airline's founder, dispatched his former tax accountant and adviser to the US to study Southwest Airlines. Michael O'Leary returned and recommended that they adapt and improve the Southwest model for the European market by providing a no-frills, low-fare service on an extremely low cost base. Working with Conor Hayes, the new chief executive of Ryanair, they began to implement the new strategy in 1992. In 1994, O'Leary became the CEO. Once the new business model was firmly in place, Ryanair began to grow rapidly, and by 2008, it had a fleet of over 160 Boeing 737 planes, carried 51 million passengers and had revenues of €2.7 billion and after-tax profits of €480 million.[44]

Value proposition is crystal clear

Many Ryanair customers used the airline to visit friends and relatives, take a holiday or pursue other leisure activities. For others, Ryanair was an important, even essential, element supporting their daily lives. Some passengers flew Ryanair to make frequent trips between jobs (sometimes relatively low-paying) in countries like the UK to see their families living in Eastern or Southern Europe. Other wealthy passengers might have their primary home in one part of Europe and commute to relatively high paying jobs in other parts of Europe, perhaps on a weekly basis.

The Ryanair value proposition as articulated by CEO Michael O'Leary was a good fit with these customer segments:

> We guarantee to give you the lowest airfare. You get a safe flight.
> You get a normally on-time flight. That's the package. We don't and
> won't give you anything more on top of that … We care for our
> customers in the most fundamental way possible – we don't screw
> them every time we fly them.[45]

Ryanair's service was delivered by the fleet of very new Boeing 737s operating largely out of secondary or regional airports in Europe and North Africa. Its prices were consistently the lowest of any airline flying the same routes. All tickets were sold over the Internet or by telephone. The company made limited use of advertising but the advertising was sometimes crude, "cheeky" and quite controversial. Often easyJet, Ryanair's largest competitor, was targeted in the ads that focused on Ryanair's low prices. Michael O'Leary and his team were very effective at public relations and at exploiting every opportunity to generate free publicity, often positioning Ryanair as fighting the Establishment on behalf of the consumer.

Business model is innovative and focused

Ryanair copied many of the elements of the Southwest Airlines' business model, including using a single type of aircraft (the Boeing 737 – the 800 series by 2007), a point-to-point service and no assigned seating. The planes had no reclining seats, window blinds or seat pockets, which collectively contributed to lower maintenance costs, faster cleaning of planes and shorter flight turnaround times. The use of one type of aircraft resulted in savings and efficiencies in many areas, including spare parts and maintenance, training of flight crew and cabin attendants, standardization of ground services and the ability to replace any plane that was delayed, or had maintenance problems, with any other available plane (particularly easy since all of the Ryanair planes had identical 189 passenger capacities). Unlike the hub and spoke service operated by most major airlines, point-to-point service meant that there were no flight delays caused by waiting for connecting passengers from incoming flights. Passengers who booked "connecting" Ryanair flights through a "hub" had to do the bookings separately and did so at their own risk. They were also totally responsible for getting their baggage from the first flight to the second flight.

As mentioned earlier, Ryanair used, almost exclusively, secondary or regional airports rather than primary airports – many of these were located at a considerable distance from the city they were named after and nominally served. For example, Ryanair served Frankfurt through Frankfurt-Hahn airport, located over 120 kilometers by road from the center of Frankfurt. Hahn had originally been a NATO airbase. With the end of the Cold War, the US Air Force withdrew from the base in the early 1990s, creating local unemployment but leaving some very good airport infrastructure. The local state and municipalities banded together to launch a civilian airport. The airport had some success in the cargo area but very limited success as a passenger airport, attracting only a small number of charter flights. However, in 1999, the airport offered an attractive ten-year package to Ryanair and the company began operations there. Largely as a result of attracting Ryanair passengers, traffic grew from less than 30 000 in 1998 to more than four million in 2007 – about 95% of these passengers in 2007 were using Ryanair.[46] To a large degree, Ryanair "created" Frankfurt-Hahn airport. The same scenario was repeated at several other locations in Western Europe; Ryanair's expansion into Eastern Europe often leveraged airport facilities that were originally built for the Warsaw Pact air forces.

In order to attract Ryanair and create jobs, the airport authorities often offered the company very low landing fees, low cost ground services and money to support Ryanair's marketing efforts. In some cases, this marketing support was substantial. In the case of Charleroi (Brussels), the airport paid Ryanair €4 per passenger brought into the airport for up to 26 flights per day, for a period of 15 years.[47] The airline also aggressively played one secondary airport off against another in order to extract the best possible terms.

Where possible, Ryanair preferred to use remote gates at airports because they were often cheaper, as well as gates without air bridges. The absence of air bridges meant that a Ryanair plane could unload passengers using stairs at both the front and rear of the aircraft. Avoiding air bridges not only saved money but also speeded up the loading and unloading of passengers. It was not uncommon for all the passengers on a full Ryanair flight to disembark within five minutes.

Another key element of Ryanair's business model was outsourcing as many activities as possible to credible suppliers. The servicing of engines was outsourced to General Electric. CAE, a manufacturer of aircraft simulators for pilot training, provided training services to Ryanair standards for prospective pilots; the pilots were responsible for paying for their own training. Recruitment and training of cabin crew was outsourced to staffing agencies and again, the cabin crew was expected to pay for its own training. With the exception of Dublin, most ground services were outsourced to specialist firms or the airport authority itself.

Like many other low cost carriers, Ryanair had only one class of service and all tickets were one-way tickets. There were no "frills" such as frequent flyer programs, free drinks and snacks on the plane or assigned seating. The absence of assigned seating encouraged passengers to check in early since boarding order was based on the time the passenger checked in for the flight.

The air carrier did not use travel agents; almost all the tickets were sold over the Internet while the remainder were sold through Ryanair call centers. There were no physical tickets – passengers just received a confirmation number to check in at the airport if they were not using Internet check-in.

Ryanair did not use a typical yield management system. In an effort to optimize the revenue yield from a given flight on a particular date, yield management systems adjust fares for a particular flight, up or down on a daily basis, depending upon actual bookings relative to expected bookings. Instead, Ryanair used a simpler system. Each flight had perhaps half a dozen fares associated with it. The first x% of the passengers booking the flight got the lowest fare; the next y% of the passengers booking the flight got the next lowest fare and so on. Ryanair offered 70% of the seats on every flight at one of the two lowest fares.[48] The final few per cent of the passengers paid the highest fare, which could be as expensive as €250. This, of course, encouraged passengers to book as early as possible. In some cases, passengers booked flights very early at a low fare, even if they knew there was a probability that they might not use the flight; the cost was that low. Since Ryanair had a strict policy of no refunds, and it was expensive to switch to a different flight, there was a "no show" rate that averaged about 8%. This meant that Ryanair "pocketed" the fare plus any fees and taxes, even though it had not delivered the service for which the customer had paid.

One of the pricing moves that Ryanair used to great effect for many years was periodically offering "free seats" where there was no charge for the flight itself – the passenger was only responsible for paying the assorted taxes, fees and charges. In some years, about 25% of its seats were "given away" in this manner. In late 2007, after the authorities required airlines to show all-inclusive fares in their ads and on their websites, Ryanair offered 500 000 seats at no charge at all.

While there was no "free" food or beverages on the flights, the airline did sell food, beverages, scratch cards and a variety of other products and services. It earned a commission on all mobile phone calls made during a flight and sold a variety of complementary products and services over its website – one of Europe's most frequently visited Internet sites. Ryanair offered other services such as flight insurance, rental cars, ground transportation tickets, Ryanair-branded credit cards, car insurance, airport parking and access to an online casino. They also had very limited baggage allowances, stringently enforced with high charges for excess weight. Collectively, these were called ancillary revenues. By 2008, Ryanair was generating ancillary revenues of € 10 per passenger, the highest in the world. Many of these ancillary revenues had very few associated costs and were an important contribution to the bottom line.

In 2006, Ryanair became the first major airline to eliminate a free checked baggage allowance. Passengers had to pay £ 5 to check a bag, if they did so when booking the flight, and £ 10 if they decided to check it later at the airport. This fee was later raised to discourage customers from checking bags at all.

The company's employee compensation system and incentive system for contractors was an important element in Ryanair's business model. Most of its employees received a significant proportion of their compensation through incentive payments. Reservations agents, check-in agents, cabin attendants, pilots and Ryanair ground services personnel were all incentivized in ways that would encourage them to enhance revenues and/or control costs. For example, about half of the cabin crews' total compensation was based on incentive payments for such activities as on-board food and beverage sales and the number of flight segments they had flown in a month. This policy of incentive payments based on achieving objectives, such as turnaround time and charging for overweight baggage was also extended to Ryanair contractors. By 2007, about 56% of Ryanair's payroll was productivity based.[49]

Another important element of Ryanair's business model was very low advertising and public relations expenses. The air carrier's advertising focused heavily on price and seat sales. Both the advertising and website were generally quite amateurish in appearance but they screamed "low price". Ryanair and Michael O'Leary were famous for creating publicity stunts and irreverent advertising that attracted extensive media coverage. In one case, Ryanair ran an ad that apparently featured the Pope revealing the fourth secret of Fatima to a nun. The "secret" was that "only Ryanair.com guarantees the lowest fares on the Internet". The ad created a furor among the general public, the press and the Catholic Church in Ireland. Even the Vatican press office got involved by firing off a press release that reverberated around the world. For Ryanair it meant about $ 8.5 million of free publicity for an investment of less than $ 1000.[50] While this "cheeky", controversial, low-budget advertising and public relations seemed to be quite effective with many customers, others, particularly customers from certain cultures where this approach was less acceptable, found it distasteful and offensive.

Extreme focus on cost control

Ryanair had an extreme focus on cost control and cost minimization, as the discussion above suggests.

Ryanair also attempted to minimize its fixed costs. Through a combination of luck and shrewd planning, most of its plane orders with Boeing were placed when the market for new aircraft was extremely depressed, such as after the 2001 terrorist attacks in New York and during the Iraq crisis in 2003. Some industry analysts estimated that Ryanair extracted discounts of more than 50% from Boeing for large aircraft orders during these time periods.[51]

Once the airline had made fixed cost investments, it tried to leverage these investments to the maximum. By utilizing airports that were relatively uncongested, it had very fast plane turnarounds, so planes spent more time in the air generating revenues. Ryanair also leveraged the planes by selling the exterior to advertisers as flying billboards and seat back space to other advertisers. It also eliminated many fixed costs by converting them into variable costs through its various outsourcing activities.

In some cases, it also off-loaded costs in unconventional ways. As mentioned above some groups of employees, such as pilots and cabin crew, paid for their own training. This perhaps not only saved money but also increased the motivation of the employees to learn.

The cost control culture at Ryanair was emphasized in many ways, some of which, on the surface at least, were quite petty. For example, employees were reportedly prohibited from charging their personal mobile phones at work because the power usage would increase Ryanair's costs.[52] While many of the individual cost reduction and revenue enhancement measures taken by Ryanair seemed fairly minor, the cumulative impact on the company's revenues and costs were significant. Figure 3.1 compares the per passenger revenues and costs of Ryanair with easyJet, the other major low cost carrier in Europe for the year ending March 2008. A very successful airline in its own right, easyJet was one of the world's top 30 airlines in terms of operating profit margin. At the time of the comparison, easyJet and Ryanair had similar geographical coverage with a significant percentage of their revenue from flights originating or terminating in the UK or Eire. easyJet focused on leisure and price conscious business travelers and its airports were more likely to be primary airports than were Ryanair's. Even with these considerations, the cost differences between Ryanair and easyJet in the figure are

	Ryanair year ending 31 March 2008	easyJet ending 31 March 2008	Difference
Operating revenue	€	€	€
Scheduled revenues	43.70	62.14	18.44
Ancillary revenues	9.58	8.42	-1.66
Total revenues	**53.28**	**73.01**	**17.28**
Operating expenses			
Staff	5.60	8.26	2.66
Aircraft ownership and maintenance	5.99	9.16	3.17
Marketing and distribution	0.34	2.50	2.16
Route charges	5.09	5.78	0.69
Airport and handling charges	7.78	18.37	10.59
Fuel and oil	15.54	18.03	2.49
Other	2.48	4.00	1.61
Total operating expenses	**41.57**	**66.10**	**23.36**
Operating profit before non-recurring items and goodwill	**10.55**	**4.46**	**6.09**

FIGURE 3.1   Comparison of per passenger revenues and costs for Ryanair and easyJet
Note: Author's estimates based on Ryanair and easyJet published financial data.

quite dramatic with Ryanair having operating expenses per passenger almost 40% lower than easyJet. With this extremely low cost position, Ryanair's operating profit per passenger was more than two times higher than easyJet's, despite easyJet's average fare being over 40% higher.

As Figure 3.2 suggests, Ryanair was also very successful in driving down its controllable costs year by year. Despite the significant increase in fuel costs during the period between 2004 and 2008, Ryanair's average fare remained virtually unchanged, while its ancillary revenues grew.

Created a virtuous cycle

By 2008, Ryanair clearly had become the dominant low cost carrier in much of Europe. Despite facing more than 50 low cost competitors scattered across the continent, it seemed to be going from strength to strength. In fact, it benefited from a "virtuous cycle" (see Figure 3.3). Its low prices attracted more customers. The sheer number of customers and the scale of its operations gave it economies of scale that resulted in lower costs. The number of customers, and its high and

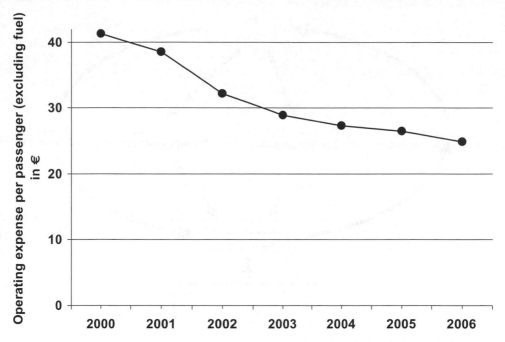

FIGURE 3.2   Ryanair's cost per passenger (excluding fuel) from 2000 to 2006
Source: Based on chart "Ryanair effect – Low Cost Focus (excluding fuel)" in presentation made on Ryanair Investor Day, 29 September 2006, New York City.

consistent growth rate, gave it a lot of negotiating power with suppliers like Boeing, General Electric and the airports. Given its track record, potential new airports for Ryanair bases would often offer attractive terms to get Ryanair to use their facilities, especially since the airline had shown that it could build passenger traffic quickly and create many jobs in the region. Similarly, complementors, such as its car rental partner and the other companies that provided services through the Ryanair website, were willing to offer relatively generous terms to Ryanair because of the volume of business it could deliver. Again, these better terms and prices either enhanced revenues or lowered costs and they all contributed to the excellent operating profit margins. Some of the lowering of costs was passed on to customers in the form of lower fares (after adjusting for inflation) that helped to generate more customers, making Ryanair even more attractive to complementors and giving it more bargaining power with suppliers, thereby perpetuating the virtuous cycle.

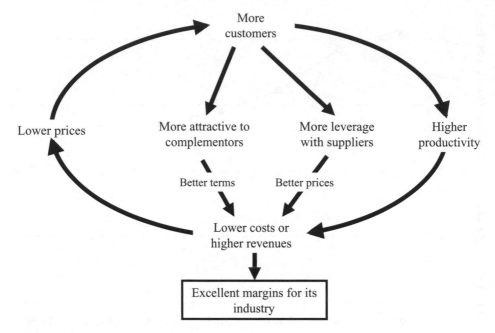

FIGURE 3.3   Ryanair's virtuous cycle

So far ... so good

By 2008, in the markets it served, Ryanair was firmly positioned in the minds of most customers as having the industry's lowest airfares. Many customers believed that if Ryanair served a particular route, its fares would be the lowest – in many cases, they would just book with Ryanair and not even check the prices of competing airlines.

Ryanair, however, was not universally loved. It stimulated both strong positive and strong negative reactions from customers. Most believed that it delivered on its value proposition and that on objective measures, such as fares, punctuality, lost bags and flight cancellations (see Figure 3.4), it was well ahead of its major European competitors. But the company's rigid adherence to its own rules created some ill will among passengers, generating word-of-mouth publicity and comments on websites and blogs that could be quite negative. The negative stories about enforcement of rules, however, did have a silver lining for Ryanair. Passengers quickly recognized that check-in rules, baggage allowances and the no-refund policy would be rigidly and uniformly applied. Therefore, it made no sense to argue with the staff; it was just better to oblige and adjust to the rules. The

Airline	Average fare €	% of flights on time	Bags missing per 1000 passengers	% of flights completed
Ryanair	44	88	0.5	99.6
Air France	267	84	17.5	97.6
Lufthansa	235	81	15.1	98.4
easyJet	66	80	Not available	Not available
Aer Lingus	94	72	Not available	Not available
British Airways	324	58	28.9	96.1

FIGURE 3.4 Comparison of average fares, flight punctuality, lost bags per thousand passengers and percentage of flights completed for major European airlines
Source: Based on chart "Europe's No.1 for Customer Service" in roadshow presentation of Ryanair's full year results, 31 March 2008.

publicity about unfortunate passengers who had gotten into difficulties with the airline over the rules helped to "train" other customers. Inconsistent enforcement of rules, such as the maximum size and weight of carry-on bags, at other airlines encouraged passengers to take a chance and test the limits. This led to more arguments between passengers and staff, created slowdowns at airports, less efficiency and both passenger and staff dissatisfaction.

Financially, Ryanair performed very consistently and very well during a period when many other airlines struggled to achieve acceptable returns; by 2006, it was the world's largest international carrier in terms of passengers carried, though obviously not in terms of revenues.[53]

ING DIRECT USA

Borrowed with pride

ING DIRECT is the direct banking business unit of ING Groep, a global financial services corporation headquartered in the Netherlands. ING DIRECT originated in 1995, when ING executives were looking for ways to expand into retail banking outside of the Netherlands.[54] They were aware of some initial successes with a direct banking business model in such countries as the Netherlands and the UK.

After some internal discussions, Canada was chosen as a pilot market to see if ING could develop a successful direct banking model that could later be exported to other countries.

In 1996, ING hired Arkadi Kuhlmann, who had previously worked for a few other financial services companies, as President and CEO to lead the initiative in Canada. The new bank faced some significant challenges. Five large banks dominated the retail banking market in Canada and the ING brand was both foreign and largely unknown in the market. Some observers expected that it would be a major challenge to develop a credible product, with an easily communicated value proposition, attractive enough to motivate Canadian consumers to move their savings to ING DIRECT.

ING started out with two products in 1997: an Investment Savings Account and Guaranteed Investment Certificates, both of which paid high interest rates with no minimum balances, fees or service charges. There were no retail branches and the accounts did not have ATM access; customers were served by a call center that was open 24 hours a day, seven days a week. Internet access was added in 1999. The company launched the product in the country's largest and wealthiest regional market with an outdoor advertising and print campaign with memorable hard-hitting ads. The advertising stressed the interest rate advantage that ING offered relative to the leading Canadian banks (sometimes with direct comparisons) and the lack of fees and service charges. ING also ran a forceful, product-oriented TV advertising campaign in Canada featuring an unknown Dutch actor, again stressing ING's superior interest rates and the absence of fees and service charges. ING's direct banking operation was an immediate success in its initial market and the bank began a regional rollout. ING Bank of Canada became the first successful retail bank launched in Canada in over 30 years and became profitable in 2001.

Arkadi Kuhlmann and his team had little time to savor their accomplishments. In September 2000, with initial success in Canada assured, Kuhlmann and most of his top management team moved to the US to prepare for the launch of ING DIRECT USA.

Appealing value proposition

ING DIRECT's target customers in the US were middle-income customers interested in increasing significantly the interest they earned on their savings and/or benefiting from lower interest rates on mortgages or loans. As in Canada, the value proposition emphasized these benefits and the absence of fees and service charges.

The ING brand attributes emphasized simplicity and straightforwardness. The color orange (a link to ING Groep's Dutch heritage) was distinctive and stood out from the conservative blue or green employed by many other traditional banks. In 2000, the initial product offered in the US was a high-interest savings account with no fees, no service charges and no minimum balance. Later in 2000, the product line was extended gradually to include Orange Certificates of Deposit with terms from six months to five years. Then, in 2002, ING DIRECT made available its Orange Investment Accounts initially offering six mutual funds, a number that increased over time. On the asset side, Orange Mortgages were offered beginning in 2001 and an Orange Home Equity loan product followed later the same year.

In all of these cases, the product pricing was straightforward with no fees or service charges and they were generally more attractively priced than similar offerings from traditional banks.

Following the Canadian model, accounts could not be accessed through ING branches or ATMs but rather through mail, Internet and telephone call centers available 24 hours a day, seven days a week. Customers could transfer money electronically to and from their traditional bank accounts as needed and use their accounts at these banks to access cash, make deposits and pay bills. Following a tactic that had been used in Canada, ING DIRECT did open four ING Cafés in Los Angeles, New York, Philadelphia and Wilmington, Delaware (where the head office for ING DIRECT USA is located). The cafés were open to customers and potential customers; they were a place where they could have a coffee, surf the Internet, buy ING-branded merchandise and get information about ING DIRECT or any of its products. From Kuhlmann's perspective, the cafés drove the point home to customers that ING DIRECT was not a traditional bank but one that was simple, easy to use and human in approach.

The ING DIRECT marketing approach was unique and was implemented with great flair. Some of its marketing was educational – Planet Orange was a site where children and their parents and teachers could learn about earning, saving and investing money. In addition to on-line advertising and simple TV advertising, ING DIRECT used unconventional marketing tactics such as providing free gasoline in Los Angeles and organizing marketing events like "Movie on the Beach" day in California, "Freedom Ride" in San Francisco (with Harley Davidson to raise money for a children's fund) and a "Hot Air Balloon Ride" in Phoenix, Arizona. The idea behind these marketing events was to create face-to-face experiences where people could get to know the ING DIRECT brand. All attracted a lot of free media attention. Despite the fact that some of these events were quite expensive, ING DIRECT's acquisition cost per customer was well below the industry average ($100 vs. $300 to $400 for other banks). The sense of "theatre" that accompanied all of its marketing events helped set ING DIRECT apart from traditional banks. Kuhlmann also positioned the bank as one that was dedicated to bringing the American customer "back to savings".

ING DIRECT strove to be an operationally excellent company. It put a lot of emphasis on having a very user-friendly website where customers could find the information they needed and complete their transactions as quickly and effortlessly as possible. In fact, Kuhlmann believed that IT and marketing were so interlinked in the business that he put one executive in charge of both to ensure a high degree of integration. An enormous emphasis was placed on creating satisfied customers. Kuhlmann recognized that when a customer called his or her bank, being transferred from one person to another was a major source of customer frustration and dissatisfaction. He instituted a policy of calls never being redirected at ING DIRECT (one touch, only touch). The associates answering the phones were encouraged to create a spontaneous, or "principle-driven", experience rather than a "rules-based", or scripted one. ING DIRECT's efforts to satisfy customers seemed to be successful. In a study done in 2003, about 80% of its customers in the US reported that customer service at ING DIRECT was "much better" (51%) or "somewhat better" (31%), in comparison to other financial institutions.[55] Not surprisingly, some 40% of new customers were the result of recommendations from existing ING DIRECT customers.

Early success

In 2000, when ING DIRECT opened in the US, there was still a great deal of skepticism about whether direct banking would work there. Citibank and Banc One had both opened direct banks in the late 1990s, but they decided to merge them back into their traditional physical banks in 2000. ING DIRECT, however, was a huge and immediate success. Within six months of launch, it had 100000 customers and $1.3 billion in assets, and it became profitable in its second year of operation. By 2006, it had 4.6 million customers, $47 billion in deposits and almost $350 million in pre-tax profits. While $47 billion in deposits represented only a 0.7% market share of all bank deposits in the US, ING DIRECT had 52% of Internet bank deposits.[56]

Competition finally responds and ING DIRECT raises the stakes

The competitive environment in the US banking market had intensified by 2006 and ING DIRECT was under increasing pressure. This pressure was coming both from new entrants and from the traditional banks. Credit card companies, some brokerage firms (particularly e-Trade) and banks with strong lending operations all saw direct banking as a relatively cheap source of deposits that could be loaned at good rates. Traditional banks, which had the primary banking relationship with ING customers, were increasingly offering a good rate (often matching or exceeding the ING DIRECT rate) on high-yield savings accounts and thus causing some customers to question the value of having an ING DIRECT savings account.

ING DIRECT decided on a very aggressive response to the deepening competitive challenge. In late 2006 it decided to introduce a high interest rate checking or payment account called Electric Orange. Customers had access to the account through a MasterCard debit card, "electronic checks" (electronic transfers between two accounts) and an electronic bill payment service. There were no paper checks, but customers were able to request electronically that ING DIRECT print a check and mail it free of charge. The customers also had "free" access to their accounts through a third-party nationwide network of 32 000 ATMs. A tiered and high interest rate was paid on all balances. In mid-2007, customers with less than $50 000 earned about 1% less than they would with an Orange Savings Account. However, those customers with high balances in their checking account (more than $50 000) actually earned higher interest rates than they would in an Orange Savings Account. As usual, there were no fees or minimum balances for the basic account, although there were fees if a customer wanted to do something out of the ordinary such as a stop payment on a check.

This new checking account product clearly was more complex than the earlier products and departed somewhat from ING's traditional very simple value propositions for its products. However, relative to the products of most traditional banks the ING payment account was simple and straightforward. It also was a very difficult challenge for ING DIRECT's competitors to respond to. Traditional banks typically paid almost no interest on the balances in their customers' checking accounts and many had minimum balances and/or charged handsome fees. At a typical traditional bank, with about 20% of its deposits in checking accounts, the cost of matching the ING checking account offer would have been huge. For the new non-traditional players, such as credit card companies and brokerage firms, the operational challenges of matching the ING offer were equally great. It was clearly an expensive product to offer and most of the non-traditional players lacked the years of operational experience that ING DIRECT had in the direct banking market.

The new Electric Orange product got off to a good start. Within 18 months of its launch, customers had opened over 350000 checking accounts and deposited over $11 billion. About 30% of the accounts were opened by customers new to ING DIRECT.[57]

LEARNING FROM LOW COST COMPETITORS

The above discussion of Ryanair and ING DIRECT suggests that there are some common principles that these two low cost competitors share. Several of these principles are shared across a broad range of low cost competitors in both business-to-consumer and business-to-business markets.

Question every element of the traditional business model

Many of the best low cost competitors with a relatively sustainable competitive advantage are the ones who don't just try blindly to adopt the traditional business model and then attempt to cut costs to the lowest possible levels. Rather they re-think the traditional business models and perform some business activities in fundamentally different ways. Both ING DIRECT and Ryanair are good examples of this.

Arkadi Kuhlmann of ING DIRECT once commented that it was a useful exercise to question every single element of the traditional business model and ask, "What if I did the opposite?" While not all his ideas were original, he did end up with a business model that was quite different from that of the traditional Canadian retail banks (see Figure 3.5).

Ryanair has also broken many of the traditional rules of the airline industry. Only the basic transportation service was included in the price and almost everything else cost extra. Even Southwest Airlines, the airline Ryanair modeled itself after, offered free non-alcoholic beverages and peanuts and had a free checked baggage allowance. Over time, Ryanair found opportunities to reduce the basic

Traditional Canadian Retail Bank	ING DIRECT in Canada
Relatively low interest rates on savings accounts and high interest rates on loans	High interest rates on savings/low interest on loans
Fees and service charges (which were a significant source of revenue and profits)	No fees or service charges
Minimum balances (if customer wanted to avoid certain fees)	No minimum balances
Full range of retail products	No checking or payment accounts
Negotiation of interest rates on products such as loans and mortgages (for some customers)	No negotiation of interest rates with customers
Wants a relationship with its customers	Doesn't want a relationship with customers
Advertising focused on image building brand advertising	Advertising focused heavily on product benefits
Discourages unprofitable customers with fees and minimum balances	"Fires" unprofitable customers

FIGURE 3.5 ING DIRECT: Breaking the conventional rules

fare through productivity improvements or by eliminating what had been up to this point "free" bundled services. It also created new revenue streams by offering new services or by charging customers for services that had formerly been free. But since the overall price of the "package" was still lower than that charged by other airlines, most customers, albeit reluctantly, accepted the new charges. Southwest had been unable to grow its ancillary revenues as rapidly as Ryanair because part of its credo from its early days was not to "nickel and dime" its customers by charging for such things as drinks, snacks and itinerary changes. Essentially, by making this philosophy a key part of its value proposition, it became very difficult for Southwest to add many of the new revenue-generating products and services that other airlines adopted. This has impacted both its competitiveness and its profitability.[58]

Ryanair also broke the rules of traditional airlines by creating new airports, offering free seats, making heavy use of incentives for staff and suppliers, and pioneered offering new services to its customers.

IKEA, the well-known Swedish home furnishings retailer, is another example of a company that broke many of the traditional rules of its industry. Traditional furniture companies had stressed brand, a handcrafted and often sophisticated image – furniture for a lifetime and high prices. They often expected customers to wait for months while their particular pieces were being made. IKEA de-emphasized the brand and promoted simple, clean designs, more of a mass-produced image and low prices. Customers felt that they could replace the furniture as their needs or tastes changed. There was immediate product availability – customers assembled the pieces themselves. The IKEA strategy seriously undermined many manufacturers of the more affordable traditional furniture. Later, many of the surviving traditional furniture manufactures in developed countries came under additional competitive pressure from manufacturers in low cost countries, such as China, who made traditional furniture that sold at very low prices in North America and Europe.

Have very simple and straightforward value propositions

Companies that play a price value leadership game generally emphasize good enough products and services at very low prices (or high interest rates on deposits in the case of a bank like ING DIRECT), as we discussed in Chapter 2. The value proposition of Ryanair, as articulated by Michael O'Leary, could not be clearer. Ryanair is about guaranteeing customers the lowest price for a safe and generally on-time flight. And the air carrier has historically delivered on this promise. Its prices are the lowest on the routes it serves, its flights are safe and it regularly turns in the best on-time performance of any airline in Europe. In another industry, ING DIRECT's value proposition is equally clear – simple products, very good rates, convenient service and no minimum balances, fees and service charges.

Similarly, the German hard discounter Aldi (actually two independent companies originally led by the two Albrecht brothers – Theo (Aldi North) and Karl (Aldi Sud) – with similar business models), which operates in a number of European countries as well as North America and Australia, has a very clear value proposition. It offers a very limited range of regular products (less than 1000 in Switzerland in 2008) of "optimal quality at everyday low prices".

Avoid complexity at any cost

Great low cost competitors avoid complexity at any cost. Both Ryanair and ING DIRECT have very simple business models that avoid complexity. The introduction of the checking accounts at ING DIRECT in the US could have destroyed that simplicity but they did everything they could to simplify the checking account business and remove the complexities.

The most successful hard discounters, such as Aldi and Lidl, are other very good examples of companies that have tried to keep complexity out of their businesses. The hard discounters' typical operating model is shown in Figure 3.6. Aldi and Lidl carry a very limited range of SKUs (typically somewhere between 700 and 3000) but they have very high turnover on these SKUs. They are skilled at picking the right set of SKUs that will appeal to customers, which aids shopping

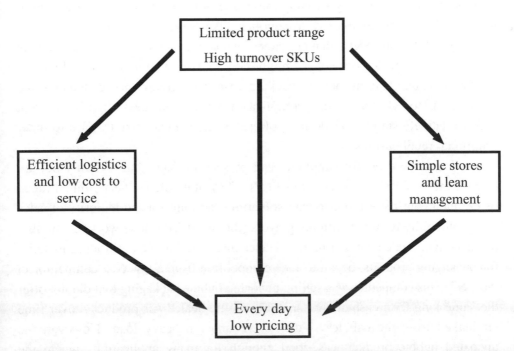

FIGURE 3.6 Hard discounters' typical operating model
Source: Based on slide in Hervé Cathelin's, "European Discount Initiative" presentation at Nestlé Investor Seminar, 8–9 June, 2005.

efficiency and helps the customers to get out of the store quickly. Their stores are very simple in layout with totally functional fittings, they have few staff members, and company-wide, they have a very lean management structure. Their logistics systems are very efficient, and they are able to serve their stores at very low cost. Products arrive at the store on standard pallets and customers serve themselves directly from these pallets. The hard discounters, particularly Aldi, put a strong emphasis on everyday low prices, but they frequently have "special purchases", such as personal computers, consumer electronic products and bicycles, that are offered at extremely low prices. These specials build excitement and generate significant amounts of store traffic. Each store gets a specific number of these items, and they typically sell very quickly. Once the product is sold out, it is not re-stocked.

This tremendous focus on avoiding complexity by limiting the number of SKUs has limited the ability of Aldi and Lidl to compete in certain product categories like baby food, culinary products and chocolate. Some shoppers for these kinds of product categories want a broad selection from which to choose. Lidl eventually moved more aggressively into some of these product categories, but it tried to offload the complexity to suppliers like Nestlé. In 2004, Nestlé began offering Lidl logistic SKUs that contained two or more consumer SKUs. A single SKU (from a logistic perspective) might contain two or more different kinds of Nestlé chocolate bars in the one packing case, thus giving the consumer some product variety. Of course, this complicated Nestlé's business slightly but kept Lidl's relatively simple. Nestlé later offered some similar mixed SKUs to other traditional retail customers.

The same drive for simplicity can be seen in many, but certainly not all, business-to-business low cost competitors. They often offer a very limited range of products, but these products can sometimes account for the majority of sales and profitability for the traditional players (the old 80/20 rule at work). A number of years ago, Sealed Air, the market leader in coated bubble cushioning material for packaging products, began to face competition from a low cost competitor in the US.[59] This competitor was selling uncoated bubble packaging that did not offer the same long-term cushioning capability as the Sealed Air product – over time air leaked from the bubbles if they were under a heavy load. However, the uncoated bubble product was good enough for many applications where the product being protected was light, involved a relatively short shipment and storage cycle, was rugged or was inexpensive to repair or replace if damaged. Sealed Air offered eight different combinations of bubble height and plastic film thickness to meet the varied needs of its customers. Its low cost competitor entered the market with a limited line of two products, priced between 25% and 45% lower than Sealed Air's. These two products were well-positioned to replace three of Sealed Air's eight products – three of which accounted for about two-thirds of Sealed Air's sales and almost 70% of its profits. We will return to the Sealed Air story in Chapter 4.

More recently, a large global chemical company faced a similar situation with an Asian competitor that had lower costs. The global company manufactured a film product that it sold in a wide variety of widths to meet its customers' needs. Since the film was originally produced on machines that had a particular width, this led to some wastage. The low cost competitor decided to offer its film in only a very limited range of widths and at low prices for those customers who would find one of the standard widths acceptable. Presumably, the use of a few standard widths resulted in less wastage, longer runs and lower costs. Of course, over time more and more customers began to design their products to take advantage of the cheaper, standard-width materials. This left the large chemical company in a position of increasingly serving those customers with the most non-standard applications, many of which were relatively low volume. If it increased its prices too much on these products, more customers would defect to the low cost competitor. It was in a trap from which it was difficult to escape.

Break through the communication clutter

Some low cost competitors operating in business-to-consumer markets make very effective use of low cost advertising and public relations and as discussed, Ryanair has been a master at doing this. It designs all its advertising in-house and takes advantage of current events to develop effective, memorable, often irreverent advertising. Over the years, it has taken advantage of wars, sporting events and even the prospective marriage of French President Nicolas Sarkozy to Carla Bruni to create memorable and controversial advertising. It reveled in its publicity, whether the response was positive or negative. With its outrageous ads, the company hoped to provoke an angry response. If the campaigns offended someone, were seen to be misleading, led to complaints directed towards the Advertising Standards Council in the UK or Ireland, or even resulted in a lawsuit, so much the better. This would provide news coverage at both the time of the complaint and at the time that the Advertising Standards Council or the court made its ruling months later. O'Leary claimed that seat reservations increased every time he got news coverage; it didn't matter whether it was positive or negative.[60]

ING DIRECT, Aldi and Lidl have made much greater use of advertising than Ryanair.[61] Aldi and Lidl are typically among the heaviest advertisers in Germany.[62] ING DIRECT's advertising has often been bold and memorable and, like Ryanair, ING DIRECT has not been afraid to use comparative advertising in markets where that is acceptable. In markets such as the US and Canada, it has made effective use of outdoor advertising, often with a humorous twist ("Ever checked your bank statement and smiled?"). ING DIRECT has also made quite heavy use of Internet advertising, utilizing many of the same lines that it created for its outdoor campaigns. It has also used television advertising, often emphasizing the value of saving at ING. The distinctive orange color of ING DIRECT has always been emphasized and the value proposition has been very clear – "great rates, no fees, no minimums". Where many traditional banks have promoted their image, ING DIRECT has emphasized its products and its core value proposition.

In many business-to-consumer situations, the low cost competitors either implicitly, or explicitly, play the role of a consumer advocate against "big bad" companies or government agencies that want to take advantage of customers and their vulnerabilities. Positioning itself as bringing low cost airline service to the masses, easyJet targeted expensive flag carriers like British Airways, who they said "bribed" customers with frequent flyer points. Ryanair, on the other hand, claimed that easyJet was trying to mislead customers when it claimed it had low fares. Both Ryanair and easyJet have attacked the UK government for raising airport taxes and the British Airport Authority for trying to build a second runway and a new "gold-plated Taj Mahal" terminal at Stansted airport near London that neither low cost airlines nor their customers wanted or needed.[63] ING DIRECT focused its advocacy on "leading Americans back to savings" and encouraged Americans to "save your money" and get back on the road to happiness.

When euro notes and coins replaced local currencies in several major European Union countries in 2002, many consumers perceived, and some studies provided evidence, that some retailers used the conversion as an opportunity to raise prices. Aldi, unlike some other retailers, scrupulously made a point of displaying posters in all of its stores with the before and after prices for many products to show that it was not taking advantage of its customers during the euro conversion.

In fact, in many cases it rounded down its euro prices earning customer respect and loyalty. Contrary to many grocery retailers, Aldi charged the same price for a product in all its stores in any given European country. Again, many customers viewed that as being customer friendly since Aldi was not taking advantage of customers in areas where there was less competition and where the chain might be able to "get away" with charging higher prices.

Be a cost innovator

Many low cost competitors are highly innovative in terms of cutting costs and/or passing costs on to other players in their value chain, including their suppliers and customers.

Ryanair has been highly innovative in this regard, as discussed earlier. It did not just do the obvious things such as eliminating travel agents and their commissions. By flying to secondary airports that had little or no passenger traffic before Ryanair's arrival, it was able to extract very advantageous terms for things like landing fees, ground handling charges and even contributions to the expenses of opening up new routes. Suppliers of labor, such as the pilots and cabin crew paid for their own training and some of their other employment expenses. By linking their compensation to various performance indicators, employees and suppliers were incented to speed turnarounds, control costs and increase ancillary revenues. The passengers also played a major role in reducing costs; if they did not change their behavior to support a low cost operation, they were subject to additional fees and charges. Ryanair increasingly added more and more self-serve options and then either incented, or forced passengers, to use them. Passengers generally did their own bookings over the Internet. If they used a Ryanair call center, they paid an additional fee.

To encourage passengers to arrive early at the airport and reduce last minute crowds at check-in and security, seating was based on time of arrival. Later, passengers were encouraged to check-in online or check themselves in at self-service kiosks. Over time, Ryanair changed expectations about how much luggage a passenger could carry on the plane at no charge by reducing weight limits and finally charging the passengers for all checked bags. Even if they paid for checked bags, they were subject to additional charges if the total weight of the bags exceeded 15 kilos. Less luggage meant fewer and faster check-ins and fewer bag drop desks (lower airport rent and fewer staff), lower ground handling costs and faster turnarounds. If the passenger insisted on checking and paying for luggage, then it was a profitable transaction for Ryanair. It was particularly profitable for Ryanair, if the passenger decided to check a bag at the last minute and paid twice the normal checked bag rate.

Overall, during the period from 2000 to 2006 Ryanair was able to drive its costs per passenger (excluding fuel) down quite dramatically. Every time the cumulative number of passengers doubled, nominal (not adjusted for inflation) costs were reduced by about 20%.[64] That is, the 100 000 000th passenger cost less than 80% of the 50 000 000th passenger – a very commendable performance.

ING DIRECT US even went one step further. ING DIRECT's website is designed to make it very easy for customers to find the information they need and to complete their transactions quickly and effortlessly. Because ING DIRECT sells a very basic set of products at very attractive rates and has no significant fee income and no minimum balances, it has to have customers who can be maintained at a low cost. With its business model, it can't afford to have customers calling the call center every few days enquiring about balances or asking other questions. ING DIRECT's staff did nothing to encourage customers, who might be expensive to serve, to open accounts or keep them open. In fact, ING DIRECT even "fired" customers (over 3000 in 2004) who did not fit its business model; they were too expensive to maintain or asked to be treated in ways that did not fit the bank's standard operating procedures.[65] With over 7 million customers in 2008, ING DIRECT US simply could not afford to make exceptions for individual customers. The net result of all of its cost reduction activities, and the growing scale of its operations, was that ING DIRECT was able to drive down its operating expenses as a percentage of client retail balances from 1.5% in 1999 to 0.37% in early 2007 on a global basis.[66] The company believed that this operating expenses ratio was more than 2.0% less than a typical retail bank with branches, giving it a tremendous competitive advantage.

Outsourcing is one way many low cost competitors lower their costs. This allows companies to have specialist companies that are focused on innovation, infrastructure or certain kinds of customer relationship activities to handle certain non-core activities, as we touched on in Chapter 2. Ryanair was a heavy user of outsourcing, which together with its very high employee productivity, gave it an employee-to-customer ratio that was very low by airline industry standards (about one employee for every 11 350 passengers versus one employee for every 700 passengers at BA in 2007).[67] By using these best-in-class strategic partners, a company can often outperform a more traditional competitor at substantially lower cost. Very clearly, as we saw with Bharti Airtel, extensive outsourcing of non-core activities can allow a company to grow much more rapidly than it could otherwise.

In many business-to-business situations, offloading costs and investments to suppliers can be an important way to control costs. This is clearly one of the benefits of outsourcing activities. Many low cost competitors exploit this source of cost reduction and pursue it aggressively, looking for any opportunity to shift costs and investments to suppliers if it makes economic sense. Earlier we discussed how Chinese motorcycle manufacturers relied on their supply chain to design, as well as manufacture, many of the key motorcycle systems and subsystems. By giving a lot of latitude to design within broad parameters, they offloaded the detailed design work to networks of suppliers who had a big incentive to meet the performance requirements at the lowest possible cost.

In several other industries, many of the competing low cost players in China buy many of the parts and sub-systems from the same suppliers. That creates economies of scale for the suppliers and lower costs for them. This allows some quite small Chinese manufacturers to be quite cost-competitive with much larger companies who have captive sources of supply for some of the key sub-systems, even though their sales volumes are much lower.

Retailers like Wal-Mart routinely assign management responsibilities for various product categories, such as feminine hygiene to a supplier like P&G. By doing this with leading suppliers for most of the major product categories it carries, Wal-Mart takes advantage of the suppliers' knowledge about how best to achieve profit and other objectives for the category, as well as offloading what could be a significant cost item. Similarly any time a company pushes the management of complexity back into its supply chain, it is shifting costs. If the supplier is able to manage these costs more effectively than the company can, then the company should benefit. As we saw with the hard discounters, they essentially push the complexity and the costs back to the supplier when they require them to provide variety within a single SKU (say by mixing two flavors of yoghurt in one shipping container).

All these different mechanisms for eliminating costs or shifting costs to customers, often by creating self-service options, or suppliers have been important mechanisms that have allowed low cost players to compete effectively with the more traditional players in their markets. In addition the relatively simple business models mean that most successful low cost players have very lean organizations that are much lower cost than those of their traditional competitors. This is particularly true for low cost competitors based in developing markets.

Remember that the customer is not always right

Another thread that goes through much of the preceding discussion of common themes among low cost competitors is that the customer is not always right. Over time, many of these companies re-shape customer expectations about what is an acceptable value proposition. Customers seldom ask to do more of the value creation themselves (assembling IKEA furniture is not most people's idea of fun). Generally, customers think that they want more choices rather than fewer, but in the US, ING DIRECT often only offered them two terms for mortgages. Customers don't like being charged to use their credit card, check a piece of baggage or get a drink of water on a plane but on Ryanair they pay for these and many other things. In business-to-business markets, customers don't always want a very limited range of sizes, no technical support and delivery at the supplier's convenience within a wide time window. But in all of these situations given a stark choice between these options and paying significantly more for the product or service from a traditional supplier, many choose the low cost competitor's limited product or service quite willingly. And not unimportant is the fact that having limited choice speeds up decision-making and saves the customer time.

Customers not only get used to the low cost supplier's product or service over time, but they also find it quite acceptable. In some cases, they recognize that there are significant benefits that they had not anticipated. One paint manufacturer in China decided to move to a once-per-week delivery in order to reduce its costs related to serving small retailers in smaller cities. All orders received by the cut-off time would be delivered a couple of days later. If the cut-off time was missed, the delivery would not occur until the following week. Some of the retailers began to prefer the new schedule, in part because the lead-time gave the manufacturer time to make, assemble and deliver the total order on the designated delivery date. Prior to this system being implemented, many orders were only partially filled with the balance being delivered two or three days later. The uncertainty about when all of the items in the order would be received bothered some of the small retailers and caused some of them to carry more buffer stock. The predictability of the new system was seen to be a significant benefit. It worked in a similar way for many consumers who initially resented having to do their banking, or order their plane tickets, over the Internet – in time gaining control of the process coupled with the added convenience appealed to many consumers.

Have the courage to drop prices significantly below competition

ING DIRECT Bank and Ryanair are both companies that have had the courage to drop prices significantly below the competition; they work on the assumption that if prices are low enough, significant demand will be created. Although the margins will be low on each transaction, the overall business will be profitable. In the case of ING DIRECT in Canada, it initially offered interest rates on checking accounts of over 4%, when all the major retail banks in Canada were offering rates much less than 1%. This quickly got the attention of customers, particularly those with large balances in their checking accounts. Unsurprisingly, the business got off to a quick start.

When Ryanair enters a new market, it typically offers prices that undercut the lowest fares of the existing airlines on the route by about 50%. This quickly helps to establish its image as the airline with the lowest prices.

Customers often need a noticeable and significant price reduction to give them the "wake-up call" to take a serious look at a new low cost player's offering. A 10% or 20% reduction in price relative to the incumbent supplier may not be enough to get people to try a new and unproven supplier. In some markets, where the risk of trying a new supplier is very high, even a 50% price reduction might not be enough to get a significant number of customers to try the service.

If the overall market is quite price-elastic, the strategy of a significant price reduction works particularly well. This was the case with the leisure air travel market that Ryanair tapped into in the UK and Ireland. Air travel had become a very attractive substitute for travel by car and ferry and a variety of other sorts of leisure time activities. For instance, instead of having a pre-wedding celebration at a local venue, people started celebrating by spending a weekend in Ibiza.

Dropping price substantially makes the choice of following suit much more problematic for the industry incumbents. A 5% drop in price might be contemplated seriously but to drop prices by 30%–40%, with a more than proportional hit to the bottom line, takes a very courageous management team. And generally, they don't think the margin on the increased volume will compensate for the loss in contribution margin. Generally, management will think it much better to give up a small percentage of market share, which may not be missed in a growing market. This temptation is particularly strong in large markets where a tiny percentage of the overall market will meet the short-term aspirations, and capacity, of the new or existing competitor that is dropping its price.

One of the biggest challenges facing a management team that is considering offering a product or service at a substantially lower cost is finding the courage to do so. Barbara Cassani, CEO of Go Airlines, the low cost airline set up by BA to compete with easyJet and Ryanair, said that this was one of the biggest challenges her company faced in setting prices. She quoted one of her executives, Stephen Horner, as saying: "We have been trying to maximize profitability. At first, we thought that by making our lowest prices hard to find would help push our average prices up. Instead, it means you fly around with half-filled planes and develop a reputation for being only lowish-priced. But if we keep our costs low and fill our seats, then revenues and profits will follow. It is an act of faith. Customers need to know we're always low-priced."[68]

TRADITIONAL PLAYERS CAN LEARN FROM LOW COST COMPETITORS

Traditional companies can learn some valuable lessons from low cost competitors, but whether it's because of ignorance or arrogance, they often don't.

Since the earliest days of low cost airlines, the carriers realized that there was a significant benefit in turning planes around quickly. Southwest Airlines opened for business in 1971 but by late 1972, it was in a precarious financial situation. After adjusting its flight schedules, the airline was able to sell one of its four original Boeing 737 planes generating a capital gain and cash. Fast turnaround of its planes was absolutely essential in order to make the new schedule work. An important element of a speedy turnaround was minimizing the amount of time spent cleaning a plane between flights. Ground staff boarded the plane immediately when it docked at the gate and began replenishing supplies. Flight attendants helped with the cleaning by following the last passenger as he or she walked down the plane, cleaning up any discarded papers or other garbage and straightening seat belts as they went. As soon as the last passenger was off the plane the next group of passengers could be boarded. Amazingly, some of these fairly rudimentary moves to speed up turnarounds were just being introduced by some major US airlines almost 30 years after they became common practice at Southwest Airlines.[69] This and a number of other practices that low cost carriers adopted decades ago seem to have been ignored by many mainstream airlines. Yet fast turnarounds allow an airline to use its most expensive assets more intensively, lowering its costs significantly per available seat mile or seat kilometer.

Lufthansa also found that by taking a page out of Ryanair's book it could both cut costs and improve service. Facing market share erosion due to competition from low cost carriers like Ryanair, Lufthansa began experimenting with ways to counter their growing threat. In late 2005, Lufthansa launched "Operation Hamburg" offering up to 3000 low-fare tickets per day on 23 European routes from Hamburg. In order to pare down costs and compensate for the lower prices, it based seven planes in Hamburg instead of using planes from the central fleet based in Frankfurt. The planes returned to Hamburg every night and the flight crews no longer spent the night in other cities. Because the planes returned to their base every night, maintenance crews got to know the planes better and could more accurately predict maintenance needs, heading off future problems. This resulted in 25% lower maintenance costs per plane. In addition, having the flight crews spend every night at home saved hotel and restaurant costs. Overall, the cost savings were estimated to be about 20% when compared to the typical short-haul Lufthansa planes and crew that often spend successive nights in different European cities. In addition to the hard cost savings, there were softer benefits. One such benefit was that now that the cabin crew were more often on the same flights, they began to get to know some of the frequent passengers, improving both customer and employee satisfaction.

Companies like Nestlé, Proctor & Gamble and Unilever have also learned from their low cost customers like Lidl and Wal-Mart. While probably none of the knowledge they garner is "rocket science", they often drive home some basics that companies all too often forget. The simplicity of the Lidl business model, and the impact it can have on costs, is one important learning point. Lidl strives for an extremely efficient and low cost supply chain; the company does everything it can in order not to increase the complexity of its operations. The chain tries to push the complexity back to its suppliers. All the successful low cost retailers are focused on having the lowest possible costs in all areas; it causes the FMCG manufacturers to question whether all of the marketing and sales activities they engage in really add significant value, or could some of these activities be cut and lead to significant savings. For example, many FMCG companies spend money on various in-store activities. Lidl doesn't want this kind of support – both the chain and its FMCG partners seem to do quite well without it. Do in-store activities really add value in traditional grocery retailers or do they do it because they always have? Does the consumer really need the variety of brands, products and package sizes in certain product categories? Or are all the additional brands, flavors and package sizes just adding to cost and complexity while not improving the consumer value proposition? As mentioned, many hard discounters, including Aldi and Lidl, achieve variety at lower cost and complexity by mixing two or more varieties of a product in one box. This way the consumer gets some variety but logistically it represents only one SKU to be handled. Are there similar innovative practices and opportunities that other more traditional retailers, or their suppliers, can benefit from?

While it is important to try to learn from low cost competitors, it is also important not to copy them blindly. Rather, a company should try to leverage any resources and capabilities it has if they will help gain competitive advantage. The full-service Australian airline, Qantas, set up Jetstar to compete with Virgin Blue (a low cost carrier that had significantly impacted the Australian market). Jetstar copied many of the attributes of Southwest, Ryanair and Virgin Blue. It set up a separate operating unit to avoid Qantas' unionized pay rates and work practices[70] and offered a very basic, but friendly, service with low prices. It focused on keeping costs low by high asset utilization through fast turnarounds and by trying to return crews to their base at the end of each day. However, where it could, Jetstar also took advantage of Qantas' economies of scale in purchasing planes and a variety of other products and services. By leveraging Qantas' resources and capabilities it was able to develop a cost structure that some analysts believed was lower than Virgin Blue's, which allowed them to "bracket" Virgin Blue. With its Qantas branded service, the airline focused on the business traveler, offering full service on premium routes and providing the connectivity that allowed these travelers to reach a wide range of domestic, regional and international destinations. With its Jetstar service, the company focused more on the leisure traveler. Through its low cost structure, Jetstar could profitably serve some routes that the branded Qantas service could not. Its low fares also stimulated market growth and helped feed additional passengers into some of Quantas' long-haul routes.

CHALLENGE QUESTIONS

Are there opportunities for you, or new competitors, to radically change the business model in your industry or in a segment of it?

Have you reviewed your value propositions recently? Are they still relevant to your targeted customer segments? Or, have they become out-of-date as a result of changes in customer needs and competitive developments?

Have you added unnecessary complexity (and cost) to your business over recent years? Do you have brands, products and product variants (sizes, flavors, colors, grades, etc.) in your product line that no longer meet real customer needs and are not truly valued by customers? Are you providing services that are not needed or valued? Would it make sense to bundle or unbundle some of your offerings so that you can offer customers a solution that is more attuned to their needs (and perhaps reduce the complexity of your business at the same time)?

Do your marketing communications convey your value proposition effectively or might a less conventional approach, perhaps taking advantage of the new digital media, be more effective?

Are you being innovative enough in controlling your costs? Are there ways you could make a step-change reduction in your costs? Could you move significant activities to other players in your value chain (perhaps even by re-configuring your value chain), who might be able to manage them more efficiently and perhaps even more effectively?

Could you benefit from being less customer-driven? Are you listening too much to your customers (or to the wrong customers) and responding too enthusiastically to their articulated needs that may not be well thought through? Are your customers always right? Should you perhaps try to lead them to new offers that, in the longer run, may deliver more value and/or lower costs to both of you? If your current customers are not interested, are there other segments of existing users, or potential new users, who might be interested in your new offers?

Are you in a business that potentially has very high price elasticity? Should you consider a radical drop in price to stimulate primary demand in your market before a competitor sees this opportunity and gains competitive advantage by doing it?

Have you ever sat down and tried systematically to understand your low cost competitors' business systems in real depth? What ideas would you come up with, if you gave yourselves the objective of identifying five (or ten) key learning points from low cost competitors? Could you significantly improve your competitive position by implementing some of the ideas without threatening your core business model (if you still believe that you have the right one)?

CHAPTER 4

Realistically assessing the threat

One of the toughest decisions executives in traditional companies face today is whether to respond to their low cost competitors and, if so, what should be the timing of that response. A response can take several forms, but the fundamental question is: should the company's management adjust its strategy in recognition of the low cost threat, or should they continue business as usual with no change in strategy or tactics? If the decision is made to respond, the options range from directly confronting the competitor in the segments they are targeting to adjusting strategy in an attempt to isolate the business from the low cost threat. This might include "moving away" from the segments most vulnerable to attack by low cost competitors, focusing on the market segments that show less interest in a good enough, low price offering, and then developing and executing a strategy to meet the needs of these segments.

We will start this chapter by emphasizing that not all companies and industries are equally vulnerable to low cost competition. However, many are vulnerable, or will become more vulnerable over time. Many companies that are at risk often initially underestimate the threat posed by low cost competitors. This is sometimes the result of complacency or arrogance or because the company is so focused on competing with other traditional competitors that it does not even recognize the threat developing from low cost competitors. Perhaps Nokia, for example, focused too much attention on Motorola and, for a while, not enough on the low cost competitors emerging in China. Likewise, Caterpillar concentrated on Komatsu and paid insufficient attention to low cost players emerging in some of its markets. Companies such as Ericsson, Alcatel, Lucent and Nortel were perhaps too focused on competing with one another in the mobile telecommunications infrastructure business, to recognize the threat from the Chinese low cost competitor, Huawei. Within a dozen years of first dipping its toes in the waters outside China, however, Huawei was one of the four largest global players in the industry, and it was rapidly growing its market share.[71] In 2007 it won more new contracts for one particular type of third-generation mobile phone technology than any other company and ranked fourth in the world in the number of international patent applications.[72] Traditional players often underestimate the size of the segments the low cost competitors are addressing and how quickly they may grow. The rapid expansion of these segments is the result of not only the efforts of the low cost players themselves, but also the efforts of suppliers, customers and complementors that support, and profit from, the activities of the low cost players. In addition, traditional companies may sometimes fail to recognize how low cost competitors might use these market segments as a base for launching an attack against the traditional players' core markets.

We will also look at some approaches that companies might use to appraise the low cost threat realistically and determine how it might evolve over time. We will emphasize the point that this analysis should not be a static one. Rather it should be dynamic in the sense of anticipating how low cost competitors might overcome gaps in capabilities and resources and how they might use a series of often neglected market segments as stepping stones to strengthen their market position, while avoiding head-on confrontation with the traditional players. Sometimes there are few, if any, limits on how far a low cost rival might "move up" in the market by evolving its strategy over time. In other cases, the business model of the low cost competitor might only enable it to occupy certain segments of the market. Moving beyond those segments may require such a fundamentally different business model that it would be unlikely that both business models could be successfully executed simultaneously. However, even in these cases, the company might have to watch for new low cost competitors using different business models going after market segments that the first generation of low cost players could not address successfully.

One useful way to summarize all the analysis and to develop a platform for change is to build a tough but realistic worst-case scenario. This usually represents a situation where the company or business unit moves ahead with a "business as usual" strategy and does nothing to respond to the low cost threat.

Finally, we will look at the financial analysis that is often used to support these types of choices. It is important to compare the analysis that many managers use versus those they *should* use if they are to make sound business decisions. We will also see how shortsighted equity analysts can sometimes encourage companies to make choices that sustain performance in the short run but that jeopardize the company's long-term strategic and financial position.

SOME INDUSTRIES ARE LESS VULNERABLE TO THE LOW COST THREAT

Not all industries are equally vulnerable to the threat of low cost competition. An industry, or product category, that is at the early stage of its product life cycle is generally less susceptible than a more mature one. As we discussed in Chapter 2, product performance is often inadequate in the early stages of a new product. Many customers are not yet happy with the product's performance, whether that dissatisfaction is based on product functionality, quality, reliability, ease of use or style. At this early stage, the main basis of competition may be performance leadership, whereby performance often improves significantly from year to year. It is usually only when the performance of the product on the relevant dimensions is good enough that some customers then start turning their attention to products that offer good enough performance at a more attractive price. This is when the low-cost competitors have an opportunity to gain significant share and scale.

Low cost competitors may also be challenged when trying to penetrate industries where strong brands, intellectual property, established relationships or access to particular distribution channels are key success factors; the emphasis, however, is on "may". Again, as we saw in Chapter 2, some of these barriers are easier to overcome than they used to be. Intellectual property can be purchased, or it might be available from third parties for a royalty payment. Or competitors may emerge in markets where intellectual property rights are not fully respected or enforced. A credible brand or access to distribution can sometimes be acquired at relatively low cost, perhaps by buying a respected company that wants to exit a market. Of course, several of the low cost competitors we have discussed, including Ryanair, easyJet and ING DIRECT, have used the Internet to deal directly with customers and bypass the traditional channels, which are often expensive and inefficient.

The most challenging situations for low cost competitors are perhaps industries or product categories where success depends on coordinating and integrating a highly complex network of activities in an effort to create and deliver customer value. Large commercial aircraft manufacturers, pharmaceutical companies and fast moving consumer goods firms, where brand is a critical influencing factor in the purchasing decision, all have substantial barriers to entry. However, even here, modularization and the growth of focused players in these industries are making them much more vulnerable to low cost competition than they used to be. For example, retailers with respected brand names are often able to source food products from high quality private label manufacturers who work closely with sophisticated suppliers of ingredients, flavors and fragrances. The resulting products often successfully compete with those from leading fast moving consumer goods manufacturers.

If there is particular concern about low cost competition from developing countries, then those industries where little of the global demand is in the developing world have less to fear. Thus, at the moment, many sophisticated service businesses, such as complex financial services, have less to fear from competitors in developing markets than those industries where more than half the global demand is in such markets.

WHY COMPANIES FAIL TO RESPOND TO THE LOW COST THREAT IN A TIMELY MANNER

We often observe that traditional companies are slow to respond to the threat from low cost competitors. Sometimes they seem to underestimate the threat or do not anticipate how the threat may evolve over time.

The low cost threat is underestimated

Traditional companies sometimes exhibit complacency or arrogance and manage to convince themselves that very few customers would want to buy "crap like that" or use an "obviously inferior" service when they could buy their own company's great product or service. Their skepticism can often be reinforced by the apparent lukewarm, or even negative, initial response to the value player's product or service. Traditional market leaders often pay particular attention to the responses of their existing customers who, of course, may not be in the low cost competitor's initial target segment. This is particularly true in the case of truly disruptive products and services. As Clayton Christensen has noted, disruptive technologies often initially do not perform as well as traditional technologies in the mainstream markets and the customers in these markets reject them.[73]

A classic example described by Christensen was the hydraulic excavator. Initially, it was a very poor fit with customer needs in traditional excavator markets such as digging ditches for large sewers and water mains or moving rock in mines and quarries. The hydraulic excavators had limited reach and were underpowered; they could not handle the large buckets, which were needed to handle many traditional tasks efficiently. The mechanical excavator was a much better fit and was able to move cubic meters of material and deposit the material several meters away. Existing customers for the mechanical excavators, therefore, had little interest in these new hydraulic products and discouraged their mechanical excavator suppliers from "wasting time" on developing those products that they perceived as having little value to them.

The little hydraulic excavators or backhoes did, however, find acceptance among contractors who had to dig ditches from the water and sewer mains to individual buildings, where the alternative was manual digging – mechanical excavators were over-engineered and too expensive to use for such small, simple jobs. However, these new customers were difficult and expensive to reach and educate. The margins on these products were also unattractive relative to those on the mechanical excavators, particularly if the manufacturer tried to use the same business system – including the distribution channels – that was used for the traditional product line. The hydraulic backhoes were often sold as attachments for the back of industrial or farm tractors through the same channels that sold this type of equipment. These channels were used to selling to small customers. Given these factors, it was not surprising that the traditional players showed little interest in the disruptive technology. However, over the next 20 to 30 years, the performance and capacity of hydraulic excavators improved steadily to the point where they became a totally acceptable solution for excavation of sewer and water mains and tasks that were even more demanding. Most of the manufacturers of mechanical excavators failed to make the transition to hydraulic excavators and were eventually driven out of these markets.

This type of scenario has occurred over and over again for both products and services. Initially, tax preparation software for individual taxpayers was a very poor substitute for the services of an accountant or a tax preparation service like H&R Block. Over time, however, products such as Intuit's TurboTax and QuickTax have become much more sophisticated and user-friendly; they now meet the needs of many North American taxpayers. Fastcase, an on-line legal research service, is challenging the on-line research services of Westlaw and LexisNexis, big divisions of the large multinationals Thomson Reuters and Reed Elsevier, respectively.[74] By using sophisticated computer algorithms to analyze the online filings of courts all over the US, Fastcase is increasingly able to do the case indexing done by thousands of human editors at the two traditional services at a fraction of the cost. This allows them to offer a much lower price service that is particularly appealing to small firms that cannot afford the offerings of Westlaw and Lexis-Nexis. Fastcase and similar companies are rapidly improving the quality and comprehensiveness of their service, so that over time the challenge to the traditional players will increase steadily.

The low cost threat often takes time to gain momentum

The initial sales impact may be very muted if the new low cost entrant is moving into untapped and undeveloped markets on the fringe of the incumbents' market, as was the case with the initial applications of the hydraulic excavator. In some cases, the incumbents may continue to grow quite rapidly, even though their share of the overall market is falling, lulling them into a false sense that everything is going well.

This happened to Saurer, the Switzerland-based leader in textile manufacturing equipment, in one of its market segments in China.[75] As late as 2003, the company believed the market in China for one type of textile manufacturing equipment (staple fiber twisting machines) was about 500 units per year. Saurer Volkmann, the business unit that manufactured this type of equipment, had a small sales force that had relationships with the top 250 customers for twisting machines. The potential customer base was believed to number between 1000 and 1500. There was no good data regarding the overall size of the market because customers were spread across many of China's provinces; some of these customers were very small with only one twisting machine. Based on a market of 500 machines per year, Saurer had a very healthy share of this market by value. In 2003, however, management realized that the market in China was much bigger than they had realized and had grown to about 1000 machines per year. Many of the twisting machines were basic, low cost machines being produced by local or regional low cost competitors. However, some of these local competitors were beginning to invest in R&D and beginning to produce equipment that was more sophisticated. Moreover, the local machine manufacturers were developing relationships with customers who themselves would be attempting to make more sophisticated products over time. These more sophisticated products would require machinery that was more sophisticated and the local competitors with the relationships with the customers would be well positioned to provide these machines. With this new development, Saurer Volkmann's position in the staple fiber twisting market was not nearly as strong as management had imagined. Consequently, the management team faced some tough decisions about how to respond to the rapidly growing threat.

This problem is not unique to Saurer Volkmann. Jorgen Clausen, CEO of Danfoss, a world-leading Danish manufacturer of industrial controls, has admitted that they made the same mistake.[76] The firm had been growing in China at 35% per annum compounded, and it had been very happy with the results. Clausen decided to investigate the Chinese market more carefully (this is explored in more detail in Chapter 7) and found that the company was just skimming the surface in most markets with just a few percentage points of market share. He also discovered that there was a large low-end market that, in many cases, the company hadn't even realized existed. This led to a very ambitious effort to develop products and services attuned to the needs of the Chinese market that would result in China becoming Danfoss' second "home" market after Europe.

Too often, this story is repeated for a number of products and services. It is a particular issue for companies operating in developing markets, where market data is often much less transparent than it is in more mature markets. This is especially true in a developing country if a significant portion of the market is in second- and third-tier cities, as well as in rural areas that are less frequently visited by the employees of Western companies. It is not uncommon for companies to underestimate the size of the market by a factor of two – the market in units being twice as large as believed. Companies are lulled into a false sense of security by having growth rates in countries like China that are many times higher than the growth rates they are accustomed to in Europe, North America or other developed markets. It's only later that they find out that the market growth rate was much higher than their growth rate, meaning they were blissfully unaware that they were rapidly losing market share.

In some cases, low cost players tap segments that take time to develop; they may require significant changes in peoples' behavior and the development of new infrastructures to support growth. Typically, these types of changes do not happen overnight. This has certainly been the case with low cost airlines. The dramatically lower prices that companies like Southwest Airlines, Ryanair and easyJet have brought to the air travel market have led to customers adopting new forms of behavior. More people in Europe now routinely take weekend breaks in countries that are further afield; whereas, prior to the rise of the low cost airlines, they would have traveled locally, or regionally, to go away for a weekend. Some customers now own weekend homes, or even their "permanent" homes, in areas that would not have been viable before the advent of the low cost carriers. Some business people working in the UK even have their primary home in Italy, France or Spain and commute on a weekly basis to their jobs. Initially, this practice was quite rare but once a few pioneers showed that it could be done, word of mouth and media spread the idea and services began springing up in support of the practice. It took time for realtors and developers in these markets to recognize the opportunity and begin offering products and services that would meet the needs of this new type of weekly "commuter".

Similarly, the growth of low cost airlines has also made it feasible for a broad cross-section of other workers in parts of Europe to take advantage of numerous labor markets opening up across the continent. Some doctors who live in other countries in Europe now have part-time practices in the UK to help meet the doctor shortage in some regions. Other relatively low-income workers, such as construction workers and flight attendants, "commute" between their homes and families in Central and Eastern Europe and their jobs in Western and Northern Europe. Again, complementary services appear that support the transportation service provided by the low cost airlines. Employment agencies see opportunities to link workers in one part of Europe with jobs in another; local stores, restaurants and bars start stocking national food and drink that make life for the Central and Eastern Europeans working in other parts of Europe more pleasant and more like "home". Even the public libraries in some parts of the UK have begun to stock books and newspapers in languages such as Polish. All of these things "lower the barriers" and make it much more feasible and attractive for a broader group of people to participate.

In some cases, "new" low cost airports or terminals were required to open up geographical markets that would be attractive to these types of commuters or other customers. For example, in late 2006, Marseilles opened a new low cost terminal called MP2 (Marseilles Province Terminal 2) designed exclusively to meet the needs of low cost carriers. There are no carpets or expensive air-conditioning. The floors are plain concrete, the walls are painted in bright pink and green, and passengers have to carry their checked in baggage through security and walk to the planes. However, the low cost approach results in significantly lower costs for the airlines – €1.50 per passenger versus €6.00 in the regular terminal. In other cases, as already discussed, obtaining a new terminal may require converting an abandoned military airport into a commercial one.

As barriers drop, and new behaviors are established, growth begins to accelerate rapidly. Ryanair began its switch from a more traditional business model to the low cost model in 1991. It took almost four years for it to grow to two million passengers per year, but the absolute growth in passenger numbers accelerated very quickly after that. In 2007, Ryanair grew by over eight million passengers in one year! The slow initial growth had become a tidal wave!

Sometimes it is the second-order effects that have the biggest impact

The initial impact of low cost players on the traditional, incumbent companies may not be the most important consideration from a long-term perspective. In many markets, if the barriers to entry are relatively low, there are usually a number of low cost competitors that enter the market. There may be enough business for everybody initially with little direct competition between the low cost players. But as the direct competition intensifies, some of the low cost competitors, usually a few of the "losers", try to escape the hypercompetitive market segments by differentiating their offerings and moving "up" in the market. These "losers" often pose a much more direct and formidable threat to the traditional players than the original low cost players since they typically offer an enhanced product or service built on a competitive low cost base. Their total costs are often well below that of the traditional players; thus they are able to offer customers a price that is relatively very attractive.

Wal-Mart, Kmart and Target all entered the US general merchandise discount retail market in 1962. Initially, however, there was little direct competition between the three companies because they competed in different geographical markets. Wal-Mart developed from its base in the rural, southern US, and as late as 1980 had stores in only one region of the country. Kmart started in Michigan and focused much more on locations close to major urban areas. Target began in Minnesota and focused more on suburban and urban areas.

Clearly, these discount retailers had an impact on traditional general department stores – chains like Sears and J.C. Penny – in the geographical areas in which they operated. They had a more limited impact on the more upscale department stores. Over time, as they expanded from their bases, the three began to compete more directly with one another. By the early 1990s, over 80% of Target and Kmart stores faced competition from Wal-Mart,[77] and as time passed, the competition between the three intensified. Because of the geographical location of many of its stores in suburban areas, Target had a customer base that was younger, better educated and more affluent that those of its two competitors. In an effort to avoid head-to-head competition with Wal-Mart and Kmart, Target began to strengthen its position as an upscale discounter that provided high quality, on-trend merchandise at attractive prices in relatively clean, spacious and customer-friendly stores. With this emphasis, it reinforced its position with its customer demographic and was able to attract even more of them. Although the initial impact of general merchandise discount retailers on mid-market and upscale department stores was somewhat muted, it intensified as Target began to move up market and compete much more directly with traditional department stores. Battle-hardened and efficient from competing with Wal-Mart, the new "fashionable and on-trend" Target posed a much more significant threat to the upscale retailers than Wal-Mart ever had.

A similar, second order impact is occurring in the airline business in both the US and Europe. In Europe, the two largest discount carriers, Ryanair and easyJet, had largely managed to avoid direct route competition for the first decade that they were in business, even though both of them had their major bases in the London area. This started to unravel in 2004 when Ryanair launched service from London Stansted to two Spanish cities that were already being served by easyJet from London Luton. easyJet retaliated by opening up three routes to the Irish Republic from London Gatwick. Up to this point Ryanair had been the only major low cost carrier offering service between London and the Irish Republic. Over the next few months, Ryanair matched easyJet's London Gatwick to Shannon, Cork and Knock services at lower prices. Historically, Ryanair had only one route to London Gatwick (from Dublin) – London's second most important and expensive airport after Heathrow. Dublin–London Gatwick was one of Ryanair's busiest routes and provided service to price sensitive business travelers and leisure travelers who valued either Gatwick's location south of London or the flights they could connect to at Gatwick. But because Gatwick was an expensive and busy airport, Ryanair had decided not to use it to serve other cities. With easyJet's challenge to its Irish quasi-monopoly, however, Ryanair felt that it had no option other than to compete directly with them on the three additional Irish routes. Ryanair was better able to offer lower prices than easyJet due to its significantly lower cost structure.[78] As a result, Ryanair captured most of the business on the routes and almost certainly made the routes unprofitable for easyJet. In 2006, about two years after the launch of its services to the Republic of Ireland, easyJet quietly withdrew from the market. Soon afterward, Ryanair reduced service to two of the cities and eliminated the Gatwick service altogether for the third. The air carrier not only continued to serve Dublin from London Gatwick but also actually increased the flight frequency.

Perhaps as a result of the increasingly direct competition between Ryanair and easyJet, the latter has increasingly been focusing its efforts on the more price sensitive segments of the business travel market – travelers who either pay out of their own pockets or work for companies that are cost-conscious. They may also be travelers who find that the airports used by easyJet are more convenient than those utilized by the full service airlines. By 2008, easyJet was the largest carrier at London Gatwick (a more business-oriented airport than either London Luton or London Stansted), and it was serving more than 30 cities in Europe from the airport with flight frequencies of up to five flights per day. Cities serviced included such major business travel destinations as Madrid, Milan, Cologne, Berlin, Barcelona, Geneva, Athens, Amsterdam and Glasgow. To increase its appeal to business travelers, easyJet also added flights at prime times for business travelers, matched BA's business class carry-on baggage allowance, offered Internet check-in with 15-minute arrival time at the gate and, for additional fees, offered lounge access and priority boarding. It also allowed passengers on early morning flights from Gatwick to check in the night before, and for those passengers whose meetings finished early, they provided the opportunity to transfer at no fee to an earlier flight if space was available.

These moves by easyJet resulted in the airline becoming a much more direct and formidable competitor for British Airways and other European flag carriers than the typical low cost carrier. Its costs, while high relative to those of Ryanair, were very low compared to those of the flag carriers. easyJet was even running ads in business-oriented papers comparing the frequency of its service to BA's from London Gatwick to major European business centers. These moves by easyJet were generally good news from Ryanair's viewpoint. The new services that easyJet were offering added significantly to the complexity of its operations as well as to its costs. This left Ryanair with an even stronger relative cost position, and it had less competition in its core leisure market. Both Ryanair and easyJet benefited from the easyJet changes, but BA and the other full service carriers were under increasing competitive and cost pressure on many of their

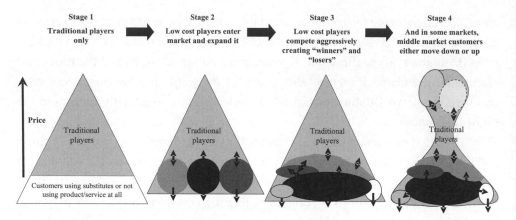

FIGURE 4.1   Market dynamics in the European airline industry over time
Note: Arrows indicate areas of growth and/or competition.

European routes. By 2008, several other Ryanair competitors seemed to be attempting to move up market to escape Ryanair's relentless low price competition.

The evolution of this market is shown in Figure 4.1. In Stage 1, the flag carriers and other airlines with similar business models had the market pretty much to themselves. The low cost carriers such as Ryanair and easyJet appeared on the scene in Stage 2, and took some business from the traditional airlines but grew primarily by developing the untapped airline market at the bottom of the "pyramid". Over time price competition developed between the major low cost carriers as their route structures began to overlap. Ryanair won many of these battles while other low cost carriers went bankrupt during this period and dropped out of the market. In Stage 3, easyJet, avoiding some of the direct competition with Ryanair that it was unable to win because of its higher cost structure, moved up the pyramid by focusing more on primary airports and business travelers. Other smaller, low cost competitors filled in some of the niches around the major players. This started to have a much bigger impact on the intra-European part of the flag carrier's business. In addition, easyJet was now more vulnerable to being "squeezed" between Ryanair and the resurgent flag carriers. The dynamics in many markets, both business-to-consumer and business-to-business, follow a similar pattern over time.

In some markets, there is also a Stage 4. If we continue with the airline example, the continuing loss of market share by traditional airlines to the low cost carriers results in many of them trying to make their prices more competitive to slow the loss of share. This leads to a squeeze in margins and cost-cutting to try to improve margins. The cost-cutting often results in reductions in service, perhaps fewer flights between city pairs to try and increase average load factors, and/or charges for products and services that were formerly free, e.g., charging for snacks and checked luggage. Some of the traditional airlines' customers finally rebel at paying high prices and suffering from service cutbacks. Some decide that they will switch to the low cost carriers and save money. Others may decide to "upgrade" to an option that they see as better meeting their needs or providing better value for money. This may mean switching to a "business class" only flight, such as those offered by Lufthansa and KLM on selected routes, or perhaps even using a corporate jet or a private air service. There has been rapid growth in executive jet services in all parts of the world in recent years as companies see growth opportunities in the premium segment of the market. NetJets, which specializes in fractional ownership of planes, has grown rapidly and even Lufthansa set up its own fleet of business jets to complement its traditional scheduled airline service.[79] If significant numbers of customers choose either to upgrade or downgrade there will be a "hollowing out" of the middle market as shown in Stage 4 in Figure 4.1. This has been the core market of traditional airlines.

The phenomenon of the "disappearing middle market" has been happening in many product categories and is a big issue for traditional appliance manufacturers, like Electrolux or General Electric, who are experiencing increasing competition from Asian players at the low end, and high-end specialty manufacturers, like Viking and Sub-Zero, at the high end.[80] In some industries there is a balanced polarization (leading to the "dumbbell" structure shown in Stage 4 in Figure 4.1), in others the migration is primarily to the low end or the high end.

In some business-to-business markets intense price competition at both the supplier and customer levels makes the suppliers' good enough products acceptable to almost all customers and the premium segment of the market disappears altogether. This can leave either a truncated pyramid, or a large good enough segment and a smaller low-end segment (see Figure 4.2).

FMCG companies also initially underestimated the threat posed by private label products that were introduced by retailers. Private label brands have existed for many years but were not a major factor in many product categories until much more recently. Marks & Spencer's St. Michael brands, as well as some of A&P's grocery brands, have existed for decades. When hard discounters like Aldi appeared on the European scene and began offering high quality private label products at

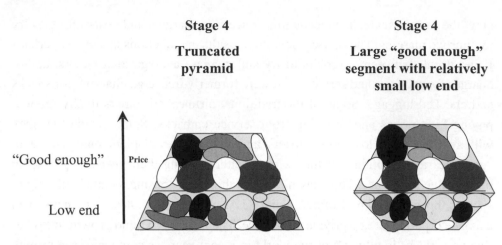

FIGURE 4.2   Other Stage 4 market structures

low prices, they were not initially seen as much of a threat. The hard discounters had only a few stores and were only a factor in a few countries, notably Germany. Some manufacturers saw them as a passing phenomenon. Some executives argued that the hard discounters were serving the many consumers who were living at a subsistence level after World War II. Once these consumers became more affluent, the executives argued, they would abandon the private label products and "graduate" to the manufacturer-controlled brands. But as we discussed earlier, this did not happen. Instead, their appeal broadened and they captured a high and growing share of the market in many countries, particularly in Europe.

In many European and North American countries, the first major thrust into private label products came from retailers such as Carrefour, Sainsbury's and Loblaws, when they introduced their lines of generic products. Usually, the packaging for these products was one color, often white or yellow, with the product being labeled simply "shampoo" or "spaghetti" in bold, black type. The products were usually quite cheap, of indifferent quality and did little to encourage consumers to switch from the manufacturer-branded products. Typically, they appealed to a small, very price-sensitive segment of the market, and they were not seen as much of a threat by branded products manufacturers. In time, some retailers started to see the benefits of higher quality, higher priced retailer-branded products as an important tool for building customer loyalty and gaining more bargaining power with the branded good manufacturers. Loblaws, the Canadian retailer, was a leader in North America in this area. It introduced a growing line of high quality products, some of them unique, under the President's Choice brand. This attracted an almost "cult" following in Canada, which contributed to Loblaws gaining market share. Other chains followed but not always with the same degree of success. The President's Choice brand built such brand equity that some US retailers started to carry the line, much to the consternation of some branded good manufacturers.

In Europe, it was the second-order effects from the hard discount revolution that probably had the biggest impact on the manufacturer-branded products. In order to counter the real, or perceived, danger from the growing hard discounter threat, many major and minor grocery retailers moved to a much more sophisticated portfolio of private label products. Perhaps the most typical approach was for a retailer to have three major sub-brands under the retailer's store brand. Typically, the lowest price line was a successor to the generic brand – a good basic quality line designed to be reasonably competitive at least on a price basis with the hard discounters' offerings. Generally, the range covered a few hundred to just over a thousand products and the sub-brand name communicated value or low price such as Tesco's Value line, Migros' (Switzerland) M-Budget line or Safeway's generic no-name line.

The second line was typically designed to match, or exceed, the quality of the manufacturer's branded product but at a lower price. Costco in North America had its Kirkland Signature line and many of the grocery retailers standard private label products were at this level. Generally, the products were simply branded with the retailer's store name.

The third sub-brand was the retailer's premium line that aimed to offer more unique products that matched or exceeded the best manufacturer brands, often at premium prices. Tesco's Finest line and Coop's (Switzerland) Fine Food line were examples of companies employing this strategy.

A growing number of retailers had also developed additional sub-brands for lines of specialized products targeted at particular market segments. These might typically include brands that focused on organic, fair traded, healthy, for children, etc. By 2008, one Swiss grocery retailer had over a dozen of these sub-brands.

So again, what began as a minor threat from hard discounters led to a series of reactions from traditional retailers. In many countries, their response of developing a more sophisticated private label strategy may have posed a more significant threat to the FMCG companies than the original challenge from hard discounters.

Similar developments have occurred in most branches of retailing, from clothing to furniture and housewares to some kinds of appliances and personal computers. Most retailers now have quite a sophisticated array of private label products that provide a very formidable threat to the brands of established manufacturers.

REALISTICALLY ASSESSING THE THREAT ... AND THE OPPORTUNITY

Clearly, what the management of a company would like to do is anticipate the potential threat that low cost competitors (including the second-order effects that might emerge over time) might pose to its business model before any competitor has actually entered the market. Then it at least has the possibility of acting pre-emptively, rather than reacting to the moves of a player, or players, that has already entered the market. This rarely happens, although some companies have seen a low cost threat emerge in one geographical market and pre-emptively have decided to take advantage of the low cost opportunity in other geographical markets where they may or may not already compete with a traditional offering.

As we discussed earlier, ING saw the potential for a low cost banking service in the results achieved by other direct banks in the Netherlands (its home market) and the UK. It decided to test its own direct banking concept in Canada in 1997 and rapidly became the country's first successful launch of a new retail bank in more than a quarter century. ING rapidly rolled out the new concept in the US, the UK, France, Spain, Australia, Germany, Italy and Austria with impressive results.

Few companies move as quickly as ING DIRECT did and even then it took them some years to act! The more likely situation for a management team is that one or more low cost competitors have already entered its market; or they have established a presence in a neighboring market segment that could provide a base for a later move against the traditional player's core business. In this case, it is important for the management team to develop a good understanding of how the low cost players' strategies might evolve over time and whether, in the long term, they could tap into some very attractive markets – perhaps even pose a clear threat to the company's core business. As part of this assessment, it is important to develop a deep understanding of the low cost players' business models and their potential limits. This will help determine how serious a threat they truly represent.

"Beat My Business" exercises can be a useful tool

A useful exercise for a management team trying to anticipate potential threats to, and opportunities for, their business is to periodically play "Beat My Business". The task given to small cross-functional teams of managers is to imagine that they are the management of a new entrant, or of a particular existing player, in the general market space within which the company already competes. While some companies use this approach for their traditional competitors, they don't always include existing or new low cost competitors in the exercise. They should! Each team is then assigned the task of developing a strategy and tactics to significantly strengthen the position of their competitor by exploiting the weaknesses of their own company, the resources and capabilities of the low cost competitor, as well as additional ones that it might develop or acquire.

One company that has used this approach effectively is Electrolux.[81] When Hans Straberg took over as CEO in 2002, one of the first things he did was travel around the world looking at the products new manufacturers, mostly Asian, were selling in their markets. Most of these products were not yet available in Western markets. He then shipped some of these products back to Europe for evaluation by Electrolux management and staff. Shortly afterward, Straberg and his management team held a series of workshops designed to shed light on the strategy of such Asian competitors as Samsung and LG from Korea. In one of the workshops, a team of Electrolux executives was asked to role-play the LG executive team with the assignment of developing strategies to beat incumbents like Electrolux. This thinking was then taken into serious account as Electrolux developed its own strategies.

In these types of "Beat My Business" exercises, the team is generally asked to develop a conventional or an unconventional strategy that will allow them to strengthen their competitive position and capture a significant market share. Having the teams go through a disciplined but creative process can improve the quality of the analysis and the usefulness of the results. A six-step process is shown in Figure 4.3.

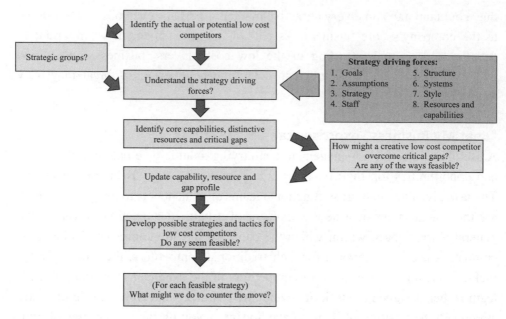

FIGURE 4.3   Flowchart to help anticipate the low cost competitive threat

Identifying actual and potential low cost competitors is key

The process of attempting to identify actual or potential low cost competitors is an important start. In some markets, there are a large number of actual, never mind potential, low cost competitors. In the wind energy business in China, for example, it was estimated that in 2007 there were over 50 competitors, many of them low cost. Clearly, it is unrealistic to try to assess the threat posed by each individual player. However, the analysis process can be simplified by organizing these low cost competitors into strategic groups – a strategic group is comprised of a set of companies that have similar resources and capabilities and compete in the market in a similar way.

As an example, the global airline industry has two major strategic groups: The large, full-service airlines that are often members of global alliances such as Star Alliance, and the low cost regional airlines that compete on the basis of low fares. The former group includes such airlines as American Airlines, Singapore Airlines, British Airways and Lufthansa. The latter group includes Air Asia, Southwest Airlines, JetBlue, Ryanair and easyJet. Similarly, there are strategic groups, even among low cost competitors. For example, there are a number of airlines in Europe that compete in relatively narrow geographical markets in a way similar to Ryanair. Like easyJet, others provide a higher level of service at higher prices with more service options.

By placing the actual and potential low cost competitors in relatively homogeneous strategic groups, the analysis task can be simplified. Since the low cost competitors within a strategic group frequently have similar strengths and weaknesses, value propositions and business systems, their strategies may evolve in similar ways over time. Even if there are a large number of low cost competitors, it may be possible to focus on the two or three major ones that might have distinctive profiles and strategies and then use a representative competitor from each of the remaining strategic groups in the market. Instead of looking individually at 25 or more players, a good insightful analysis may be done by focusing on four or five key or representative players.

Understanding what is driving the strategy of the low cost competitors

The next step is to assess some of the major factors that might influence the strategy or tactics of the low cost competitors. Some of the factors that might be relevant are shown in Figure 4.3. A company's goals or objectives can influence what it does. Does it have a stated goal, such as becoming the market share leader in a local market, becoming a global player, developing new technology, etc.? What are its assumptions about itself, the other players in the industry, the market (such as its growth rates, unmet needs) and the like? If a company knows, for example, that a large American player in the market is under severe shareholder pressure to generate better returns from its business, it might assume that if it put that competitor under severe pricing pressure in a peripheral market, the American competitor might withdraw from the market rather than see its margins decline to untenable levels.

A company will tend to follow its past strategy if that strategy has worked well in the past. Go, British Airways' low cost subsidiary, launched a service between Edinburgh and Dublin in the winter of 2001. Ryanair did not serve this route at the time but it did not want another low cost carrier serving the low fare market between the UK and Ireland. It therefore launched its own service between the two cities undercutting Go's fares. Given that Ryanair had a substantially lower cost structure than Go, it was better able to sustain the resulting price war. After almost three months of intense competition, Go finally admitted defeat and withdrew from the market leaving Ryanair victorious. Despite Go's unfortunate experience, easyJet also tried to enter the Irish market in 2004, as we saw earlier in this chapter. Not surprisingly, Ryanair matched the easyJet routes and another price war erupted. Again, Ryanair was the victor. Other competitors can probably expect the same treatment if they try to challenge Ryanair in one of its important markets.

Staff can be another important strategy driver or strategy inhibitor. What are the backgrounds of the key executives, particularly the CEO or the head of the relevant business unit? In what part of the business did they grow up? What past accomplishments have propelled them to their current position? Again, having an in-depth understanding of these kinds of things might provide useful insights into the strategies and tactics that a low cost competitor might utilize. For low cost competitors expanding from bases in countries like China, talent – or the lack of it – may influence their strategic choices. In one McKinsey survey of executives in Chinese companies with global ambitions, 44% of the respondents mentioned a shortage of managerial talent as being a major barrier to growth outside of China.[82] This is likely to be a particular issue for those companies trying to move into more sophisticated segments where strong brands, deep relationships with customers and cultural understanding are important. The talent shortage could well influence a competitor's growth strategy.

A low cost competitor's structure and systems can also suggest what direction it might take or how it might respond to competitive or market developments. There are companies that might be better able to offer their customers value-added services, if that becomes a competitive necessity. And companies, like individuals, have a style, often reflecting the personality of the chief executive – some are quite rational and only seem to make decisions after a careful and reasoned analysis; others seem to react much more impulsively and aggressively, if they are confronted or challenged by a competitor.

A thorough assessment of the strategy driving forces for each of the major low cost competitors, and strategic groups of competitors, can be an important first step in developing an understanding of their likely future actions and how they might respond to competitive moves in the market. An important area to monitor over time is change in any of these strategy driving forces. Has a new CEO been appointed or have they added new members to the executive team or board of directors? Has there been any change in their stated objectives? Have they restructured the company in any way? Any type of change may signal that an alteration in strategy is in the works. For example, Vueling, the low cost Spanish carrier, appointed Barbara Cassani, the founding CEO of Go, to its board in June 2007. At that point in time, Vueling, which had a business model very similar to Ryanair's, was experiencing heavy losses. Go had competed as a "nicer, more friendly" low cost carrier and was having some success when BA decided to sell it. Was the appointment of Cassani a signal that Vueling was going to try to move up market to escape the competitive pressure of Ryanair? If so, this might have been good news for Ryanair but bad news for Iberia, the Spanish flag carrier.

Core capabilities, distinctive resources and major gaps are often key drivers of a low cost competitor's strategy

Clearly, a major factor influencing the strategy and tactics of low cost competitors are their resources and capabilities, particularly those that help them stand out from their competitors. For example, a low cost competitor based in India might have access to high quality, low cost engineering talent. It's useful then to think through how it might leverage this distinctive resource. Is there a customer segment that might prefer a product more customized to its needs, if it were available for only a small price premium? Might this be a way for the Indian competitor to break into the North American market? Or consider Digicel, a mobile operator that got its start in Jamaica in 2001 when the market was opened up to competition. The incumbent, Cable & Wireless, offered a high-priced service that was accessible only to people who were relatively well off. Denis O'Brien, founder of Digicel, decided to offer a low cost service based on a state-of-the-art network. He rapidly extended wireless coverage to rural and thinly populated areas of Jamaica where there had been no mobile service at all. With low-priced, prepaid service and cheap handsets, he became the island's largest mobile operator within 15 months. Having developed the capabilities to build, launch and profitably operate a wireless telecom company in a newly liberalized market where incomes were generally quite low, he quickly applied the same strategy in over 20 similar Caribbean markets. In 2006, he began moving into other similar island markets in the South Pacific. In 2007, private equity firms valued Digicel at $3.8 billion.[83]

While it is important to understand the distinctive resources and core capabilities of low cost competitors, it is often at least as important to understand the resource and capability gaps that might inhibit their ability to grow. Do these gaps represent an across the board limitation, or are they only constrained with respect to some market segments? For example, customers might only be willing to buy from a low cost competitor that does not have a long established quality record if the application is a low-risk one. In one particular instance, customers were willing to use a low cost Chinese competitor's product in clothing applications but not for an application in tires. The product liability risk of a tire failing was just too high for the customers; they preferred to buy higher priced products from Western manufacturers with long-established quality track records. Therefore, the Western and Japanese manufacturers knew that they were less vulnerable to low cost competition in the high risk product applications, unless, and until, the Chinese competitor was able to establish a strong quality track record.

Low cost competitors can overcome critical gaps in creative ways

Sometimes it appears that current or potential low cost competitors are severely limited by critical gaps in either resources or capabilities. In the example above, the lack of a quality track record limited the low cost competitor's ability to compete in what customers viewed as high liability risk applications. Low cost competitors, however, are sometimes able to find creative ways to overcome some of these apparent gaps. Huawei, the leading Chinese telecommunications equipment manufacturer, lacked some critical intellectual property (IP) that was required to strengthen its position in an important market. However, it was able to fill this gap by buying a bankrupt Western competitor with this IP at a very low cost. Similarly, Chinese wind energy competitors had been able to license important IP for wind turbines from German and Japanese manufacturers that were under significant competitive pressure.

This is, in fact, a common way for companies in developing countries to overcome what could be critical gaps in research and development, branding, relationships with first world customers, etc. Nanjing Automotive Company bought the bankrupt MG Rover Group in 2005 to gain access to the MG and Austin brands and certain research and development and technical capabilities.[84] For similar reasons Tata Motors bought the Jaguar and Land Rover businesses from Ford for an estimated $2.3 billion in 2008 in order to acquire the well-known iconic brands, as well as the know-how and sales networks that it would need to expand its presence outside of India.[85] Acquisitions can also help companies fill some of the managerial talent gaps they have in critical areas.

Some Indian and Chinese automotive parts companies are also starting to buy European and North American companies that have strong supplier relationships with automobile manufacturers and their tier 1 suppliers, allowing them to accelerate the development of their business with these manufacturers.

In 2005, Haier, the large Chinese appliance manufacturer, attempted to buy Maytag, North America's third largest major appliance manufacturer, to help accelerate its growth in North America. Maytag, a highly regarded brand in its own right, also owned a number of other well-known North American appliance brands. Whirlpool, the large US-based major appliance manufacturer, was so concerned about the potential impact of this move that it bid for Maytag itself. It was successful, but the company paid a steep price for keeping the brands from falling into Haier's hands – about $1.9 billion.[86]

Developing new core capabilities is often much more challenging than simply filling a resource gap. As we have seen, getting access to the latest production technology or a particular piece of IP, may not be a huge challenge. Core capabilities are bundles of skills, knowledge and collective learning that allow companies to execute critical processes, at least at the level of their best competitors. By their nature, core capabilities are based on culture, systems and processes that are not very easy to develop or duplicate. Even when a company is able to copy the strategy and match the hard assets of a company like Ryanair, it may have difficulty in executing the strategy at anything approaching the same level of excellence. Similarly, a low cost telecommunications equipment company like Huawei may, over time, be able to offer products that are comparable to, or perhaps even better than, those of Cisco, but it may still have great difficulty matching Cisco's capability to service sophisticated and complex global customers effectively.

With globalization, many Chinese and Indian companies also have access to the world's leading consulting companies, advertising agencies, legal firms, etc., and many are availing themselves of their services. As private equity investors increasingly penetrate most world markets, they can bring their expertise and connections to help these companies access and acquire the resources and capabilities they need to grow. The Blackstone Group, a large private equity firm, invested $600 million in ChemChina, China's largest chemical conglomerate in 2007.

ChemChina claims it has benefited from access to Blackstone's experience, contacts and expertise in the global chemical industry as it expands rapidly outside of China.[87]

How might a low cost competitor significantly enhance its position?

Once you have gained an understanding of your low cost competitors and developed a sense of their resources and capabilities and how they might fix critical gaps, you can start to think creatively about how each low cost competitor, or strategic group of competitors, might best enhance their company's market position. The following questions and examples will help a management team jump-start its analysis:

- **Are there disruptive technologies or business strategies that the low cost player could use to improve its market position, particularly ones that it is best positioned to leverage?**

There is a pressing need in many Chinese and Indian markets for affordable products or services that hundreds of millions of consumers, with limited ability to pay, might be able to afford. It is no surprise that many companies in these markets have focused on low cost technologies that provide good enough solutions such as Tata's World Car. In some cases, this has led them to focus on disruptive technologies.

A good example of this occurred in the digital radiography market in China.[88] Traditionally most diagnostic X-ray images were captured using analog technology where an exposure resulted in an image on a film. However, this analog technology was being replaced in the late 1990s by direct digital radiography (DDR), allowing an X-ray scan to be captured electronically and viewed immediately and directly on a screen. There were two leading technologies for digital radiography. Flat panel imaging was favored by the leading diagnostic imaging companies such as GE and Philips. Despite relatively poor image quality and high radiation dosages for the patient, it could be used for real time applications such as imaging a beating heart. The second imaging technology – line scanning – had better resolution but it took about ten seconds to do a scan and the patient had to stay completely still during the procedure. It was obviously not suitable for imaging hearts or other moving organs but it was appropriate for routine radiography applications in a hospital or clinic.

The cost of line scanning machines was estimated to be about 10–15% of the cost of flat panel imaging machines.

A Chinese company, Zhongxing Medical, developed the line scanning technology, leveraging the original work on the technology done by Philips, a Dutch company, and a Russian research institute, and launched it in China in 1999. It was particularly successful in second- and third-tier hospitals in China; within five years, Zhongxing Medical had captured 50% of the Chinese DDR market. The company continued to invest in product development and over time, it came closer to matching the performance of the flat panel machines sold by GE and Philips. Increasingly, as is typical with disruptive technologies, they are displacing the mainstream technology in more and more demanding applications.

Some additional questions that a management team assessing competitive threats should ask itself are:

• **What could a company do if it had access to very low cost R&D, engineering or production?**

It could, for example, afford to customize products to better meet customer needs. Haier has used this approach in some of its markets to gain competitive advantage. The company has been willing to do minor customization of some of its appliances to meet the particular needs of certain retailers.

• **What would happen, if the competitor dramatically dropped prices? Is the market likely to be very price elastic?**

This has been a common tactic of low cost competitors, and again, Haier has used this tactic to its advantage. The home wine cooler market had existed in the US for many years, but the wine coolers were so expensive that they sold in relatively low volumes to sophisticated, and relatively wealthy, wine consumers, usually through specialty stores. Haier decided to introduce wine coolers to the US at a price that was about 50% less than the existing manufacturers were charging. At this price point, its refrigerator offerings became attractive to mass merchandisers, as well as to middle-class consumers, and the market exploded. Within two years, Haier had captured a 55% share of the US market.

Low cost competitors often follow similar strategies to improve their position

Low cost competitors are often able to improve their market position by targeting segments that have traditionally been of little or no interest to the mainstream players. On the surface at least, these market segments are often unattractive and promise little or no profit or threaten to cannibalize profitable, existing business if they were developed. Frequent targets of low cost competitors in many industries have been:

Unexploited niche markets. Looking back to the home wine cooler example, we see that, as is often the case, the niche market turned out to be much bigger than anticipated when there was a product with a low enough price point. Similarly, the low cost airline market was initially also seen as a niche market. Today Ryanair carries more passengers than BA.

Peripheral markets. Successful low cost competitors often start on the path to success by exploiting peripheral markets that are not seen as being attractive by the mainstream players. Wal-Mart started in the Deep South. Komatsu's strategy in the heavy equipment industry was to encircle Caterpillar before challenging it in its core markets. Huawei has followed a similar strategy. The Chinese company first ventured outside the mainland to Hong Kong where it made its first sale to Hutchinson (which later became Orange) in 1995.[89] As Orange expanded into a number of countries, mostly in Europe, Huawei was able to leverage this customer relationship and gain access to more geographic markets. Under its own power, it moved from Hong Kong into a series of second- and third-tier markets including Vietnam, Russia and a large number of countries in Africa and South America. In all these markets the company leveraged, and further developed, its expertise in developing cost-effective telecom networks that could help the telecommunications network operators serve scattered, poor and rural populations profitably. Most of its Western competitors saw poor prospects for profitable growth in these types of markets. From a strong position in these market types, and with a growing reputation, Huawei was able to get a foothold in the Middle East for its advanced 3G technology in direct competition with leading Western firms. Huawei's reputation for very strong technology and intense, if not always sophisticated, customer support (leveraging its low cost Chinese engineers and technicians) helped Huawei to break into the European market in 2004 with another 3G contract with a maverick Dutch mobile operator, Telfort.[90] When Telfort was acquired by KPN, the largest Dutch telecommunications company, Huawei found itself as a supplier to one of the largest operators in Europe. Since then it has been able to capture significant business from other leading European operators including British Telecom. So in just over ten years Huawei was able to move from its base in China into the heart of Europe, the home market of some of its strongest global competitors. Although it had only made some small inroads into the North American market by 2008, it seemed only a matter of time before it established a major presence there.

Low-end segments with basic needs. Many of the low cost competitors start by serving low-end segments with very basic needs. This was, and is, the primary focus of a low cost carrier like Ryanair.

Segments where the cost of an effective response seems too high for the mainstream players. Many low cost competitors take advantage of the reluctance of the mainstream players to pursue market segments where the returns are likely to be very low and/or where there is significant potential for cannibalizing their existing high-margin business. Part of the reluctance of the large Canadian banks to move into the direct banking market in competition with ING DIRECT was due to the potential loss of hundreds of millions of dollars of profit if they cannibalized their traditional savings accounts that paid very low rates of interest relative to a direct bank like ING DIRECT.

Another common element of many low cost competitors' strategies is to move from segment to segment over time; often using the experience, reputation and relationships they have developed in the previous market segments to assist their entry into the next segment. In essence, this was how Huawei moved from China into Europe. Each of the intervening moves leveraged on its previous record to create a smooth transition. It was able to leverage the relationship it built with Hutchinson (Orange) in Hong Kong to gain business in other markets as Hutchinson entered them. The strong reputation it built, initially in China and then Hong Kong, Africa and other markets, for its willingness to tailor technical solutions to customer needs and provide very heavy on-the-ground support helped it to break into the Middle East and Europe. A frontal assault on the European market without first building its reputation in the peripheral markets would almost certainly have failed.

Haier also successfully rolled from segment to segment to gain a foothold in the North American market. Haier first entered the US market in 1990. Its initial product was compact refrigerators which due to their small size could be imported economically from China. Its primary target segment was college students.[91] To differentiate itself from its competitors, it did such things as adding hinged wooden flaps to the refrigerator, which could be folded out, making the refrigerator double as a computer table. It also targeted assisted living facilities that also had a need for compact refrigerators for each apartment or room. Targeting these kinds of niche segments meant that initially it did not need access to mass distribution channels – it could use a much more focused approach. This initial foray also started the process of building the Haier brand in the US. By 2002, Haier had captured almost 50% of the country's compact refrigerator market.

As mentioned earlier in the chapter, the next market segment Haier went after was the low cost wine cooler market. Penetrating this segment required access to mass distribution, but with the success of its compact refrigerators and the new profit opportunity that wine coolers promised, it was successful in getting companies like Wal-Mart, Lowes, Home Depot and Sears to carry these products. By 2002, it had achieved a 55% market share in this product category. The acceptance of its products and its ability to service its channels well helped Haier build its reputation with its retail partners.

With a toehold in the channels of distribution, the way was paved for Haier to move into full-sized refrigerators. It began developing models to meet the needs of the American market and opened a manufacturing plant in South Carolina in 2000. Since that time, it has steadily expanded its US presence with refrigerators and freezers and more recently other categories of major appliances. In 2007, it began a major expansion of its plant in South Carolina to accommodate more products.

It is a challenge to anticipate the moves of unconventional competitors

One of the biggest challenges of successfully applying the "Beat My Business" tool is anticipating the potential strategy and tactics a low cost competitor might use to capture a growing share of the market over time.

It's difficult enough for a management team when it is looking at actual or prospective competition operating in the same business environment as its own company. Even more difficult is trying to anticipate the moves and growth strategy of a competitor that is based in a very different business environment and has very different resources and capabilities than the team's own company, or the other companies with which it is used to competing.

Western companies often have particular difficulties anticipating the possible strategies that companies based in China or India might follow to gain competitive advantage and win market share. One approach that has proved successful for some companies is to review the approaches that companies from other developing markets adopted in the early stages of their challenges to the Western incumbents. This might be done within the company's industry, or other industries that it views as being analogous. There are often lessons to be learned from the strategies and tactics adopted by Japanese and Korean companies in the last half of the twentieth century.

However, naively adopting the lessons from these earlier generations of low cost competitors can be highly misleading.

Firstly, as discussed earlier, the Chinese and Indian domestic markets for some products and services are much larger than the equivalent markets in Japan and Korea (often by an order of magnitude). If a Chinese or Indian company is able to dominate, or own a major share of its home market, it will have better economies of scale and a much larger and perhaps more secure base on which to grow.

Secondly, as discussed at length in Chapter 2, the emergence of many focused companies concentrating on one of the core sets of business activities – customer relationships, innovation and product commercialization, or infrastructure – means a new entrant today need not master all three sets of activities; it does not have to replicate the complete set of activities in order to compete with a traditional player. Many of the Japanese and Korean companies did have to do this. Now the latest entrants can specialize and draw on the expertise and resources of best-in-class partners, not only in their local market but globally as well. As discussed in Chapter 2, the standardization and modularization of many products and processes that has happened over the last 20 years or so has made it much easier for low cost competitors to enter markets and compete effectively.

Thirdly, many Chinese and Indian companies have benefited, and are benefiting, from access to their diaspora of executives, entrepreneurs, engineers and scientists who have gained invaluable business experience working in leading companies in North America and Europe. Drawing on these resources can give these companies extremely talented and experienced people who have seen how the very best companies operate and organize, and who may have established relationships with potential customers and suppliers. Japanese and Korean companies did not have the same level of access to similar resources when they were at the same development stage.

Chinese companies, in some industries, also have privileged and low cost access to intellectual property that was originally developed in state-funded research institutes. In fact, some of China's emerging champions such as Lenovo, the third largest personal computer company in the world, and Dawning, a significant player in both high performance computing and low cost servers, were originally launched out of a government research institute.[92]

For all these reasons, the progress of Chinese and Indian competitors is likely to be much more rapid than the earlier competitors from Japan and Korea.

Another difficulty for many management teams is to imagine creatively what a smart competitor might do with the resources and capabilities available to it. Everyone recognizes that companies in developing countries have access to low cost labor, including low cost scientists and engineers. But imagining all the ways a company could take advantage of low cost engineering, for example, is much more difficult since most managers only have conventional notions about how companies should play the game.

Some Chinese and Indian companies have used low cost engineering to develop high performance products, as well as to achieve breakthroughs with low cost price points. They have sometimes been willing to trade off high performance for good performance at very low prices; or they have focused on process innovation so they could, for example, offer high variety at very low cost. Both of these strategies can have a devastating impact on typical Western companies by undermining their business models. A Chinese company may be able to offer tremendous variety at low cost through a combination of re-engineering processes – developing more flexible production systems and, in some cases, replacing automated systems with low cost and flexible manual systems. This could undermine the business model of a Western company that provides a range of niche products at relatively high prices. Normally, a Western company might anticipate that a low cost competitor might pursue the high volume segments of the market, not low volume niche segments.

Since there is a pressing need in many Chinese and Indian markets for affordable products or services to service hundreds of millions of consumers with a limited ability to pay, it's not surprising that many companies in these markets have focused on low cost technologies that provide good enough solutions, such as Tata's World Car. In some cases, this has led them to focus on disruptive technologies.

MOST BUSINESS MODELS HAVE LIMITED REACH

Business models for low cost competitors are quite different from those used by their traditional competitors – they play the game differently. As we have seen in numerous examples in this book, the target segments, value propositions and business systems of low cost competitors are different. Like any other business, a low cost competitor succeeds when it has a value proposition that:

- is responsive to the needs of its target segment;
- is differentiated from those of its competitors;
- fits with its resources and capabilities;
- is able to be delivered by the company's business system.

A company's business system must be designed to deliver the right product or service at the right price, through the right channels and with the value proposition effectively communicated to the target segment (see Figure 4.4). Ryanair targets a different segment of customers than British Airways. BA's primary target is its business customer, particularly the long-haul business customer. Thus, BA's value proposition is very different than Ryanair's, as is the business system designed to deliver that value proposition.

Most business systems have limits in terms of the range of different market segments that they can serve effectively. In the early stages of market development, early entrants often have relatively unfocused strategies. They tend to go after a rather broad range of segments with an "all purpose" solution, often built around performance value. The business model may be somewhat flexible, allowing a low cost competitor to partially meet the needs of a broad cross-section of customers. At the outset, the market segments may not be well defined and the total number of customers may not be very large. As the market develops, however, and the

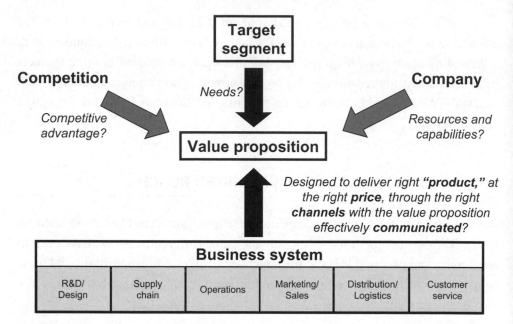

FIGURE 4.4 The business system must be designed to deliver the value proposition

segments become more clearly delineated, some competitors may refine their focus on customers with particular needs, often performance-based needs such as particular features, ease of use, reliability or style. As we discussed in Chapter 2, as progress is made in these areas the performance is more than adequate for some customers, and they now start paying more attention to price value or relational value and competitors emerge that respond to these needs.

If the market competition is intense, we will see companies that are intent on meeting the needs of their target segment and have highly tuned business systems to deliver the value proposition successfully. The low cost competitors usually develop a differentiated business model that allows them to offer an attractive price value proposition to certain segments of the market. But usually this differentiated, and specialized, business model does not allow the low cost competitor to challenge the incumbent in all market segments. Clearly, the low cost airline business model is the best fit for leisure travelers, "commuters" traveling between home and work or business people paying out of their own pockets, who are traveling within a region, have some flexibility in terms of dates and time of day, are not very time sensitive and are satisfied with a basic level of point-to-point service. The business model provides the low cost carrier with its greatest competitive advantage on relatively short route lengths, where the airline is able to use one type of plane and is able to achieve very fast turnarounds as a result of minimal checked baggage, use of uncongested airports and so on.

However, the typical business model of low cost airlines has clear limits; it will not allow these airlines to successfully challenge the full-service airlines on intercontinental routes, where many passengers, particularly business travelers, value additional services. Many of them can make a strong business case to their employers that they need a comfortable seat for sleeping in order to be rested and productive when they get to their destination. They do need some schedule choices, more flexibility to change flights, as well as someone to look after them if there are major disruptions to their travel plans as a result of bad weather, flight cancellations, missed connections, lost bags, etc. While there may not be enough of these travelers on most routes to fill a plane, there are often enough of these passengers to provide a solid business base. If the airline is able to fill the rest of the plane with less-demanding economy passengers, making some contribution above their variable costs, this can provide a profitable foundation. Thus, while many of a traditional carrier's local and regional business might be threatened by low cost airlines, its core intercontinental routes and some of the feeder routes that support the intercontinental business may be insulated from this type of low cost competitor.

Unfortunately, this does not mean that the traditional carriers are off the hook! They might still be faced with other low cost carriers that decide to focus on the profitable core of their business – the highest-volume, intercontinental routes servicing a large number of first- or business-class passengers. Routes where a high proportion of the travelers fly point-to-point and have no need for connecting flights make a particularly attractive target. In 2005, this started to happen on a few key routes, particularly the high traffic ones between Europe and the US, such as London–New York, London–Washington and Paris–New York. A couple of new all-business carriers, such as Silverjet, began competing with BA, Virgin Atlantic and the major US carriers by offering a similar service at significantly lower prices than the incumbents. These carriers generally used secondary airports at both ends of the route (such as Newark in the US and London Stansted or London Luton in the UK). Most of these airlines collapsed when fuel costs soared in 2008.[93] However, this does not mean that a low cost competitor won't eventually successfully challenge the traditional airlines on selected long-haul routes.

Ryanair even threatened to enter the North Atlantic market in 2006 by targeting price sensitive customers. The carrier expected to offer a two-class service using secondary airports in Europe and North America; Michael O'Leary suggested that this North Atlantic service would be operated by a business unit that was independent from Ryanair's traditional European business. Air Asia, which modeled its low cost company on Ryanair, moved in this direction in late 2007 in its region. Through an affiliated company Air Asia X, it began offering a two-class, low cost long-haul service with its first route between Kuala Lumpur, Malaysia and the Gold Coast in Australia.

DEVELOPING A WORST CASE SCENARIO CAN PROVIDE A "BURNING PLATFORM"

After the various teams have developed their "Beat My Business" strategies, it's often useful to bring the various low cost competitor strategy scenarios together to see what it might mean for the traditional company. It may also be advantageous to think through the possible strategies that the other traditional players might take to counter the low cost threat. In some cases, their reactions to the threat may be more damaging to the company's business than the combined impact of the low cost competitors. The combined scenario might provide the "burning platform" for change that will be needed to get the organization to respond quickly and appropriately to the low cost challenge.

To develop a motivating scenario for the organization, one approach is to take the collective inputs and build a "worst-case" or NO GO scenario about what would happen if a company did not respond at all to the threat posed by low cost competitors (and any second-order effects from the company's other traditional competitors). It may be unrealistically pessimistic but it may be just what is needed to jolt the organization into a serious analysis of the alternatives and possible action.

A good example of a company facing a very unattractive NO GO scenario was Sealed Air with its AirCap line of bubble packaging, mentioned in Chapter 3. Bubble packaging or bubble wrap was initially a high-end packaging solution for customers. It fulfilled a need for high performance protection of fragile or easily damaged products that were in storage or transit for extended periods of time. Sealed Air was a leader in this market in North America and Europe, and its leadership products incorporated a barrier coating that reduced air leakage from the bubbles; the product was quite expensive and sold based on the value it offered customers in terms of less damage and less breakage. In the early 1980s, however, Sealed Air was increasingly challenged by competitors that were marketing less sophisticated, uncoated bubble products for less demanding applications. These competitors had captured a significant share in several European markets and were gaining momentum in North America.

The Sealed Air situation looked quite bleak. But to bring the NO GO scenario to life it is important to try to understand the approach that a competitor, or competitors, might use. One viable scenario might be that one or more uncoated bubble competitors developed a line of uncoated bubble products that complemented Sealed Air's line of higher quality, coated bubble products. With this as leverage, they might have been able to penetrate Sealed Air's distribution channels and build relationships with these distributors. The distributors would be attracted to the uncoated bubble player's products because they could better service a number of customers that had needs for both coated and uncoated bubble applications. Then, over time, the uncoated players might improve their products, or work around Sealed Air's patents, to develop a line that challenged Sealed Air's coated bubble product in terms of performance. If a manufacturer of uncoated bubble products had been able to develop significant volume at the lower end, it would have been able to go to the distributors (if the distributors were willing to concentrate their bubble packaging purchasing with the manufacturer) and offer attractive terms such as volume discounts based on total purchases of both coated and uncoated bubble packaging. At the very least, this would have placed Sealed Air in a more difficult position. At worst, Sealed Air might have found itself locked out of some of the key channels for its products that it had at one time "owned".

Sometimes these vivid NO GO scenarios can end up painting such a bleak picture that the management team realizes it has to respond to the threat, even if the short run financial results are not as attractive as it might like.

Ultimately, Sealed Air did respond to the competitive threat with its own line of economical, uncoated bubble wrap packaging called PolyCap for application types at significantly lower prices than its traditional product line. The lower prices made it feasible for customers who had previously used cardboard, paper, peanut shells and pieces of foam to consider using bubble wrap packaging. This significantly expanded the overall size of Sealed Air's packaging market. If it had not responded and left the "bottom end" of the bubble wrap packaging market to its competitors, these competitors might have been able to build up a large base of business in that market segment and ultimately pose a threat to Sealed Air in its own traditional market. By offering PolyCap to its distributors, it also made it more difficult for low cost competitors to get access to an effective distribution channel.

GE Healthcare is another company that has been very concerned about leaving opportunities in the lower performance segments of the diagnostic imaging markets to low cost competitors. It developed a line of good enough, reliable and less costly MRI machines targeting hospitals in Chinese second- and third-tier cities. By 2004, GE was reported to have a 52% share of this growing market – almost $250 million a year – and seemed to be successfully defending its position against low cost, local competitors.[94]

FRAMING THE FINANCIAL ANALYSIS AS A COMPARISON OF TWO FUTURES IS CRITICAL

One of the major barriers to an effective and timely response to low cost competitors is in the minds of the executives; they must make the fundamental decision about whether they want to react. For simplicity's sake, let's assume that the best way for a particular company to respond to its low cost competitors is to introduce a new product that will compete directly with the competitive offerings at a competitive price. As Figure 4.5 suggests there are three financial perspectives that might be relevant to the decision – the present, the future with the new product and the future without the new product.

In the "present", the company often has good volumes at attractive margins and is making attractive profits in the business. The "future with the new product" while often adding some incremental volume, albeit at significantly lower margins, often results in the company cannibalizing some of the sales of its existing high-margin business. At first glance, this does not look like an attractive proposition for the shareholders. However, the third perspective, "the future without the new product", is usually even less appealing. Here the low cost competitors have

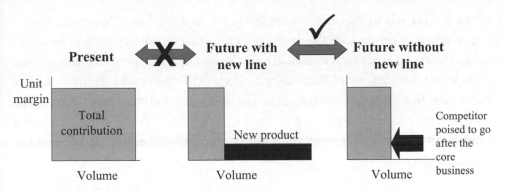

FIGURE 4.5 Always compare two futures

eroded some of the company's existing business and are now well-established and often well-positioned to go after the company's core, high-margin business.

Clearly, the relevant comparison should always be the one comparing the two futures: the future where the company challenges the low cost competitors with truly competitive offerings versus the future where it ignores them, which might jeopardize its future prospects. However, too often we see management teams debating the merits of the present versus the future with the new product. The present was wonderful while it lasted but it's now gone forever. The real issue is which of the two "future" perspectives leaves the company better positioned.

While the need for this kind of analysis seems obvious, many management teams resist doing it. When making its decision on whether to launch a low cost subsidiary, Barbara Cassani, CEO of Go, described how BA had never really analyzed the likely impact of that on its core business.[95] Many of the executives worried about peripheral issues such as the impact of Go (which would not pay commissions to travel agents) on BA's relationships with its travel agents, or whether Go should ever be allowed to compete with BA on major profitable routes like London–Milan. But they never seemed to have the discipline to look realistically at the two options for the future: one future with Go and one without it. Eventually, the BA board approved the launch of Go largely because the CEO at the time, Bob Ayling, was firmly behind the move.

Another barrier to facing the hard reality and acting on it is the concern that many management teams have about how the analysts will react to their strategic moves. In some cases, meeting the low cost competition threat requires the company to either pre-empt or confront the low cost competitors in segments of the market where the margins are likely to be quite low. This could have a negative impact on some of the financial metrics that the analysts might be monitoring closely on a quarterly or annual basis. Ironically, good performance on some of these metrics may mean that a company is unwilling to make the hard choices about how best to deal with the challenge of low cost competition. So, in fact, weaker performance on the metrics in the short run may be good news as a company improves its long run strategic position but at the expense of short run financial returns.

CHALLENGE QUESTIONS

Are you in an industry, or the stage of an industry life cycle, where you are less vulnerable to a low cost threat? Why do you feel this way? Will it change? What might be the early indicators of change?

Are you underestimating the low cost threat to your business? Is there a disruptive technology or business model already in the industry, which will become a threat in more and more segments over time? Are you in an industry where the low cost threat, by its very nature, will gain momentum over time? Is there a potential "second-order effect" in your industry as the competition among the low cost competitors intensifies, creating "winners" and "losers", with some of the losers becoming value-added players that will compete more directly with you?

Would a "Beat My Business" exercise be a useful one for your company? Which low cost competitors or strategic groups of low cost competitors should you focus on? When profiling these competitors, are you taking a dynamic enough view and recognizing that they might take active steps to acquire new resources and capabilities to accelerate their growth? Are you being sufficiently creative in anticipating the strategic moves they might make to enhance their market position, perhaps by rolling through a series of segments over time? Are you fully anticipating the possible moves that less conventional low cost competitors might take, particularly those from the developing world?

Have you thought about the limits of the business models of your low cost competitors that might limit the segments of the market they address? Could they leapfrog into a new business model or add a business unit with a new business model that might hurt you in additional segments?

Would it be worthwhile to develop a worst-case scenario of what might happen if you don't challenge your low cost competitors? Would it be even worse news for you if you didn't challenge them but some of your other traditional competitors did? What would this scenario look like?

Are you considering the right financial scenarios as you assess the impact of low cost competition on your business? Are you falling into the trap of comparing the present with the future, instead of two or more futures?

CHAPTER 5

Confronting low cost competitors in the price value segment of the market

The task of realistically assessing the threat, particularly the long-term threat, from low cost competition is often a challenging and contentious one for the management of a traditional company. If the assessment is done at the early stages of the development of low cost competition in the industry, the debate will be even more contentious because many executives will still be in denial. To them the threat is not material. They will have difficulty imagining how a few "fly by night" operators, perhaps based in distant markets, with shoestring operations and "crappy" products could ever be a threat to their formidable company, its strong market position, great products and apparently satisfied customer base. Later, the threat will be more visible and real, since a few tentative low cost winners will probably have emerged and, at least in some markets and some segments, the traditional company will now be feeling that a real battle is shaping up.

Once management has realistically thought through and assessed the long-term threat posed by existing and potential low cost competitors – and if it has decided the threat is real and pressing – it must decide how to respond. One of the toughest choices any top management team has to make is whether to enter the price value segment of the market and directly confront low cost competitors in their market space. In making this choice, management must weigh the advantages and disadvantages of such a move in the context of its particular business. Companies that serve their end user indirectly must consider the complete downstream value chain, such as distributors and retailers, and the likely evolution of this value chain in arriving at a decision.

A second important issue that management must deal with in many situations is how far "down market" it should go. Does it mean confronting the low cost competitors at every level in the market? As we will argue, in many situations it is not necessary, or even advisable, to try to compete at all price points in the market. The major benefits of confronting low cost competitors, if deemed advisable, can often be achieved by coming up against the low cost competitors in the mid-tier market segments. It is not always necessary, or advisable, to confront those operating at the very bottom of the market.

If the decision is made to move into the price value segment, or segments, of the market then the management team faces a new set of more tactical decisions about the best way to do so. One of the key issues is whether to enter the price value market with an independent business unit – through an acquisition, joint venture or organic growth – or to do it with products and services marketed by the core business unit. Clearly, there is a continuum of choices from two totally independent business units to one totally integrated business. Again, there are no simple answers but each clearly has its advantages and disadvantages; the choice depends on the objectives of the company and the particular market situation. We will look at several examples of how different companies have made these decisions and what seems to have driven their choices.

In some business-to-business markets, a number of companies have chosen to meet the needs of the market's price value segment by offering these customers re-manufactured products. This is one way to respond to customers who do not need the latest technology, but who do need to find economical solutions.

We will end this chapter by taking a look at three case examples of companies moving into the price value segment of their markets. Nokia is one company that has developed a strong position in the entry segments of the market in almost all countries around the world. Perhaps its biggest challenge to date has been China. In the case of Dow Corning, we will see how a leading chemical company set up a focused business unit to compete very directly for customers seeking low prices and willing to settle for "bare bones" service and no technical support. In a third case study, we will look at Aer Lingus, an airline that is in the unfortunate situation of sharing its home market with Ryanair, making price differences between the two airlines very visible and challenging. The company has learned many lessons from Ryanair and has ended up converting its short-haul business into a reasonably price competitive operation designed to co-exist with Ryanair while undercutting many of the flag carriers with which it also competes.

Ultimately, many companies, after weighting the pros and cons of the various options for meeting the needs of the price value segments, decide not to enter these arenas. However, they still face the challenge of how to manage the competitive threat posed by their low cost competitors. We will turn our attention to this issue in Chapter 6.

COMPETING AT ALL LEVELS IN THE MARKET IS USUALLY NOT NECESSARY

An important issue for most companies that are considering entering a market's price value segment is how far down market should they go to compete. In many markets, particularly those in the developing world, there is a wide range of price points. At the very bottom of the market, there are very basic products that may or may not deliver even the most basic functionality. These products may be made from sub-standard or even unsafe materials, have poor and inconsistent quality, may not be reliable and may offer no or very limited after sales service or support. The producers of some of these products or services could be "here today, gone tomorrow", giving the buyer no recourse if the product or service fails to perform. Referring to our earlier discussion, these are *not* good enough solutions for the vast majority of reasonably informed customers. But these kinds of product and services do exist, particularly in developing markets where customers may have little or no experience with the product category and few enforceable rights. Clearly, for most established companies, this is not a part of the market that they would be interested in participating in, and there is generally no need for them to have a presence there. The companies that do compete in this segment are typically small and pose very little competitive threat to the traditional players in the market. However, some of these companies learn from working with their customers and move up, over time, to compete in the good enough segment of the market, where they can pose a growing threat. But most do not survive.

When we talk about entering the price value segment of the market, we are talking about the world of good enough products and services – products that provide basic functionality, are safe and acceptably reliable and usually have some basic level of service and support (which may be largely self-service). In many

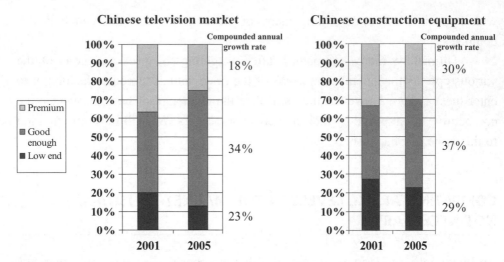

FIGURE 5.1   Fast-growing good enough segments exist in many markets in China

Source: Based on Till Vestring, "The Battle for China's Good-Enough Market – audio slideshow with text transcript", Results Brief, Bain & Company, 19 September 2007.

developing countries, in both business-to-business and business-to-consumer markets, this may be the mid-range or mid-performance segment of the market. In countries like China and India, this is often the fastest growing segment of the market, sometimes growing twice as fast as the overall market.[96] In China, many markets, including those as diverse as televisions and construction equipment, have fast-growing good enough segments (see Figure 5.1).

P&G is grappling with the challenge of good enough products as it tries to grow its business among very poor customers, most of whom live in the developing world. In designing products for low-income shoppers in developing countries, companies know that their products must sell at affordable prices, which are sometimes tied to the "coins" these shoppers are most likely to have in their possession. For example, in Mexico a product might have to be designed to sell for 10 pesos, because that is a coin shoppers are likely to have in their pockets. This is why, in developing world markets, P&G often begins with what the consumer can afford and then works backwards to adjust the product ingredients and manufacturing process to meet that pricing target. P&G emphasizes, however, that the products that emerge from this process must "delight not dilute" the quality. That must still be there because, as one P&G executive said, "You cannot trick a low-income consumer because they can't afford to buy products that don't work. (If it doesn't perform) they won't ever buy you again and they'll tell everyone they know about it, too."[97]

THE CHALLENGE DECISION REQUIRES THINKING THROUGH MANY ISSUES

It is useful to break up the decision about whether to enter the price value segment of the market into two sub-decisions: the strategic decision of whether to enter or not and, if the answer is affirmative, the tactical decisions about how best to do this. While there is certainly no one right answer to the first question, there are a number of arguments, pro and con, that typically come into play. It is the weight of these arguments in the particular context that should drive management's decision.

We will start this discussion with some of the typical arguments for entering into the price value segment and then consider some of the possible arguments against adopting this strategy.

ARGUMENTS FOR ENTERING THE PRICE VALUE SEGMENT

Good enough products can meet a real market need

As we discussed in Chapter 2, there is, in most markets, a significant segment of customers who are seeking basic, good enough products or services. If such a segment does not currently exist, or it is not large enough to support a viable business at the initial stages of market development, it will usually develop as the market moves towards maturity. Managers are sometimes in denial about the existence of such a segment because they feel that such a basic product or service could not possibly meet the needs of a significant number of customers. As has been demonstrated in market after market, however, there is usually such a market – perhaps not among existing customers but among current non-users for the product or service. And, if the incumbent company does not cater to this need, other companies will.

Opportunity to engage price value customers and develop better solutions to their needs over time

One of the challenges in moving into the price value segment of the market is designing a product or service that will really meet the needs of this segment. Not all companies feel they understand enough about the elements of a good enough solution. And sometimes the initial efforts are not totally successful. However, in business-to-business markets in particular, one of the arguments for moving into this market area is to improve the opportunities for meaningful dialogs with customers in the segment – in this way, a company can better understand what their customers are willing and not willing to pay for. The initial product or service offering might not be optimal, but it provides a starting point; the company now has a better opportunity, if it really engages with these customers, to build closer relationships with them and deepen its understanding of their needs. This should allow a company to design good enough solutions that really do meet the needs of this market segment.

Sometimes if a company feels that it must enter the market as quickly as possible, it may take an existing product and try to cost reduce it by removing features and lowering specifications. This usually does not result in a truly cost effective product, but it can speed up entry. At that point, the company will probably be in a better position to gather, and benefit from, customer feedback as it designs a second-generation product from the ground up.

Opportunity to grow with customers as their strategies evolve

Consider a Western company that is supplying equipment to customers in a rapidly growing business-to-business market in Asia. Assume, for the moment, that the equipment it supplies is only competitive in market segments with the most demanding applications – it's a typical developed country, high-end or premium player. The rapid growth of the overall market is attracting a number of new customers for this type of equipment. However, many of these new entrants, which are now potential customers, lack experience in this kind of business. They will probably start by focusing on the least demanding segments of their market. The Western company's equipment will be over-engineered and over-priced for these kinds of applications, so the new customers will not consider buying its equipment.

For these less demanding segments, the low barriers to entry often mean that the new entrants face intense competition from incumbents and other new entrants, resulting in low margins. In time, in an effort to escape this fierce competition at the bottom of the market, some of these recent entrants will try to move up market to a more demanding and profitable set of customers. The requirements of these more demanding customers may mean that the recent entrants must buy new, more sophisticated equipment to meet the more demanding quality requirements. At this point, they have become potential customers for the Western equipment supplier but at this stage, many of the entrants will have built relationships with their suppliers of basic equipment. If they have been satisfied with the equipment and service, and if the supplier also has equipment that will allow them to produce the products needed by some of the more demanding segments, they may stay with this supplier. Thus, the Western equipment supplier might have difficulty selling its product to these upwardly mobile customers, even if it provides the best solution. The Western supplier simply lacks the relationship with, and even has trouble getting a meeting with, the prospective customer.

This was exactly the situation that Saurer Volkmann faced in China (discussed in Chapter 4). Volkmann's twisting machines are used to twist spun cotton and wool fibers into yarns. These yarns are then woven into textiles. For an inexperienced Chinese entrepreneur entering the business of making yarns for the first time, the easiest way to enter was by twisting medium cotton yarns. But since the barriers to entry to this segment of the business were low, the competition in this market segment was fierce. To escape this competition, some of the more experienced and sophisticated players were tempted to move up market to twist fine or very fine cotton yarns, or even wool or wool blend yarns. These represented applications that were more demanding and required more sophisticated and expensive twisting machines. Volkmann decided to move into the less sophisticated twisting machines market, in part to help build relationships with new entrants and other low-end customers; thus, it created the potential to grow with its customers as it became bigger and moved into more demanding market segments. Volkmann did not want to leave this opportunity open only to its low cost Chinese competitors. One of these local competitors was already investing in R&D to develop more sophisticated equipment for the higher-end applications.

May provide an opportunity for "up-selling"

Another reason for entering the price value market segment is to have a low price offering in the product line. With the knowledge that a particular supplier has an entry-level product or service, some customers are willing to talk to them to get more information about the product and its price point. Once the dialog has begun, the customer may recognize that the low cost offering is not the best solution for him and is then willing to entertain the possibility of buying a higher performance solution that might better meet his needs. But without offering the initial price value, the selling company might never have been able to get its "foot in the door".

This was another of the major arguments that the Saurer Volkmann management used to support its decision to enter the mid-performance segment of its market. In Saurer's case, customers were attracted to its mid-performance product, priced about 25% above the reasonably good quality Chinese twisting machines. But Saurer Volkmann's salespeople were usually able to convince customers that the 25% price premium was justified by the machine's 20% higher productivity, lower energy usage and higher German reliability. Having concluded that the lower performance product was good value, some customers were then willing to consider Saurer Volkmann's high-end twisting machine, about 50% more expensive than Saurer's mid-performance offering. If they bought the higher-end machine, they would be able to twist very fine cotton yarns and wool yarns. Because there was less competition in these market segments, margins were higher. Some customers believed that even after paying the higher price for the high performance Volkmann machine, they would make more money with it. As a result, many of them bought the high-performance product giving a significant boost to Saurer Volkmann's sales.

If Saurer Volkmann had not had the lower performance product in its product line, it would probably never have had the opportunity to start this conversation with most customers. Management felt that in this particular case, it actually led to an increase in the sales of its high performance product, rather than the cannibalization that it had feared.

Many life insurance companies have found that having low cost term insurance products in their agents' portfolios has helped the agents get their "foot in the door" and initiate a discussion with potential customers.[98] Sometimes, as a result of this first discussion, the agent is successful in persuading the customer that a more expensive and profitable policy, such as permanent or whole life insurance, is a better solution for their needs.

Opportunity for synergies

Synergies between the value-added business and the price value business might benefit both. In many businesses, there may be significant synergies between the high-end solution and the lower performance solution. Fixed costs, such as research and development, may now be spread over a broader base of business. In some cases, both products might be made in the same production facility and the combined businesses may help ensure high-capacity utilization leading to lower overall costs. This benefits margins across the whole product line. In the case of some other products, it is possible that both solutions are based on a common platform and through increased volume on the platform, costs per unit may be significantly reduced. Even if the products do not share a common platform, it's quite likely that some of the components can be shared across the product line, driving up production volumes and driving down the costs of these components. If purchased materials or components are shared across the product line, procurement should be able to negotiate better prices based on the higher combined volumes. There may also be opportunities for both products to share the same sales and distribution infrastructure, again benefiting the total business as well as making it more difficult for the low cost player to tap into existing distribution channels.

In some cases, the high-end and lower performance products may be physically identical but the "performance" of the low-end product is diminished by disabling, or degrading, some of its functionality and/or features. However, this might be an expensive way to create a lower performance offering.

One business where significant costs can often be easily shared across several products in the product line is computer software. This strategy, sometimes called "versioning", is widely used to tap into different market segments where consumers are looking for different performance levels and are willing to pay different prices.[99] For example, Intuit, the developer of the personal finance software Quicken, is one company that has done this quite effectively. In 2007, Quicken offered four versions of its product, Basic, Deluxe, Premium and Home & Business, with prices varying from about $30 to $80 in the US. As the customers moved up the product hierarchy, they received more functionality and tools that allowed them to manage their personal finances in increasingly sophisticated ways – from tracking spending in the basic version to tracking spending, financial planning, managing investments and even managing a small business in the most advanced software version. In addition to functionality differences, a company can differentiate one version of a product from another by speed, user interface, flexibility of use and after sales service and support.

Gives traditional players some "control" over low cost competitors

Another major argument often made for entering the lower end of the market is that it gives the traditional players some control over their low-end competitors. This has a couple of major benefits. Rather than conceding a whole segment of the market, if a company offers and effectively markets a competitive product at a competitive price (but not necessarily the same price), it forces the low-end competitors to fight for every sale and to work to capture market share.

It also gives the traditional player some control over the pricing and profitability of the low-end competition. It usually does not make sense to match the low cost players on price because this will usually precipitate a price war that could severely impact the traditional player's profitability and brand image. A price war also typically leads to an increased price differential between high-end and low-end products, encouraging more customers to switch from the firm's high-end offerings to one of the low-end products.

Even if the traditional player does not match the price of the low cost competitors, whatever price it does set for its lower performance products essentially puts a ceiling on what the low cost players can charge. Because they usually lack the credibility and brand equity of the traditional player, and because their product or service may not have as good functionality and support, they will usually have to sell their product at a discount compared to the traditional player's product. Putting a ceiling on the price that the low cost competitors can charge has a very direct impact on their profitability and cash flow. This impacts their ability to invest further in the business – in R&D and marketing – and even in their willingness to invest in the business. If the traditional player can make the business look unattractive enough, the low cost player may well decide that there are "softer" targets and focus their investment in one of these other markets.

ARGUMENTS FOR NOT ENTERING THE PRICE VALUE SEGMENT

Conflicts with the traditional value proposition of the business

One of the major arguments for not entering the price value segment of a market is that it may go against the traditional value proposition of the business – one that may have been based on either performance value or relational value. If the company's value proposition has been based on performance leadership, it will often find it very difficult to start marketing a product or service that is clearly not a leadership product. This is made even more difficult, in some cases, if the company has actively marketed its product or service against that of its low cost competitors and essentially either directly, or indirectly, disparaged their offerings – in effect, saying, "Why would anybody buy that inferior, 'stripped down' product when they can buy our great products?" It then becomes more difficult to do an about-face and start saying to customers that while they shouldn't buy the competitor's inferior product, they should buy the company's version of it. Employees sometimes also have difficulty accepting the change. Of course, companies that do decide to take the plunge find at least somewhat plausible reasons why customers should buy their offerings, such as "designed by the world leader in ... for those customers who have less demanding applications".

Encourages cannibalization of high-end products

A second major argument often used to support the decision not to enter the price value segment is the cannibalization argument, discussed at the end of Chapter 4. The argument is that, in many cases, if a traditional company introduces a low cost offering in the market, some of the existing customers that were buying its higher performance products or services will now buy the new lower cost offering. Perhaps they did not really need all the performance provided by the high-end product for their particular applications but bought it because they wanted the sense of security of buying an item from a leading supplier. As discussed in Chapter 4, the cannibalization may very well occur anyway, with sales lost either to the low cost players or to another traditional player that decides to add a low cost offering to its product line. If we don't eat our own lunch, then somebody will eat it for us!

Lacks resources and capabilities to successfully compete

A third argument, and in some cases a valid one, is that the company lacks the resources and/or capabilities to develop a truly competitive product for the price value segment of the market. This is a particular challenge for companies that have been the market performance leaders with a focus on trying to develop evolutionary or even revolutionary advances in the product or service. Success in the price value segment often requires totally re-engineering the product or service from the ground up and then relentlessly executing cost reduction programs over time. This often requires a very different set of capabilities, mindset and motivation than was, and is, required in the core business. At the very least, it is frequently a major challenge to develop a culture of trying to continually find opportunities to drive cost out of the total delivered cost of a product or service. Nokia faced this challenge when it got really serious about developing a highly competitive and profitable entry-level phone business. As the culture developed within Nokia, it was able to drive tens of million of euros of savings to its bottom line by such things as simplifying and reducing the cost of its mobile phone packaging.[100] Once the culture is established, some people in the organization start to see cost reduction as being just as challenging and fulfilling as developing the next new handset.

As we will see later in the chapter, some companies set up separate business units to allow each business unit to be more focused and to develop its own culture. In other cases, companies will buy products from third parties and sell them under their own brand; they may use either their primary brand or a sub-brand.

While some firms are successful in developing an acceptable new product or service for the lower performance segment of the market, they may have difficulty in cost-effectively marketing and selling the product or service to their customers. In cases where the company is selling directly to the end customers, the effectiveness of the sales force may be the issue. Using salespeople who are used to a value-added sell may not be the best or most cost-effective strategy. Some companies operating in China, India and other developing countries find that their lower performance products sell into very different market segments than their more sophisticated products. In the case of business-to-business products, the customers may be first time buyers and live in more remote geographical areas than the customers of the more sophisticated products. The sales force of the Western company might employ college educated and well-trained salespeople who are quite sophisticated. Asking them to go into relatively remote rural areas and sell products to small, poorly educated entrepreneurs, who a year or two ago might have been farmers, may not be well received by either the salespeople or the customers. This can result in lower sales force morale and, at the extreme, some salespeople leaving the company. Even if they are able to reach the target customers and sell effectively, they might be far too expensive a resource to use in this way. In one specific situation, a North American company found that the "all-in" cost of its traditional salesperson was more than four times the cost of a "local" salesperson. In addition, they were often less effective than the local salespeople at selling to the target customers for the low-end products.

Since the role of the salesperson is quite different for the value-added products than it is for the price value products, it often makes sense to separate the two roles. In this way, the company salespeople will be less schizophrenic. Each group can be recruited, trained, compensated and managed in the most appropriate manner, encouraging them to execute their targeted role in the best way possible. However, in some cases this may result in two salespeople calling on the same customer and perhaps competing with each other for an order. The company will also need to put in place the appropriate incentive policies and management structures to ensure that if a salesperson selling the price value solution sees an opportunity to sell a value-added solution, he or she passes the lead on to the other sales force, rather than trying to sell the customer the wrong solution. If this sharing of leads doesn't happen, it could provide an opportunity for a competitor to move in and sell the customer a more appropriate solution.

Of course, in some situations, if the product is suitable, it may be possible to sell the lower priced products through a distributor. Again, there may be a challenge to ensure the distributor passes on leads for the higher priced products to the direct sales force. An appropriate financial incentive program for the distributors can help here.

But perhaps one of the biggest challenges is to develop a culture that "eats, drinks and sleeps" low cost in one part of the company, when the rest of the company has very different and, what may be perceived as, more exciting priorities. Clearly, it is easier to build such a culture if the low cost business is housed in a separate business unit.

VALUE CHAIN MEMBERS CAN IMPACT DECISIONS

In the discussion above, we have looked at several examples where the company faced with responding to the low cost competition threat deals directly with its customers. Of course, in many situations there may be one or more intermediaries, such as distributors, retailers or sales agents, which come between the company and its end-users. This can influence the decision to introduce a product targeted at price value customers and how best to implement the strategy.

Intermediaries can be very responsive to the needs of their customers. If these customers articulate the need for a lower price offering, they may respond to it. Even if a traditional company has a strong relationship with these intermediaries, if it does not respond positively to the end-user demands, the intermediaries may well seek out another source for a lower price offering. If, however, the traditional company does respond positively with a competitive offering, and the intermediary agrees to carry it, this may effectively block this channel of distribution for other competitors, including low cost players.

Some companies do develop good solutions for customers seeking low cost, good enough products and services, but then face issues with their traditional channels. These traditional channels may be "over-engineered" and too expensive for the company's low cost offerings. The company may be much better off developing new channels and bypassing its traditional channels. Even when the current channels are over-engineered, or inappropriate in some other way, they may want to still be the exclusive or semi-exclusive channel for the new good enough product. This can lead to significant channel conflict.

Caterpillar faced this issue when it developed products for customers with less demanding applications than its traditional customers. These products are often smaller and much less expensive than its traditional construction and mining equipment. But in some cases, the company has used its traditional distribution channels partly because these channel members see the product affording them the opportunity to serve new customers. These dealers, often with exclusive franchises for large geographical areas, can have revenues in the billions of dollars; they are very good at selling, servicing and supporting the traditional large pieces of equipment sold to construction companies and mining companies. They have massive service bays for servicing the huge pieces of equipment, highly trained personnel and substantial inventories of spare parts. This has been a huge barrier to entry for competitors in Caterpillar's traditional business.

This great infrastructure, however, is not very good at selling and economically servicing relatively low cost, simple machines. It is simply "over-engineered" and too expensive. It has been a major handicap to Caterpillar as it tries to compete with its lower cost competitors.

AN ALTERNATIVE WAY TO PROVIDE A PRICE VALUE SOLUTION TO THE MARKET

In some businesses, there is an alternative way to provide a price value solution to customers. This involves either buying, or taking as trade-ins, components or products and re-manufacturing them or re-conditioning them so that they can be resold. Typically, these products are sold at significantly lower prices than new products, yet may have working lives close to those of the original product. They may deliver 80% of the performance of a new product but only cost 50% as much. They often carry warranties that are similar to those on original new equipment. In some businesses, where technology is advancing quickly, these re-manufactured products will not have the capabilities or performance of new products, but they might well satisfy the needs of a customer who does not have applications requiring leading edge performance. However, these solutions might still be over-engineered and too expensive for less demanding applications.

The sale of remanufactured components and products does provide a company with an opportunity to reach customers that might not normally have been able to afford its products. This can be a vehicle for building a relationship with a customer which may, over time, grow and can provide an opening for the sale of new products and services as the customer's needs evolve.

MAKING THE DECISION IN A TIMELY MANNER

Probably one of the biggest challenges for many companies that ultimately decide to move into the price value segment of the market either for opportunistic reasons, or defensive reasons, is to make the decision in a timely manner.

Sometimes, a proactive management team can determine early on that a significant price value segment will emerge in a market where it competes. Additionally, if its analysis suggests that it makes sense in the long run for the company to enter that market – acting for either offensive or defensive reasons – then an early, pre-emptive move might be advisable. By doing this, the company makes the market less attractive for price value competitors to enter and it might well become the dominant player in the segment before other traditional players realize that there is a real market opportunity there.

GrandOptical was a company that saw an opportunity in a lower price segment of the market and moved early to capitalize on it.[101] GrandOptical, a division of GrandVision based in France, was founded in 1989 and operated a chain of high-end optical stores. Its traditional stores were large (about $300 \, m^2$) and furnished with high-quality displays and fittings. About one-third of the floor space in each store was taken up with a laboratory that could "manufacture" the eyeglasses in one hour, once the customer had selected his or her frames. Each store carried a very broad selection of about 3500 frames from the leading eyewear brands, some of which cost more than €500. Each store also stocked about 10 000 lenses. The staff members were well-trained professionals, and the customer service level in the stores was very high. A typical sale in the 1990s was about €300–€400 but prices could go much higher. The chain had a very strong customer satisfaction guarantee. The stores appealed to a fairly affluent clientele who were willing to pay for the stylish products and the high level of customer service. The management of the chain recognized that there was an opportunity for a more mass-market offering below GrandOptical with good quality products, lower prices and good service. It also recognized that by having a strong mid-market offering, GrandOptical would be less vulnerable to competition that might use the mid-market segment as a launching pad to go after its customer base.

The new chain, Générale d'Optique, was launched in 1994 and was positioned to offer eyewear at very reasonable prices. Its stores were smaller, about 200 m², and they did not have an on-site laboratory. The stores carried about 2000 frames, all under the chain's private label. When the customer ordered a pair of glasses, they were "manufactured" at a central location and available for pickup at the store three days later. The glasses were sold at three price points (basics, trends and creations) and the prices were all-inclusive for standard lenses. There were additional charges for special lenses. The lowest price was about €100 per pair. The chain ended up being successful and soon had more stores than the original GrandOptical chain.

An interesting question to ask managers who have made the move into the price value segment of the market, is: "What would you have done differently, if you had it to do over again?" At least part of their response is almost invariably that they would have made the move much earlier and more aggressively. No matter how quickly a company moves, in retrospect, it usually feels that it didn't move fast enough!

SHOULD THE PRICE VALUE BUSINESS BE INDEPENDENT?

If a company decides to serve a market's price value segment, it then faces a difficult decision about the degree of independence that should be given to the managers responsible for developing and implementing the strategy for this market segment. Usually the advantages of operating the business reasonably independently outweigh the disadvantages. Most successful price value businesses within larger companies are independent business units with their own management teams and control of their own strategies.

However, there are a number of arguments that have been advanced as to why the price value business should be more closely integrated with the value-added business. We will explore these arguments and then turn our attention to some of the very practical reasons why, in reality, the advantages of independence often outweigh the advantages of integration. As we will see, this does not mean that all opportunities for achieving synergies between the two businesses should be ignored.

Integration has several potential advantages

Integrating the price value and value-added businesses will ensure that there is no unnecessarily intense competition between the two businesses resulting in excessive cannibalization of the value-added businesses' products and services. The argument is often articulated as "we should be attacking our common enemies, the other competitors in the industry, rather than each other".

If the price value and value-added businesses are able to leverage a common brand, this will provide a number of benefits. Use of a brand associated with the value-added business often has the advantage of allowing the price value offering to command a premium price relative to what it might command with a new, unknown brand. By utilizing the same brand across the full product line, it may also make it easier to up-sell the customer, particularly if a common sales force is used across the full line. It also makes it easier to move customers smoothly up the product line as their needs evolve, or to get them to use both types of products if they have needs that span both the price value and the value-added product spectrum. Nokia is a company that has done an exceptional job to date in employing one brand that covers the full range – from entry-level products to very upscale, multimedia handsets. Even its lowest priced products have a reputation for being very high quality and reliable, and maintaining their value (an important issue in emerging markets where there is often a good market for second-hand phones). The entry-level phones are not simple, utilitarian, commoditized devices. They are products that are designed to meet the needs of particular market segments, including those segments that are highly involved in the choice of handset and want a product that has the technology and style to meet their aspirations, albeit at a price of less than $80.

There are, however, possible downsides to using the same brand across a range of products covering the range from good enough basic products to industry leading performance and/or high style products. On the one hand, some customers might not even consider a low-end offer from a high-end brand – they might simply assume that it will be too expensive for them. On the other hand, there is the potential of damaging brand equity by associating a high-end brand with a basic product. This issue is likely to be more pronounced with business-to-consumer products or services rather than those in the business-to-business arena. It will be a particular issue in those product categories, both with business-to-business and business-to-consumer, where many consumers base their purchase decisions heavily on emotional and image considerations, rather than more objective performance factors. Therefore, it is not surprising in the watch industry where image and emotional value are often paramount, that the major players have a stable of brands, each of which is carefully positioned in the market. The Swatch Group alone has about 20 different watch brands in its portfolio. The performance differences between these watches are sometimes minor. In fact, when it comes to accurate timekeeping, some of the less expensive brands with watches that have quartz movements might keep more accurate time than the more expensive brands and watches with mechanical movements.

Another major argument advanced for integrating the price value business with the value-added business is that it will result in better coordination between the two and lead to more synergies between the businesses. The businesses can share resources and capabilities, such as research and development, production facilities, a sales force, IT infrastructure, management, etc. In businesses that involve physical products, they may be able to be built on a common platform, share components and so on. By sharing such resources, it is argued, money is not wasted on needless duplication. In cases where customers may use products or services from both business segments at the same time, or over time, having a common user interface may represent an important synergy from the customer perspective. This will be particularly true in products and services where the user interface is an important choice element and a barrier to switching from one supplier to another. Having the user interface, for example, is quite important to some customers in selecting mobile phones, as well as in many types of business-to-business equipment and some types of software products.

In some cases, the economic arguments for combining both the price value and value-added product lines in the same business are quite strong. For example, as we discussed in Chapter 4, grocery and general merchandise retailers facing competition from hard discounters, such as Aldi and Lidl in Europe, often decide to respond by offering a limited range of SKUs that closely match those of Aldi and Lidl at comparably low prices. Tesco in the UK began offering a line of 600 "value" products in the mid-1990s, and in 1996, it launched an "Unbeatable Value" campaign that promised customers who found these products cheaper elsewhere a refund of twice the difference in price.[102] Coop, one of the two leading grocery retailers in Switzerland, pre-emptively introduced a similar range of "everyday products at guaranteed permanently low prices" under the Prix Garantie label shortly after it became clear that Aldi and Lidl would be entering the Swiss grocery market. Clearly, in this situation, it would have been a very expensive proposition for Tesco or Coop to set up a totally separate chain of hard discount stores to compete with Aldi and Lidl. It might also have diverted top management time away from more strategic priorities. In addition, management might have felt that embedding these price value products in their full service stores would help differentiate these low cost offerings from Aldi's and Lidl's. Some customers attracted to very basic, low price products would still have the opportunity to get the low prices on these products, while being able to pick up other value-added (and presumably more profitable) products on the same store visit. Some, but not all, consumers would have viewed this as a convenience.

Not all retailers have adopted this strategy. Carrefour, the large French retailer, has chosen a different strategy. In some of its markets, including its home market, it has its own hard discount chain (called Ed in France) that competes head to head with Lidl and the other hard discounters. To many shoppers, it is not obvious that Carrefour and Ed are both part of the same company.

Advantages of independence often outweigh the advantages of integration

Unfortunately, in practice, the advantages of integration are often oversold and most of the advantages have significant downsides. Many companies support a more integrated model to ensure that they obtain all the potential synergies between the value-added business and the price value business. They don't want to "re-invent the wheel". In too many cases though, this means sharing a high-cost, over-engineered infrastructure that is simply not competitive with that of a focused price value player. Often the infrastructure required to support a value-added business must be quite flexible to support the range of customers, products and services that need to be sustained. However, this can often mean that it is over-engineered and much more expensive than it needs to be (even when the cost is shared between the two businesses) for a price value business with a very limited set of products and services.

Similarly, in product businesses, the notion of integrating the businesses so that components may be shared across the value-added and price value businesses may result in the value-added business having to use over-engineered and expensive parts. While the value-added business may require parts that can last 50 000 hours or 100 000 hours before needing replacement, this may be far too much for a low-end customer who is concerned about buying a machine that can pay for itself in one or two years and whose life span isn't much longer. In this type of situation, having parts that last 5 to 10 years is simply overkill.

Integrating the price value business with the traditional business can also mean adopting work practices that made sense a couple of decades earlier but are now outdated and inefficient – as a result of habit or perhaps union contracts, they are frozen. While a value-added business that has relatively high margins might be able to cope with the inefficiency and cost, a competitive price value business often can't afford to do so. Many of the airlines around the world that launched low cost carrier businesses forced those businesses to share some of their high cost infrastructure with their unionized work forces and inefficient work practices. This contributed to their new low cost carrier business being generally uncompetitive with the independent start-up carriers like Southwest Airlines and Ryanair. Even though Southwest is one of the most unionized airlines in the US, its work practices are designed to support its business model, not that of a legacy carrier.

Integration also means, in many cases, accepting preconceived ideas about the business model and how to operate the business. What needs to be done to be successful as a price value player may go against the culture and values of the value-added business. As we have discussed, Ryanair became the most successful low cost carrier in Europe. Its home page on the website was garish to say the least. It used a variety of different colors that were not coordinated, there was almost no white space and it screamed "cheap, low-price". To many people it was totally unappealing from an aesthetic point of view – it looked so amateurish it could have been designed by a pre-teen trying to use every color on the palette.

However, given the results they helped to achieve, the graphics were probably highly effective with the target audience – something that would probably never have happened if Ryanair had been an independent, low cost business unit of a traditional airline (no matter how effective the graphics treatment was). One had only to look at the websites of those low cost airlines that were owned, or partly owned, by major carriers to see the influence of their cultures. For instance, the website of Germanwings, a low cost carrier that was indirectly and partly owned by Lufthansa, had a totally different look from Ryanair's. Its website and those of other low cost carriers with similar heritages were usually much more aesthetically appealing and more "corporate". But did they generate the excitement, the image of low cost and low prices and the business results that the Ryanair site achieved?

As Clayton Christensen has noted in his book on disruptive innovation, most organizations find it easier to resource projects for the higher end of the traditional value-added business than a new, disruptive technology that will, initially at least, appeal to customers or potential customers who use the products, or technology, for relatively low-end applications.[103] Gross margins tend to look more attractive at the higher end of the market. Under these circumstances, it's much easier to build the financial case for investments in new products or services at the higher end of the market. Particularly in an integrated business, it may be difficult for the price value portion of the business to get the investments it needs to support its growth.

Another challenge when the price value products or services are embedded in the existing value-added business, particularly if they share a common brand, is that customers may have unrealistic expectations of the product or service. They may expect the same level of service and support that they receive with the traditional value-added business. This may be totally unrealistic for a price value business that is trying to be really competitive in its market space. There is some evidence that customers in the UK mobile phone business have had quite different levels of customer satisfaction, even when they used basically the same service depending upon who is the perceived provider of the service. Virgin Mobile, a VMNO, has consistently achieved higher customer satisfaction ratings than the operator whose network it uses. For example, in the 2005 J.D. Power and Associates UK mobile customer satisfaction survey, Virgin Mobile was first and T-Mobile (its host) was last in the prepaid service segment.[104] While Virgin Mobile's brand image, offers and customer service undoubtedly contribute to the difference, it's also probably due to the lower expectations customers have of a low cost mobile phone service provider.

Similarly, when consumers shop at Aldi or Lidl, their expectations are relatively modest. They realize that they are getting very good value at the store; market research suggests that Aldi and Lidl generally beat their (modest) expectations. When these same customers patronize other grocery retailers, they have much higher expectations and the other retailers are often perceived as falling short.

The discussion above suggests that there are, at first glance, some significant advantages to integrating the price value business with the value-added business. However, in most situations these advantages are not realized. In fact, there are often major disadvantages to the integrated approach that reduce the probability that the price value portion of the product line will achieve its objectives. In most situations, a company will only develop a truly effective and competitive price value business if the business is placed in a separate business unit – one with a high degree of independence to make decisions that are in its narrow self-interest, not in the corporate interest. An aggressive, offensive posture is much more likely to be successful than a defensive posture, and it is usually a defensive posture that the more integrated price value businesses take. Ironically, sometimes by pursuing narrow self-interest, the independent price value business is most likely to make the largest long-run contribution to the success of the parent company. This does not mean that all synergies should be ignored. Rather, if both the price value business and the value-added business see an attractive opportunity to work together for their mutual benefit, then they should. For example, both might see value in jointly negotiating a price with a common supplier to take advantage of their combined purchasing power or, in some cases, they can share a common IT and production infrastructure, if it is a low cost one.

Even when the price value business is set up as a separate business unit, it takes a major effort to ensure that the culture of the parent company does not jeopardize the ability of the price value business to deliver customer value in its market. BA set up Go in 1997 to capitalize on the rapid growth in the UK's low cost carrier market. Bob Ayling, BA's CEO, did his best to ensure that Go's CEO Barbara Cassani was able to operate the business independently. However, as Cassani noted in her book, there were still significant challenges: "Our early attempts at being low cost were a bit theatrical because we were not naturals. Ten years of bad habits at British Airways justifying high prices to customers by adding bells and whistles to the product don't die overnight."[105] Also, she had to spend a considerable amount of time and energy defending Go within BA.

SOME MAJOR TACTICAL DECISIONS

Once the decision has been made to enter the price value segment of the market with a reasonably independent business unit, there are then several important tactical decisions to be made. Among the most important of these considerations is the make versus buy decision and then whether to use the same brand, a separate sub-brand or a totally separate brand.

Make versus buy

Most companies that decide to enter a market's price value segment come in directly rather than through acquisition. If they are entering early in the development of the price value segment of the market, there may be few players available to be purchased and those that do exist will have a very limited track record.

When the market is at a more mature stage, there may be an increased opportunity to buy an established price value player, or to enter into a joint venture with one. In many businesses, however, where physical products that can be transported economically over large distances are involved, the price value players are increasingly likely to be based in countries like China and India. Here many of the price value players, in a number of industries, are likely to be local companies with products that might not be good enough for all but the most basic, price-driven customers. A more likely target for a Western company is a company competing in the mid-performance segment of the market – companies that often produce and sell satisfactory products at very low prices by Western standards. In 2005, Danfoss successfully acquired the Chinese company Zhejiang Haili Electronic Technology Co., Ltd. (Holip), a manufacturer of low cost frequency converters.[106] By acquiring Holip, Danfoss gained a position in the fast-growing good enough segment of the frequency converter market to complement the position it already had in the premium segment of the market. Gillette's Duracell did the same thing when it acquired a majority stake in Nanfu, the leading Chinese brand for the mass market. The Duracell brand continued to be positioned as a premium brand.

However, it is often very challenging for a Western company to find and acquire companies like Holip and Nanfu.[107] Many of these developing markets lack transparency, so identifying suitable candidates and conducting a thorough due diligence is not easy. In some cases, particularly in China, the products of these low cost competitors are copies of the products of the industry leaders. The acquiring company could face patent infringement charges soon after the purchase is completed, if it has not done a thorough due diligence. Even if a suitable candidate is identified, the deal may be quite time-consuming and may face strong local opposition, including political opposition. When the US private equity firm Carlyle Group tried to buy a majority stake in a large Chinese construction equipment company, political opposition forced it to settle for a 45% stake. But even with that concession, the deal had still not been consummated almost three years after the original agreement had been announced.[108] There may also be a culture clash between the acquiring company and the acquired company. And finally, the question is: "What has the company bought?" In some cases, the key people may only stay long enough to learn from their Western parent and then leave to set up a competing business. This does not mean that an acquisition should not be considered, but if acquisition is the chosen route, management needs to be aware of the possible pitfalls.

When a company chooses to acquire a low cost competitor rather than developing the business internally, it may face other issues. If the acquired company is in a developing country, the company standards with respect to working conditions, safety and the environment might be quite low by developed country standards. If the acquiring company applies its corporate policies and procedures, this may lead to a significant increase in costs. Some acquirers also feel obliged to raise the product specifications to higher levels to protect their reputation, even if they exceed the needs of the good enough segment of the market and what is being provided by the other companies competing in that segment. Again, costs rise and either margins are squeezed or prices must rise. Collectively, these can result in the acquired low cost business unit being less flexible than, and less price competitive with, its local peers.

ING DIRECT has used a combination of "greenfield" and acquisition depending on the particular market and competitive situation in a country. Generally, it has grown by developing greenfield businesses. However, it has usually moved into a market where the direct bank model was not widely accepted at the time of entry. Canada, Australia and the US were all examples of this. However, in other mature markets, where one or more direct banks were already quite well established, it has been willing to acquire existing players. It entered the German direct banking market, for example, by investing in a bank with a relatively large direct banking operation and ultimately acquired it. It then added to this original direct bank, ING DiBa, by acquiring the second largest direct bank in Germany and combining the two businesses under the ING brand.[109]

An intermediate option is a joint venture. Again, like acquisitions, it can be problematic in many situations; this is particularly true in developing markets.[110] Even sophisticated players can find themselves in trouble in markets like China. Groupe Danone, the leading French FMCG company, had a majority stake in a joint venture in China with a local partner. The joint venture was very successful on the surface. For example, by 2007, it had captured about 40% of the bottled water market in China. However, in 2005, Danone realized that its joint venture partner had set up a parallel business that was using the joint venture brand and was by 2008 siphoning off hundreds of millions of dollars of business.[111] By mid-2008, the two partners were in a serious, very public conflict with charges flying back and forth between them and it appeared that the joint venture was on the verge of being terminated.

Brand choice is a critical decision

As the discussion above suggests, the price value business should generally have its own brand that is distinctive from the value-added business – this might be either a sub-brand or a totally separate brand.

The exceptions to this generalization are likely to be in business-to-business markets, where the product itself is a large part of the value proposition and where the associated services, if any, are quite consistent across the whole business. This is particularly likely to be true where the product is sold through indirect channels or where the distributor or value-added reseller might provide different levels of service to meet the needs of different end-user segments. A common brand across the full line may facilitate up-selling customers, moving up the product line as customer needs evolve and even selling a broad range of value-added and price value products and services to a customer who has diverse needs.

In many business-to-business markets, where some brand differentiation is needed and is possible, sub-branding may be a good option. The company will get many of the benefits of the parent brand without having to use one brand across the whole business. The price value offerings benefit from the credibility of the corporate brand while giving the business unit the opportunity to position the price value brand in a more optimal way in its target segment. The parent brand is also somewhat protected from any negative associations that might develop from the price value brand that could damage the brand equity of the parent brand. Also, compared to building a totally new brand from scratch, this option can be relatively fast and inexpensive.

ING DIRECT is a good example of the successful use of a sub-brand. ING DIRECT stands for simple products, convenient service, very attractive prices (high rates on savings products and low rates on loans) and no hidden fees or service charges; its image is one of being fresh and innovative. While one could argue that ING might have been better off using a completely new brand, because the ING brand had little equity in the non-European markets where it was initially launched, management saw another reason to use the sub-brand in these markets. It was a relatively cheap and effective way to build brand awareness for ING among retail consumers in mature financial service markets like North America and Australia. ING hoped to be able to take advantage of this brand awareness in selling other ING-branded financial services products.

Midland Bank launched a 24-hour, seven-day-a-week telephone banking service in the UK in 1989.[112] This was the first direct banking service in the country. The front end of the bank's infrastructure – the part that provided the interface with the customers and supported the banking representatives who interfaced with the customers – was developed specifically to support the telephone bank. However, much of the rest of the bank's infrastructure was outsourced to Midland Bank. Customers could make deposits and withdraw cash from their accounts using Midland's ATMs and their monthly statements were processed and printed using Midland Bank systems.

In contrast to ING DIRECT, the telephone banking service was called First Direct and there was no mention of Midland in the bank's advertising and promotional materials. The bank made the decision to use a separate brand to give the direct bank an opportunity to develop its own distinctive image. Clearly, an obvious connection with Midland might cause customers to transfer aspects of the Midland image, both positive and negative, to First Direct. One particular concern was that Midland, like the other High Street banks in the UK, had a negative image with most retail consumers. Customer satisfaction ratings were typically quite low. First Direct made large investments in its front-end infrastructure and in training its banking representatives to provide friendly, high-quality service to customers.

It was very successful over time in developing very high customer satisfaction levels, much higher than any of the traditional banks or building societies. First Direct might not have been able to do this if it had been linked with Midland Bank in the minds of retail customers, either directly or by the use of a sub-brand.

We see, in the examples of these two direct banks, that corporate management made different choices based on their differing objectives and the differences in market conditions. In some countries, ING was using ING DIRECT to help build a positive corporate image, while Midland Bank was more concerned about damaging the brand image of First Direct by linking it with the relatively poor retail image of its parent.

British Airways also made the decision to use a separate brand for its low cost subsidiary, calling it Go. Competitors, particularly easyJet, made very sure that consumers understood that Go was owned and "subsidized" by BA and that it had been designed to put easyJet out of business.

Novartis, one of the largest pharmaceutical companies in the world, also used a separate brand called Sandoz for its line of generic ethical pharmaceuticals. Sandoz had been established in Switzerland in 1886 and merged with Ciba-Geigy to form Novartis in 1996. At the time, the Sandoz name had then been de-emphasized. But in 2003, the decision was made to convert almost all of Novartis' generic brands to the Sandoz brand. This was done for a number of reasons – a major one being to leverage the strong Sandoz brand name that had an established reputation for high quality. It would also help Novartis' various generic products stand out in an increasingly crowded but rapidly growing market for lower cost generic drugs. Novartis wanted to position Sandoz as the world's number one brand for high quality and affordable generic medicines. Novartis made no attempt to hide the fact that Sandoz was a Novartis company. Perhaps the clear focus of the Sandoz business unit, and the brand on the generics market, contributed to this business growing three times as fast as its Novartis branded drug business; in 2007, Sandoz accounted for almost 20% of Novartis' revenues.[113]

Developing new sales and distribution channels is often necessary

Earlier in this chapter, we acknowledged that good enough products and services might require different sales channels than a company's traditional products. Cummins Diesel faced this type of issue in India a few years ago. At the time, it had a 60% market share in the high-horsepower diesel generation market in India and a very low market share in the high-growth, low-horsepower (under 100 kilowatts) market, a relatively price sensitive segment.[114] End-users in the low-horsepower segment included small retailers, regional hospitals/clinics and farmers. Each end-user segment had somewhat different needs. For example, regional hospitals and clinics wanted the generators to be reasonably quiet so that patients and staff would not be disturbed. Farmers wanted the generators to be protected from dust. Historically, Cummins had used direct distribution, but direct distribution to these customers would be too expensive, so the company would have to use less skilled, third party distributors.

The solution Cummins created was to develop a series of smaller, lower-powered modular diesel engines that could be combined with generator sets. These units could be customized for different segments using add-on "kits", such as an add-on kit for noise suppression for the hospital segment. This made it very easy for a less-skilled sales and distribution channel to sell solutions that met customer needs. Within three years, Cummins had captured 40% of the Indian market with good profitability and had begun exporting the "solutions" to other markets in Asia, Africa and Latin America.

Nestlé and P&G have also had to develop new channels for their products in the developing world. As they, and other multinationals, have moved to develop affordable products for consumers that have just entered the market economy, they have been forced to develop effective ways to reach the local, traditional outlets where many of their target customers shop, sometimes several times a day. In Mexico, P&G experimented with local agents, who often employed several sales representatives, to try to build closer relationships with the over 600 000 "high frequency" stores in Mexico. These agents and their representatives earned commissions from mark-ups on the products they sold. This was a very different sales and distribution strategy from the one that P&G had traditionally used.[115]

P&G has also had to develop new merchandising approaches that will be effective with these channels. The typical store in Latin America (often located in a person's home), as in many other parts of the developing world, was just over 20 square meters in size and the competition for shelf space in the best locations within the store was fierce. Since the product categories P&G competes in only account for about 10% of the sales in each store, it had a particularly challenging task.

Need to evolve channels over time

A particular danger in some businesses is that new channels emerge rapidly as the prices drop and the level of support required to sell, install and support the product or service decreases. This is especially true in technologically intensive businesses where prices often drop very quickly over time as companies move down their experience curves. The channels can evolve rapidly from direct sales forces to specialty distributors, mass distributors and finally to the Internet. Here the challenge for a player that wants to participate in the lower performance segment of the market is to continually move products into the new emerging channels before competitors, often price value competitors, get established there.

Hewlett Packard did an excellent job of this in the printer business; which, in the space of a couple of decades, went from being primarily high-end sophisticated products sold by a skilled sales force to a mass-market product sold through a vast array of different channels, largely indirect. HP seemed to be skilled at moving into new, indirect channels just as they were becoming viable channels for printers. By moving early, HP faced less resistance from its existing channels because these were still experiencing considerable growth from their printer business, even though they might already be losing market share to the new, emerging channels. HP also moved very quickly to offer lower priced products that fit both the needs of the emerging channels and end-users. This prevented new or existing competitors from dominating the emerging, lower cost channels. These emerging, low cost channels would have been an ideal entry point for a price value player. If HP had not moved quickly, given the growth in the market and the rapid shift in the percentage of the total printer volume that was going through the lower cost channels, it might have quickly lost its market leadership position.

NOKIA DEVELOPED A STRONG POSITION IN THE ENTRY MOBILE PHONE SEGMENT

We will now turn to the first of the three case examples of companies moving into the price value segments of their markets.

Motorola was the first mobile phone handset manufacturer to set up operations in China, in the late 1980s. It was followed, a few years later, by Nokia and Ericsson and then by companies like Siemens and Samsung. These companies moved to China in part to tap into low labor costs and they used their operations there as a manufacturing base. Initially, the foreign players dominated the small but growing domestic market.

Local Chinese competitors emerged quickly

By the late 1990s, the mobile phone business was moving away from a landscape totally dominated by integrated manufacturers to one where specialized innovation and infrastructure players played an increasing role in the design and manufacture of mobile phones. One of the specialized innovation companies was TechFaith whose initial hires were engineers and designers who had worked for Motorola in China.[116] TechFaith developed ready-to-build phone designs with all the necessary hardware and software for local Chinese mobile phone manufacturers. The Chinese companies were able to focus on assembling the products and distributing and selling them. Some of the designs that these local Chinese manufacturers offered were quite different from the somewhat bland ones developed by the large multinationals for the global market. One Chinese design was a crimson heart-shaped clamshell with cubic zirconium encrustations and pulsing lights! Soon there were more than 20 local brands and some of them became quite well known in China.[117]

In 2002, Motorola and Nokia alone still controlled almost 50% of the Chinese market with Motorola having the leading share. Eighteen months later, the local Chinese players, such as Ningbo Bird and TCL, had captured over 40% of the market; Motorola and Nokia's combined share was less than 35%.[118]

Nokia responded rapidly to the threat

Nokia responded to the reversal quite rapidly. By 2005, it had introduced a number of new entry-level products, including two designed just for China that used stylus input for Chinese characters. A major reason that the local players had gained share so rapidly was that they had much better distribution than Nokia outside the major Tier 1 and Tier 2 cities. Although Nokia had several "national" distributors, most of their real coverage was in the top ten cities. Nokia ended up dropping several of the national distributors, but added 40 provincial distributors, as well as a direct sales force of 5000 persons. During peak holiday seasons the direct sales force could increase to as many as 15 000 people, many of whom were in-store promoters for Nokia's products.

Over time, Nokia has deepened its understanding of the customers who buy entry-level phones in the developing world. Many of them are illiterate, and one mobile phone might often be shared by several family members, or even shared as the "public" phone in a village, where an entrepreneur rents time on the phone to other villagers. To meet the needs of these customers, one phone might have several address books for different family members; these address books might also use symbols like snakes and soccer balls instead of names.[119] To serve the needs of the "public" phone segment, the mobile phone might have a timer that cuts off a call after a pre-determined time.

Nokia's experience in India has demonstrated that entry-level users often move up to models that are more expensive when they replace their first phone.[120] So, by having entry-level models, the company gains an opportunity to build the brand loyalty of customers who over time might move up to more expensive and presumably more profitable products.

Nokia's results to date in the entry-level business have been very good

To date Nokia's efforts in the entry phone segments of the market seem to have been very successful. By late 2007, they had captured about 35% of the Chinese market and close to 50% of all emerging markets. In that same year, entry-level handsets accounted for over 50% of Nokia's global unit sales. Nokia claims that the entry-level business is profitable. As evidence, they reported that between the third quarter 2006 and the third quarter 2007, operating margins grew from 15% to 23%, even though entry-level handsets (those selling for less than € 30 anywhere in the world) grew from 22% of all handset sales in 2006 to 41% of all handset sales in 2007.[121] In fact, Nokia claimed that the gross margin on its entry-level business was about 30% in 2007, which was about the same as Sony Ericsson achieved on its total handset business.[122]

DOW CORNING DECIDED TO COMPETE AGGRESSIVELY FOR PRICE SEEKING CUSTOMERS

As we have stressed here and in earlier chapters, a company's choice about whether to enter a price value business and if it does, how to implement that decision must be based on its objectives, resources and capabilities and its particular market and competitive situation. The situation Dow Corning faced had some similarities with the Nokia situation and some important differences. But first a bit of history.

In 1943, Dow Corning was formed as a joint venture between Dow Chemical and Corning Glass to explore the potential of silicones. Over the years, Dow Corning invested heavily in R&D to develop a range of silicone products that met very specific customer needs. The company was generally regarded as its industry leader. By 2000, Dow Corning had captured 40% of the global market and was the market share leader in what had become a multi-billion euro business.[123] Silicones were used in a wide variety of applications from hair conditioners to caulking. Dow Corning had traditionally organized its customers into six major application industry segments such as buildings, healthcare and household products. Each of these application segments had its own marketing, sales and technical service organizations.

Dow Corning faced a very tough situation in 2000

With the company under bankruptcy protection, as a result of lawsuits related to silicon breast implants, Dow Corning was in a crisis situation by 2000. Sales and profits in its traditional silicone businesses were also under increasing pressure from global and regional competitors such as General Electric, Toshiba and Wacker. It was also facing increased competition from local players with little or no R&D and low overheads in the commodity parts of the silicone business – with some of these price value competitors based in Asia.

Dow Corning recognized that its customers could be broken into two major need/benefit segments. The first group of customers, "solution seekers", wanted to take advantage of Dow Corning's technology and of its innovations.[124] An example of this might have been a health and beauty company making a new conditioner and wanting to use silicone to help achieve just the right set of product properties. The second group of customers, "price seekers", were in mature industries, or were buying products in the mature stages of their product life cycles. They simply wanted the lowest possible prices. Price seekers were present in each of the application segments (see Figure 5.2), although the share of the segment they represented varied from one application segment to another. Overall, the price seekers accounted for about 25–35% of the demand, and they were expected to account for a growing share of the overall market in the future. However, this was the least profitable segment of the market, and a considerable share of the sales force's time was spent in lengthy price negotiations with this customer group. Dow Corning faced a tough decision: Withdraw from this price value segment or find a new way of serving it profitably.

End-user application segments

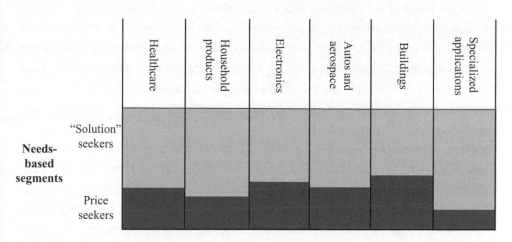

FIGURE 5.2   Dow Corning recognized that price seekers were present in each application segment. (Note: percentages are illustrative.)
Source: Based on Kamran Kashani and Inna Francis, "Xiameter: The Past and Future of a Disruptive Innovation", IMD, Case No. IMD-5-0702.

Dow Corning launched a new business unit

A task force organized by Dow Corning proposed that a low-price/no-frills Internet-based business be organized to serve the price seekers. This was done under a new brand named Xiameter. No attempt was made to hide the fact that it was a Dow Corning business unit; effectively, Xiameter was a sub-brand, which offered customers a limited range of products – initially about 350 versus the almost 8000 products that Dow Corning carried. Customers would be required to buy the product in relatively large quantities, usually in truckloads, pallet loads or tank loads. It would obtain its product from the Dow Corning manufacturing plants around the world. Customers would agree to adhere to a strict set of business rules with respect to things like on-line ordering, delivery lead times, payment terms, rush order surcharges, cancellation penalties, etc. There was no technical support available for Xiameter customers. In exchange for agreeing to adhere to these business rules, customers paid about 15% less than the prices being charged to Dow Corning's customers. Since customers were served directly, distributors were eliminated from Xiameter's value chain.

The launch of Xiameter threatened to overshadow the Dow Corning brand. This led to a major effort to renew the strategy for serving the solution seeking segments of the market. Dow Corning was able to refocus on those customers who were looking for solutions and were willing to pay Dow Corning to access its technical innovation, its proven solutions and its ability to provide cost-effective ways of meeting their technical and financial objectives. Without having to attempt to meet the needs of two very different segments of customers, the Dow Corning sales and service organization could be much more effective.

The two businesses had many synergies in areas such as manufacturing, logistics and IT infrastructure. Because Dow Corning had a very strong cost position from a product perspective, Xiameter was not at a cost advantage because it used a shared manufacturing and logistics infrastructure. However, Xiameter customers had to agree to quite long lead times or accept a significant rush order penalty, and this helped the manufacturing plants to achieve longer production runs, higher capacity utilization rates and lower manufacturing costs.

Clearly, it was very important that Dow Corning enforce its Xiameter business rules with even its best customers, some of whom purchased products from both Xiameter and Dow Corning. It had to be very clear to customers that no technical support would be provided for Xiameter products and that the strict Xiameter payment terms would be enforced. If these rules were not strongly enforced, the company's two distinctive value propositions would be at risk and profitability would be negatively affected.

And the strategy seemed to work well

By 2006, Xiameter was viewed as a major success for Dow Corning. Sales had grown at double-digit rates since 2001 and profitability had soared. While Dow Corning had benefited tremendously from the boom in many of its end-use markets and silicon shortages, most analysts believed that Xiameter had made a major contribution to the company's financial performance. Xiameter was believed to be a large and profitable part of the Dow Corning business.

AER LINGUS PLAYED A PRICE VALUE GAME IN A DIFFERENT SEGMENT

Sometimes a proactive management team sees a low cost competitor having success with a new business model in one of its markets and recognizes the opportunities that such a business model can create. For one reason or another, the management might decide not to confront the competitor in that particular market. This may be because it lacks sufficient scale or a first-mover advantage, or because it feels that the cannibalization of its core business might be extremely high and may accelerate its decline. Sometimes the fear of failure in its home market, and the visibility of that kind of failure, contributes to the decision. The management team may, however, see enough potential in the low cost business model that it decides to pre-emptively try the low cost model (or a refined version of it) in other markets before either the original low cost competitor or imitators do the same. One example of a company doing this successfully, discussed at length earlier in the book, was ING DIRECT. It has had success with its low cost direct banking model in such countries as the US and its home market, the Netherlands. ING DIRECT was launched in nine countries in 2008, achieving good results in most of these markets. The business became a significant contributor to the profitability of parent ING Groep within ten years of its launch.

In other cases, when a company is challenged by low cost competitors in its core market it realizes that it can't compete successfully with them in a head-to-head battle. Perhaps the traditional company's management realizes that no matter how aggressively it tries to drive down its costs, it may not be able to bring its costs in line with its new competitor – perhaps due to inefficient work practices and strong unions. In other cases, its brand image may be such that customers may not believe that it actually does have the best prices. It also may simply be that the business culture is so different from the one required to be a low cost player, that there is no realistic way to change it in any sort of reasonable time frame.

In some cases, the other generic options of performance value or relational value leadership may no longer be viable options for the company in the long term. Perhaps this is because low cost competitors have attracted so many of the company's customers that the company lacks the scale or scope to compete against other traditional players playing a performance value or relational value game. In such cases, one option might be to play a price value game in another segment of the market, ideally one that is protected from the low cost competitors by significant barriers to entry. For example, there may be regulatory barriers or geographical barriers, or the particular segment that it is targeting is one that the existing low cost competitor or competitors have chosen not to compete in because it does not fit with their particular business model. Aer Lingus is an example of a company that faced this type of situation.

Competing in Ryanair's home market

As the flag carrier for the Republic of Ireland, Aer Lingus had been in competition with Ryanair for 15 years by 2000. The competition intensified after 1992 when Ryanair decided to move to a price value strategy based on the Southwest Airlines model. While Aer Lingus had made some reactive changes in strategy as a result of Ryanair's entry and growth, there were no major changes in Aer Lingus' core strategy during the 1990s. The issue came to a head in 2001, however, when the air travel market was hit by a combination of the September 11 attacks in the US and a global economic slowdown. The combination of these two events, in addition to the heavy competitive pressure from Ryanair, brought Aer Lingus to the verge of bankruptcy in 2001.

Aer Lingus' business had two major components at that time: a short-haul business within Europe and a long-haul business which involved flights to North America, particularly to cities with large populations that have Irish roots such as New York, Boston and Chicago. In the two segments of its business, it faced different types of competitors. In the short-haul business, Ryanair was its most significant competitor, although Aer Lingus also faced competition from major European flag carriers such as British Airways, Air France and Lufthansa on routes to the UK, France and Germany, respectively. On the long-haul routes, it faced competition mostly from major US carriers such as Delta Airlines, American Airlines and Continental Airlines. While the restructuring plan that began in 2001 involved a number of common elements that affected the total Aer Lingus business, the company adopted somewhat different strategies for the two parts of its business. We will first focus on the common elements and then look at the different approaches used for the two different parts of the business.

A difficult balancing act between cost cutting and differentiation

The aim of the restructuring plan implemented by CEO Willie Walsh and his management team was to return the airline to profitability as quickly as possible. Aer Lingus redefined itself into a point-to-point low cost, low fares airline, primarily providing passenger transportation services but with a slightly differentiated product offering relative to Ryanair. It copied many of the basic elements of the low cost model including low, unrestricted one-way fares. It also rationalized its distribution network, reducing commission to travel agents and utilizing its own website – aerlingus.com – as its primary distribution channel. By the end of 2005, Aer Lingus generated 71% of all its bookings through aerlingus.com.

The air carrier eliminated complimentary in-flight food and beverages on short-haul flights and introduced the in-flight sale of these items – an important part of its ancillary revenue generation efforts. Additionally, it generated revenues through flight change fees and refund fees, as well as from commissions earned on sales through partners offering car rentals and hotel accommodations. It also sold travel insurance through the website. After the initial restructuring, Aer Lingus continued to monitor market and competitive conditions and adapted its strategy and tactics where necessary. In a bid to both cut costs and increase ancillary revenues, it followed Ryanair's lead and announced the introduction of fees for checked baggage on short-haul flights in 2006.

Prior to the restructuring, Aer Lingus had operated a variety of different aircraft from three different manufacturers. After consolidating the fleet, Aer Lingus operated only two Airbus aircraft: Airbus A320s on its short-haul routes and Airbus A330s on its long-haul routes. It also made a major effort to shorten aircraft turnaround times dramatically and increase aircraft utilization.

It is clear that many of the operational efficiencies that Aer Lingus was trying to make could not be achieved without the support of its employees and unions. As a start-up, Ryanair had been able to outsource to efficient third parties most, or all, of its passenger processing, baggage handling, catering, aircraft maintenance and some human resource activities. Aer Lingus' unions resisted outsourcing many of these activities. However, by working with its unions, the Aer Lingus management team was able to negotiate a significant downsizing of the work force (about 40%), wage reductions, pay freezes and higher productivity targets. In return for agreeing to these measures, the company offered enhanced redundancy payments and gave employees a significant ownership stake in the company. The negotiations with the unions took more than four years, however, and essentially became an on-going process as the company struggled to continually improve work practices and reduce costs.

From a marketing perspective, Aer Lingus developed different strategies for the short-haul European segment and the long-haul, largely North American, segment. On its short-haul routes it offered a service very similar to Ryanair's with the exception that it flew to primary, centrally located airports, such as London Heathrow, had assigned seating and promised never to leave a passenger stranded in the case of plane or weather problems. Its revenues per passenger (including both flight-related and ancillary revenues) were about twice as high as

Ryanair's. While Aer Lingus was clearly primarily targeting business travelers going to major European business centers, or passengers wanting to connect with long-haul services out of major European airports, it decided in 2004 to eliminate business class on its short-haul flights. This had an obvious impact on revenues but it also reduced the complexity and the costs associated with the short-haul business.

On its long-haul routes, primarily to the US, Aer Lingus offered a more traditional two-class service but retained some aspects of its low cost, intra-European model, such as one-way fares. It focused particularly on the 10% of Americans who claimed Irish heritage; they were the dominant carrier on the Ireland–US routes it served with a market share three times that of its closest US competitor.

Some initial successes but is it sustainable?

A majority of analysts agree that the Aer Lingus strategy change, initiated in October 2001, has been reasonably successful and represents one of the best examples of a successful restructuring of an airline in the history of aviation. Costs (excluding fuel) had been reduced by 47%. By 2005, its cost structure was highly competitive relative to peer network carriers, but it still remained relatively uncompetitive with low cost carriers, particularly Ryanair. The airline returned to profitability in fiscal year 2003. In 2004, the operating profit (before employee profit share) was € 107 million, an increase of 28.9% over the 2003 level of €83 million. The operating margin, 8.1% in 2005, was one of the best in the industry in Europe, comparable to British Airways' 8.3% but well below Ryanair's 21.6% in that year. The main drivers were the reduction in average fares (stimulating demand) combined with the resulting rising load factors and reduction in costs. The improved performance allowed Aer Lingus to complete a successful IPO in September 2006 which contributed to a strong balance sheet.

Despite its return to profitability, it remained a small airline. The trend towards consolidation of European airlines is expected to continue (Air France–KLM, Lufthansa–Swiss, etc.) and Aer Lingus' profitability and valuable Heathrow spots have made it ripe for a takeover and possible asset stripping by an airline looking to expand its long-haul business. Ironically, its relative cost competitiveness and profitability might work against its ambition to remain an independent airline.

In addition, Aer Lingus face intensifying competition from Ryanair. The two airlines overlapped on 60% of Aer Lingus' short-haul routes (in terms of serving the same cities but not necessarily the same airports) and with Ryanair's continued expansion out of Dublin, this posed a threat to the profitability of Aer Lingus' short-haul business. Its labor costs were still significantly higher than Ryanair's and its strong unions made it very difficult to close the gap. However, it was working hard on other elements of its cost structure: reduction of its airport costs through renegotiation of handling contracts and of the third-party maintenance contracts for its fleet, renegotiation of the charges levied by Dublin Airport Authority, continued focus on increasing short- and long-haul aircraft utilization, as well as further reductions in marketing, sales and distribution costs. However, the air carrier was unlikely to be able to significantly narrow the gap with Ryanair, which was successfully pursuing its own cost reduction programs and generally had more negotiating power.

Aer Lingus was clearly protected from the full force of Ryanair's competitive pressure by the latter's strategy of not serving primary airports. However, this did not protect the company from other low cost carriers, such as easyJet, who were willing to use primary airports. One or more of these low cost carriers could potentially add Dublin as a destination, particularly when a planned Dublin Airport expansion was completed, which would create more capacity there. However, in the past, Ryanair has shown that it will vigorously and ruthlessly try to prevent other low cost carriers from establishing a base in Ireland. Ironically, Aer Lingus' biggest competitor might help protect it.

In 2006, Ryanair did attempt a hostile takeover of Aer Lingus; the move was blocked by the European Commission on the grounds that it would give Ryanair too dominant a position in the Irish market. Key Aer Lingus shareholders, including the Irish government and Aer Lingus employees, were also opposed to the move. In late 2008, Ryanair made a new offer for the airline.

In conclusion, Aer Lingus successfully moved to a "somewhat" low cost model but will that be good enough in the long run? The carrier was by 2007 Europe's most cost competitive network airline, enjoying relatively high margins. It had long-haul potential, i.e. North America, South Africa, Middle East and Far East. If the Irish economy were to continue to succeed and grow, it would create increased demand for airline services to and from Ireland. Aer Lingus would be well placed to profit from that demand especially on the long-haul sector. The early success of the transition Aer Lingus made was undoubtedly one of the major factors that led the board of BA to select Willie Walsh as its new CEO in 2005. Despite this vote of confidence in Aer Lingus' strategy, it was not out of the woods.

CHALLENGE QUESTIONS

If you were to enter the price value segment of the market, how far down the market would you want to go? How far down do you think you might need to go to be well positioned to compete effectively with low cost competitors and to make it more difficult for them to challenge you in your high-end business? Are these two points the same or do you have to work to resolve them?

What arguments for entering the price value segment might be valid in your particular situation?

What arguments for not entering the price value segment might be valid in your particular situation?

How do channel considerations affect this decision in your particular case? Will you need to develop new channels? Should you consider evolving your channels?

Where do you come out, on balance, with respect to entering the price value segment of the market (as you define it)?

In your particular situation, are there alternative ways to meet the need customers might have for a price value solution? Might re-manufactured, or re-conditioned, products be a way to meet the need?

If you should enter the price value segment, is now the time to move? Are you moving fast enough?

Should the price value business be independent – what are the main arguments, pro and con?

If you do enter the price value business, should you build it yourselves, or buy? Should you use the same brand, a sub-brand or a totally new brand?

Are there any lessons for you in the Dow Corning Xiameter case study?

Are there any lessons for you from the difficult situation Aer Lingus faced in the home market of Ryanair and the strategy it adopted?

CHAPTER 6

Avoiding head-to-head competition with low cost competitors by playing a different game

After the management team has completed a review of the current and potential threat to its core business from low cost competition, it has to make some tough decisions. One, which was discussed in Chapter 5, is whether to confront the low cost competitors in the price value segment of the market. If the team makes the decision not to enter into direct competition with its low cost competitors, it needs to make some fundamental decisions about how it will distance the business from these competitors and build barriers to try to prevent the low cost players from eating into its core business over time. To do this, it has two basic options. The first option is to offer customers outstanding performance value so that a significant segment of customers will see the incremental performance of the company's products or services as being worth the incremental cost. The value should also be attractive relative to other competitors trying to play a performance leadership game. The second option is to offer customers outstanding relational value – customized and integrated solutions, fast response or something else that will result in deep and enduring relationships with its customers.

When first challenged by low cost competitors, a company usually adjusts its strategy to cater somewhat to the needs of the customer segments seeking price value. This strategy often becomes a hybrid strategy over time; it doesn't fully meet either the needs of customers concerned about price value or those seeking more value-added solutions based on either relational value or performance value. If the management team decides to compete in the price value segment of the market, it also usually has significant work to do to optimize the performance of its traditional business. If the tough choice is to compete seriously in the price value segment of the market with a focused price value offering, then the strategy for the rest of the business' target segments generally needs to be reviewed and refocused. This is what Dow Corning had to do after it set up the Xiameter business unit to focus on the price value segment. The company then had to "re-think" its offerings for the "solution seeking" segments. Again, this means developing industry leading performance value or relational value offers.

This chapter begins by examining Electrolux, a company that was facing increasing competition from both low cost competitors and high-end niche players. We will look at how it tried to deal with the threats, as well as the opportunities, in its markets, by stressing performance leadership. Then, taking a broader scope, we will discuss the issues faced by companies that choose to compete on performance leadership in many of today's fast moving markets.

Next, we will look at two companies that have tried to deal with the actual, or potential, threat of low cost competition by stressing relational value leadership. One of these companies competes in a highly commoditized business-to-business market and the other operates in a business-to-consumer space where it serves tens of millions of customers. This will give us an opportunity to look at building relational value leadership in two very different types of situations.

ENHANCING PERFORMANCE VALUE

Many companies' core value propositions emphasize performance value (previously discussed in Chapter 2). They offer customers some appropriate combination of superior functionality, innovative features, exceptional user experience, excellent quality, style or fashion leadership. Among the companies that have traditionally emphasized this approach are P&G (including Gillette), Nestlé, BMW, Bang & Olufsen, Bloomberg, Philips, Swatch, Research in Motion (BlackBerry), Grundfos and, in particular, Apple. Apple has a long history of developing a series of evolutionary, or even revolutionary, products in both established and essentially new product categories. Macintosh, with its graphical user interface, iMac, iPod, iTunes and iPhone are among the series of products that have allowed Apple to take on the market leaders in personal computers, consumer entertainment and mobile phones. Companies like Microsoft, Sony and Nokia are among the companies who have been forced to play a "catch-up game" with Apple.

Many of the companies that have been successful performance leaders in past decades now find themselves under increasing pressure from low cost companies offering good enough products and services at low prices. Electrolux, a company that traditionally emphasized performance leadership, found itself being challenged by low cost competitors.

Electrolux was not well positioned for the emerging market environment

Based in Sweden, Electrolux is a leading household appliances manufacturer. Historically it had manufactured well-engineered, solid and reliable appliances that were often the performance leaders in their segments. In the 1980s and 1990s, Electrolux grew tremendously through acquisitions that included Zanussi, Flymo and White, but it had not fully consolidated the acquired operations into its existing ones. This resulted in an assortment of brands, all needing the support of separate production and marketing operations.

Electrolux was hurt in the early 1990s by an economic downturn in its core European and North American operations and by the maturing of the white goods sectors in those same markets, combined with intensifying competition. To achieve growth Electrolux targeted Eastern Europe, Asia, South America, the Middle East and southern Africa. Activities in Asia included the setting up of joint ventures in China and the acquisition of majority stakes in factories in India. By 1996, almost 25% of Electrolux's sales of household appliances came from outside the European Union and North America.

By the end of the 1990s, the company was struggling to keep its high-cost European factories viable in a market increasingly being targeted by Asian, particularly Korean and Chinese, manufacturers. It appeared on the one hand that many consumers from all income levels were increasingly shopping for inexpensive, good enough products for some, or all, of their needs. The products of these manufacturers were rapidly closing the performance and quality gap with Electrolux, and they were less expensive. This trend was being driven partly by large, increasingly pan-European, retailers' price-led strategies.

At the same time, there was also a growing segment of consumers that were spending more money on building and furnishing their homes – this segment demanded products with more features and more customization potential, different styles, "trendy" brand names and a higher level of service from appliance manufacturers. Premium brands, produced by European and North American manufacturers, such as Bosch, Miele, Sub-Zero and Viking, were targeting these high-end market segments with differentiated products; these companies often took aim at lifestyle segments that were willing to pay significant premiums for products perceived as meeting their needs. The middle of the market, traditionally dominated by companies like Electrolux, was disappearing.[125]

Electrolux responded to the challenge on multiple fronts

Electrolux's president and CEO Michael Treschow (nicknamed "Mack the Knife") announced a major restructuring plan in June 1997. Over a two-year period, Electrolux laid off more than 11 000 of its workers (11% of the workforce) and closed 23 plants and 50 warehouses, with the reductions taking place mainly in Western Europe and North America. Restructuring charges in 1997 amounted to about $ 325 million. Electrolux further streamlined its operations in 1998, divested several non-core units and eliminated a large portion of its direct sales force. The company completed its restructuring efforts in 1999 and began to focus on maintaining a strong market position (as the global number two manufacturer after Whirlpool).

Benefiting partly from healthy markets and the restructuring efforts sales and net income grew in 2000 to approximately €14 billion and €0.5 billion, respectively. However, by the end of that year the company was in trouble again. It faced weakening demand, high costs and a portfolio of 50 brands. Operating income was down by nearly 23% over the previous year.

Hans Stråberg took over as president and CEO in April 2002. Stråberg realized that he had to do things very differently if he was to achieve sustainable profitable growth for Electrolux. Cost cutting was only part of the answer to the company's problem of stagnating sales and increasing operational costs. He had to transform Electrolux into a truly market-driven company; the company needed to differentiate its products from less expensive Asian products.

Under Stråberg, Electrolux pursued a two-pronged approach, addressing both costs and revenues. It cut costs by relocating production to low cost countries and divesting or changing the business model for units that were not profitable (e.g. air conditioners in the US). It did a number of other things in order to bring its costs under better control; the company rationalized its product mix and created a smaller number of product platforms, some of which could be used globally.

This enabled standardization of components, fewer product variants, simpler production and higher quality. It aggressively pursued cost savings in purchasing, partly by buying parts and other products and services on a global basis where it made sense. The company hoped to increase the percentage of purchases from low cost countries to 40% over a few years and drastically reduce the number of its suppliers. Electrolux also worked with core suppliers to reduce the cost of components. It moved a greater share of production to low cost countries – the goal was to move half its production facilities to low cost countries by 2008. The total cost of this move, through 2008, was estimated to be €1 billion but the program was expected to generate annual savings of €300 million from 2009 onwards.

Additionally, it increased R&D spending, focusing on brand building and increasing product innovation in the hopes of creating products that would command higher prices. In order to develop products that would be differentiated in meaningful ways from its competition, Electrolux put more emphasis on developing products based on consumer insights. Thus, the development of new products was increasingly based on comprehensive research into how consumers thought about and used the products. The new approach made much greater use of observation and user testing than the traditional customer surveys that Electrolux had relied on earlier. This led to more proactive product development and effective marketing communication once the product was launched, which was more likely to stimulate purchase. The process for consumer-focused product development was launched in 2004 and involved multi-functional teams (design, product development and marketing). To support the product innovation drive, Stråberg increased spending on R&D from 0.8% of sales to 2% annually.[126] The number of new appliance product launches rose from about 200 in 2002 to 370 in 2005.

In order to deal with the differing needs and buying behaviors at the two ends of the market, Electrolux developed different business models for the segments.[127] The company utilized different production platforms, sales forces and communication approaches for the more basic and premium ends of the market. Electrolux decided to focus on these two broad market segments because that was where it felt the biggest potential for profitable growth lay. It could draw on its brand portfolios to attempt to position products for the premium end of the market more effectively. In some cases, it used a sub-branding strategy such as AEG-Electrolux.

Stråberg was convinced that only with a strong global brand could Electrolux be successful in the long run in delivering sustained higher margins and profits. This led to an increased emphasis on the Electrolux brand with about 2% of revenues being targeted at brand-building activities. The share of products sold under the Electrolux brand rose steadily from 16% of sales in 2002 to almost 50% in 2005. The company launched the Electrolux brand promise "Thinking of you" in 2005 to emphasize its consumer focus.

Electrolux has made some progress but the challenges still loom large

Electrolux has certainly taken a number of positive steps in terms of customer-driven product development, brand building and cost reduction. Sales increased at the rate of 7% from 2004 to 2005 to SKR 129.5 billion and operating income increased by 2.9% on a comparable basis (before restructuring charges for factory closures in Europe). After the spin-off of the outdoor products division in 2006, Electrolux became totally focused on indoor appliance products for consumers and professional users. But the success of its current approach is far from assured. The path it has chosen is a long one, and there is no quick fix to its problems. The company has maintained its strong position in the appliance industry (it continues to be the number two global player after Whirlpool-Maytag). However, the company still faces many challenges.

It is not easy to attack both the mainstream and premium segments of the appliance market successfully. There isn't a precedent for a successful approach of this type in the appliance industry. GE has struggled for decades to do the same in the segments of the major appliance business where it competes in North America. Electrolux's other global competitors are also trying to do somewhat the same thing. The leading Chinese appliance company, Haier, is also in the process of building and increasing the reach of its brand, while still using its low cost base in China to cater to the market's entry-level segments. And the specialized premium brands, such as Sub-Zero and Viking, continue to do very well in their segments of the market.[128] While economical from a brand-building perspective, it's questionable whether using a sub-branding strategy, like AEG-Electrolux, is the best one for penetrating high-end niche markets against focused competitors who have brands with a strong premium image. Electrolux, however, faces intensifying competition in all of the world's major regional markets. Whirlpool's acquisition of Maytag in 2006 gave Whirlpool added leverage with suppliers and the trade, compared to Electrolux, in the very important North American market. The ultimate impact of this development will take time to play out.

Electrolux continues to have major issues in the fastest growing region in the world, Asia – a region that accounted for only about 4% of total revenues in 2005. The company has divested its Indian appliance operations, including all three production facilities, to Videocon, one of India's largest industrial groups; this reduced losses, but it also affected the company's ability to grow the brand in this high growth market. China remains unprofitable and Electrolux was reassessing its approach there. And its generally weak position in all emerging markets puts Electrolux at a competitive disadvantage relative to its major Asian competitors, Haier, LG and Samsung. All are better positioned than Electrolux in these markets, helping them achieve economies of scale that they are leveraging as they increasingly target the European and North American markets. Overcapacity in the Chinese economy, combined with falling profit margins in their domestic market, was also pushing Chinese firms to seek new markets outside China.

Electrolux will find it more and more difficult to achieve meaningful product differentiation over its Asian competitors, leading to a higher brand premium. The Koreans are already known for having well-priced, good quality products coupled with strong designs and some innovative features. The Chinese, led by Haier, are also concentrating strongly on consumer-focused products; they have great ambitions to upgrade their products and brand image. In addition, Haier has been opening factories in, or close to, developed markets, such as the US and Eastern Europe, with the aim of producing tailor made products for these regional markets. Haier had an R&D budget of almost 4% of revenues in 2004, significantly higher than the percentage that Electrolux was devoting to those efforts.

Despite all its efforts, Electrolux's operating performance has been relatively weak compared to its Asian competitors and the industry average. The industry recorded an average top line growth of 10.8% in the period 2001–2005 but Electrolux's revenues only grew at 0.8%. In addition, the company's operating profit margin was 4.7%, compared to the industry average of 7%.[129]

In conclusion, while Electrolux has made some intelligent changes in its strategy, it was still facing some huge challenges in 2008. As we discussed in Chapter 2, performance leadership is particularly difficult to sustain in a highly competitive market that is clearly quite mature. This is particularly difficult in a mature market where much of the know-how and technology is either widely available in the market or available from specialized third parties who are willing to sell or license it to any company that needs it. Also, it is particularly difficult for a broad-based supplier, like Electrolux, to do this simultaneously in a number of different mass-market product categories, as well as a series of high-end premium niche market segments where it faces strong and entrenched local competitors.

MAINTAINING PERFORMANCE LEADERSHIP IS A CHALLENGE TODAY

Electrolux is not the only company struggling to maintain its performance leadership position. Many other companies, including Bang & Olufsen, are facing similar challenges. Bang & Olufsen, the well-known Danish company, has been a performance value leader in consumer electronics for many years. Its leadership generally has been based not only on technical performance but also on its beautiful and iconic designs. For an industry where change is rapid, many of its eye-catching designs have stood the test of time; one of its CD players was still on the market 11 years after it was released. Bang & Olufsen uses highly creative contract designers to design its products, but it's difficult to find these rare, talented individuals and manage them effectively. Bang & Olufsen is also struggling as consumer electronics becomes more and more digital, combined with extremely rapid changes in the product technology.[130] By 2008, it hadn't been successful in coming up with a digital music player that could match Apple's iPod.[131] This would have seemed to be a product category where Bang & Olufsen could potentially excel.

Rising costs and shortening windows represent a significant issue

A particular challenge in many industries is the squeeze being created by the rising cost of developing new products and services and the simultaneous decline in the time to capitalize on innovative new products. The pharmaceutical industry is a good example of this. Pfizer spent about $800 million in budgeted research costs on Torcetrapib, a drug designed to raise the level of HDL cholesterol (the so-called good cholesterol) that can keep arteries clear of plaque.[132] Pfizer stopped work on the drug in late 2006 when a 15 000-person clinical trial demonstrated that it had some serious, negative side effects. If the drug had successfully completed the clinical trials and received the approval of regulators all over the world, Pfizer would have spent many additional millions, if not hundreds of millions of dollars, launching the product globally. For every drug that reaches even the final stage of clinical trials, thousands of other candidate drugs have fallen by the wayside in laboratory tests, animal tests or smaller-scale human trials. The average cost of developing a new prescription drug is estimated to be close to $900 million.[133]

Even though the new Pfizer drug would likely have had strong patent protection and any new competitive drugs would have to go through the same lengthy approval process, it would have probably had less than ten years to capitalize on the drug before generic competitors entered the market and drove prices down dramatically. While pharmaceutical R&D costs are high and the product development cycles are long, at least there are significant barriers that slow down the entry of competition. Most companies that focus on developing other types of performance leading products are not so fortunate. The hard disk drive business is an example of this. In the early 1980s, a new hard disk would typically ship for four to six years before being withdrawn from the market. By the end of the decade, the typical shipping life had fallen to two to three years, and by the 1990s, it was just six to nine months.[134] So with rising R&D costs in many industries, and shorter periods to capitalize on that R&D, many companies playing a performance leadership game feel that they are being squeezed. This is shown graphically in Figure 6.1.

One of the reasons that competition is able to follow the performance leader so quickly is the leakage of competitively useful information through suppliers and customers. Even if non-disclosure agreements are signed and adhered to, information does leak to competitors, often in innocent ways. For example, a company that buys new innovative equipment from a supplier to allow it to make industry leading products may inadvertently help its competitors. The new equipment is likely to have "bugs" in it or things that could be improved. If the company notifies the supplier about the bugs, or the product improvement opportunities, and they are fixed and adopted by the supplier, this will help any of its competitors that subsequently buy the same piece of equipment. They might be able to ramp up production more quickly and even lower their costs, since the annoying and time-consuming bugs will have been fixed; the equipment may be more efficient, or more effective, as a result of the product improvement suggestions. In highly competitive industries, these small things can be important. Sharp, arguably the technology leader in manufacturing LCD panels, tries to protect its leadership in a number of ways. It does not always report the problems it experiences with new

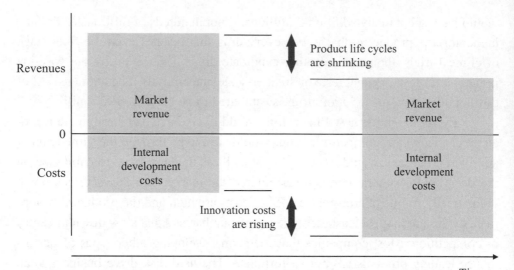

FIGURE 6.1   While product innovation costs rise, the time to capitalize on innovations is generally declining
Source: Henry W. Chesbrough, "Why Companies Should Have Open Business Models", *MIT Sloan Management Review*, Winter 2007, Volume 48, No. 2, p. 24.

equipment to the machine supplier but quietly fixes the machines itself. That way the followers, who will experience the same problems, will be delayed while the manufacturer tries to remedy the problems. The company also writes some of its own software and, in some cases, deliberately does not automate processes that might again leak through suppliers; rather they use skilled human operators for some of the tricky, critical process steps.[135] Honda also uses a number of proprietary processes and tools in its manufacturing activities; it make its own specialized equipment to prevent the leakage of intellectual property to competitors through suppliers.

Using open business models can help

One way a number of performance leadership companies are using to meet the challenge of rising innovation costs and shortening windows is to take advantage of the trend in many industries for more open innovation. This trend, discussed in Chapter 2, which results in more innovation being available on the open market,

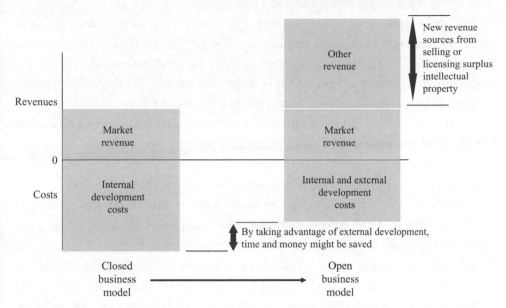

FIGURE 6.2 Creative ways to offset rising development costs and shorter product life cycles
Source: Henry W. Chesbrough, "Why Companies Should Have Open Business Models", *MIT Sloan Management Review*, Winter 2007, Volume 48, No. 2, p. 27.

is one of the factors that helps accelerate the speed with which low cost competitors enter markets; it helps them to rapidly match new products and services offered by the value-added players. But open innovation can also be used to help the value-added players gain and sustain advantages over the low cost competition. As shown in Figure 6.2, performance leadership companies can, for example, sometimes both speed up development and lower development costs by taking advantage of the innovation that might be available from external sources. A.G. Laffley, the CEO of Procter and Gamble, set an objective of having 50% of the company's innovative ideas come from external sources. By 2006, some 35% of its innovation was being sourced externally; about half of the 16500 people working on innovation were not direct P&G employees.[136]

Some companies have found that a significant amount of the intellectual property that they have developed in-house is never used; however, some of it does have commercial value. By taking advantage of the same trend to open innovation, companies can also defray some of their R&D costs by licensing, or selling, this surplus intellectual property – or even selling parts of their business based on non-core intellectual property to third parties. P&G actively does this. For example in China, it provides secret, high-value "performance chemicals" for detergents to Chinese partners who mix these chemicals with other basic ingredients, package the resulting detergents and distribute them.[137]

IBM is another good example of a company that has aggressively taken advantage of the opportunities that a more open business model offer.[138] In its semiconductor business, it established a research alliance with Toshiba Corporation and Chartered Semiconductor to share the costs, and risks, of developing new leading-edge semiconductor manufacturing processes. It is now also much more willing to license proprietary IBM process technology to third parties, which again helps to offset the very high development costs it incurs in this area. It also actively invests in and supports the open source Linux operating system. This gives IBM's customers an alternative operating system for IBM's server and storage product lines. And customers don't need to lock themselves into either an IBM proprietary operating system, or one of the proprietary systems available from companies like Microsoft or Sun Microsystems. For IBM the open source operating system allows it to serve customers who want this option at relatively low cost.

Performance value leadership requires constant innovation

Tennant, a US-based manufacturer of industrial floor cleaning equipment, is a good example of a mid-sized company that has invested heavily in R&D to maintain a performance leadership position, relative to both its traditional competitors and emerging low cost competition. In one case, it developed a new innovative carpet-cleaning machine to replace machines that sprayed a cleaning solution onto the carpet and then vacuumed the solution and dirt away. Tennant's new ReadySpace machine sprayed a cleaning solution onto brushes that then cleaned the carpet. The machine was not only highly effective at removing the soil, but also, more importantly, at reducing the drying time for the carpet. By shortening the time from 24 hours to 30 minutes, it created a lot of value for some customers such as casinos, hospitals, airports and hotels, which operate 24 hours per day. The machine was launched in 2004 and soon became Tennant's best-selling carpet cleaning machine. The company continues to introduce new and innovative products and shows good growth in a highly competitive market.

It is clear that performance leadership requires constant innovation. While most companies focus their efforts on product or service innovation, the best companies consider the total solution that customers are seeking. The success of iPod is a good example. While iPod is a competent MP3 player, functionally, it is not very different from competitive offerings. But when you also consider design and ease of use it starts to stand out. When you add iTunes – a tightly integrated, complementary service, that is also very easy to use – as an affordable, and legal, source of new music and entertainment products, the gap between the iPod and its competition really begins to widen. In essence, it becomes a new business model for the distribution and consumption of entertainment.

Apple is a moving target. Both the iTunes product and service continued to evolve rapidly after its launch in October 2001. By 2007, Apple was on its sixth generation of the original iPod and had several other models such as Nano, Shuffle and Touch. It has been a very difficult target for competition to catch. In addition to Apple's own efforts, a virtual industry of complementors has grown up around iPod. Docks with external speakers and accessories of all sorts have increased iPod's customer value, as have the host of other contributors, which create content that can be downloaded from iTunes to iPods.

Given the above discussion of open innovation, it's interesting to note that the initial concept of iPod complemented with a Napster-like music sales service did not come from within Apple but rather from an inventor/entrepreneur, Tony Fadell. The basic hardware design for the iPod was bought from a small Silicon Valley startup called PortalPlayer.[139] Fadell initially worked for Apple as a contractor. He soon joined the company and ultimately became a senior Apple executive.

Performance leadership products and services have to provide great solutions not only for their customers, but also for all members of the value chain, including key influencers and other stakeholders, including complementors that are not directly involved in the value chain. Apple's iPod would not have been as successful without the support of the organizations and individuals who created and provided the content that could be downloaded from iTunes. Sometimes deficiencies in the product can be offset by the strong support of members of the value chain who get other benefits from working with a supplier. Caterpillar has benefited tremendously from the loyalty of its distributors at times when its product line might not have been the most competitive in the industry. But these distributors recognized that, over the years, Caterpillar had worked closely with them and helped them to build large profitable businesses.

Getting beyond the strategic breakpoint can create real competitive advantage

In trying to develop and maintain performance leadership, a company searches for points of differentiation. However, many points of differentiation do not create sufficient incentive for customers to choose a new product over their existing choice or other alternatives. The strategic breakpoint refers to the degree of differentiation the product or service must have to create a powerful motivation for the customer to choose a product over the alternatives. Exceeding the strategic breakpoint can help establish performance leadership. As shown in Figure 6.3, the relationship between the differentiation a company achieves and its competitive advantage is not always a simple, linear one. Often, if a company is only marginally better than its competitors in delivering a benefit to its target customers, there will not be much of a competitive advantage and little significant change in market share because the incentive to overcome the switching barriers that encourage customers to continue using the familiar, proven solution will not be sufficient. But, at some point, if the differentiation achieved proves to be an important benefit for the target segment, it will lead to a significant competitive advantage and, hence, improved market share. The relationship is often an "s-shaped" curve as

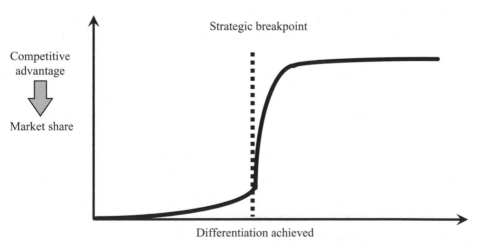

FIGURE 6.3 Strategic breakpoints can lead to significant competitive advantage
Source: Adrian Ryans, Roger More, Donald Barclay and Terry Deutscher, Winning Market Leadership, Toronto: John Wiley and Sons, 2000, p. 154.

you overcome the switching barriers for many customers at about the same degree of differentiation. This provides the basis for a strong value proposition since the product both meets the customer's need and does a better job of meeting that need than any of the competitive offerings. Finally, at some point, increased differentiation compared to competitors will have diminishing marginal returns.

When ABB entered North America's power equipment market in the early 1970s, the market was mature and dominated by such formidable competitors as GE, Westinghouse and McGraw-Edison.[140] In the mid-1970s, shortly after ABB entered the market, there was a rapid rise in oil prices causing a significant market decline. After conducting a great deal of market research on US purchasers of this kind of equipment, ABB realized that warranties were an important buying determinant for several market segments. At that time, there was no competitor who offered a warranty of more than one year. In order to differentiate itself from its competitors on this important attribute, ABB decided to introduce a full five-year warranty on its equipment. In order to be able to do this in an economical way, the company had to make major changes in how it designed and manufactured its products. Within a year of introducing equipment with the new warranty, ABB managed to increase its market share from 8% to 15% in a very difficult market environment. One could argue that if ABB had made the warranty on its equipment 18 months, it would have achieved some differentiation but it might not have achieved a real competitive advantage and, hence, a significant market share increase. Clearly moving to five years pushed it well past the strategic breakpoint.

This notion of a strategic breakpoint has important implications for new product and service development. One can argue that a good new product development strategy is sometimes to focus on a compelling benefit, or couple of benefits, that target segments are seeking, attempting to make sure that you clearly differentiate yourself. That is, the company should try to develop a product that gets beyond the strategic breakpoint for that particular attribute, or attributes. In some high-technology markets where there are significant switching costs, this might require not just a 20% improvement in performance, but perhaps a 200% or 300% improvement, or more! If the company is successful in getting beyond the breakpoint, this strategy may be much more effective than one based on trying to be a little better than competitors on each of the product specifications. Even the collective impact of being a little better on each specification may not be sufficient to create a real competitive advantage and changes in customers' choices.

By adopting a more focused new product development strategy, aimed at achieving a dramatic improvement in performance on a key attribute, both the time to market and the cost of developing the new product may be dramatically reduced. In some cases, this more focused development process also benefits product quality, particularly in products like software.

Determining the degree of differentiation you need to achieve to reach the strategic breakpoint is not easy. Hard economic analysis, from the buyer's perspective, is important in order to calculate the economic value of the benefit to the customer. This will help determine the degree of differentiation you will need to achieve before a fully rational customer will switch to your product because their economics support it. How far beyond this you need to go to give the customer the added incentive to go to all the trouble to switch, and overcome any risk aversion, may require managerial judgment or additional market research.

Apple's successes seem to be based on this (and not all Apple's new products and services are successes!). It usually seems to go well beyond its competitors on a couple of key choice attributes, often ease of use and styling. These are also attributes that competitors have difficulty copying quickly and Apple is usually a moving target. Tennant, by dramatically shortening the carpet drying time from 24 hours to 30 minutes, also seemed to go well beyond the strategic breakpoint, and in this way was able to distance itself from its low cost competitors.

STRESSING RELATIONAL VALUE

While many companies have stressed performance value as a way to gain and sustain competitive advantage and to stay ahead of the price value players, other companies have focused on relational value as their key differentiator. Companies as diverse as Tesco, Tetra Pak, Viking (a US-based manufacturer of high-end gas ranges and other kitchen and outdoor cooking appliances), Orica, private banks, IBM Global Services and Hilti, all put a heavy emphasis on building deep relationships with customers to reduce the impact of price value players on their businesses.

AES Engineering, based in the UK, is the world's fourth largest manufacturer of mechanical seals that are used in such things as pumps and other rotating equipment to prevent fluids and gases leaking out. Poor seal performance and seal failures can be both costly and lead to environmental damage. Its products come in a huge variety of shapes and sizes, and a big part of its job is helping its customers design or specify the right seal for their particular task and making sure that the seal is working properly after it has been installed. It promises very fast delivery of products to its customers. AES also offers a seal repair service to provide customers with a cost-effective alternative to new seals. Almost half of the company's employees are in service-related roles. By building close consultative relationships with its key customers and responding rapidly to the full range of their needs, AES has been able to strengthen its position in its industry and help protect itself against the threat of low cost competitors.[141]

Relational value tends to be particularly important in situations where a customer segment has, or perceives itself as having, complex and diverse needs; it sees value in being able to purchase an integrated solution from one supplier. Clearly, what an integrated solution is in a complex business-to-business situation or a complex business-to-consumer situation might be very different from what it would be in a simpler situation. Consumer expectations regarding wealth management for a high net worth individual, for example, are very different from the wealth management solutions sought by a middle-income consumer. Despite the obvious differences in these situations, a company stressing relational value tries to provide its customers with appropriate customized treatment, tailored offerings and very complete solutions – if that is what the customer wants. In some cases this requires being very fast in responding to client needs. In other instances where the needs are relatively complex, the customer and the supplier become quite dependent on one another; a relationship that often involves a great deal of mutual trust.

Several of the companies mentioned above, including P&G and Tetra Pak, used to put most of their emphasis on having the best performing products, but over the years, they have drifted more and more towards relational value. P&G, for example, has realized that having the best product is not always enough; it is no longer always possible to have a demonstrably better product that can win in a "white box" (before branding, packaging, merchandising, promotion, etc.). Some of its competitors are able to offer good enough products that are very good and fully meet the needs of many customers. The brand is obviously very important for many consumers but the question increasingly is "whose brand?" – is it the manufacturer's brand or the retailer's brand? In this environment, building deep, cooperative relationships with retailers may be the most important key success factor for P&G.

In the last few years, the company has built more than a dozen innovation centers around the world – centers that incorporate some of P&G's deep understanding of the shoppers who buy its products. P&G teams work with retail customer teams at these centers, jointly developing strategies to create more value for the retailer's customers and more profit for the retailer in the product categories in which P&G is active. Some of the innovation centers incorporate virtual stores so that retailers can quickly visualize how new shelf layouts, or displays, might be able to improve their performance.[142]

Ironically, this deep focus on building relational value often leads to ideas for improving performance value – a result of developing a deeper understanding of needs all the way down the value chain.

Building relational value can have some very significant benefits for the companies that do it successfully. Generally, if a company has a tight and intimate relationship with its customers, it reduces the number of customers that defect in a given period of time. If the company continues to add customers at a "normal" rate, it will obviously grow faster than one that has to add a lot of new customers just to replace those who have defected. For example, in 2003 Nextel, the US-based mobile phone operator, experienced a "churn" rate of about 1.5% per month. That is, it lost 1.5% of its customer base every month and had to replace them before it could experience any growth. This sounds like a very high churn rate but, in fact, it was the lowest of the major US mobile phone operators. The other players were experiencing churn rates of anywhere from 2.3% to 3.0% per month! Nextel's lower churn rate was the result of working closely with segments of business customers and private customers to develop wireless "solutions" that met their specific needs.

In one case, Nextel worked closely with complementors to develop a personal digital assistant (PDA) with voice, data, walkie-talkie and satellite positioning capabilities. This allows companies such as plumbing contractors to track their trucks, dispatch trucks to customers and bill and process credit card payments on the spot. This solution provided high value to this market segment and led to higher loyalty, less price sensitivity and higher monthly revenues per customer. In the business-to-consumer side of its business, Nextel also tried to identify segments and develop customized solutions for some of them. One of Nextel's more mass-market solutions was for NASCAR fans. The company designed packages for the fans that included special handsets and other accessories; it also provided "access" to NASCAR race events such as watching races live on mobile phones from a variety of different perspectives and listening to drivers speaking to their crews in the pit.[143] For the enthusiastic fan, this represented a very high value solution.

With fewer customers to replace, at a typical cost of $400 to $500 per new subscriber, in terms of marketing and sales costs and handset subsidies, Nextel was much better positioned for growth and profitability than many of its larger competitors. Loyal customers are often more profitable, as this example suggests, because they can be served at a lower cost and because they often buy a wider range of products and services from a supplier. If the supplier understands its customers' needs well, it is more likely to offer products and services that are more attuned to its customers' needs; this may also make the customers less price sensitive. All of these factors seemed to be working with Nextel's customers. In 2003, it had the highest average revenue per user among the five major US national wireless carriers. Combining this with Nextel's low churn rate meant that the average lifetime revenue per subscriber was $4300 for Nextel, 50% better than the next best carrier and 150% better than the weakest of the other large national carriers. Not surprisingly, Nextel's financial performance was strong.[144] By 2004, the company had a net income of almost $3 billion on revenues of just over $13 billion.[145] Shortly thereafter, it merged with Sprint, but for a variety of reasons the performance of the combined company has not been strong.

We will now look more closely at how two companies have attempted to build deeper and broader relationships with their customers in two very different industries, one in a business-to-business market and the other in a business-to-consumer market. The business-to-business market involved relatively few customers, while the business-to-consumer market involved millions. Clearly, creating relational value leadership is quite a different type of issue in these two quite different situations.

Orica was facing total commoditization of its core products

In the 1990s, the fierce competition in the explosives industry was seriously affecting Orica Mining Services (then ICI Australia) profitability. At one time, there had been significant product differentiation in the commercial explosives business, but by the 1990s, it had become largely commoditized. If one of the explosives' companies wanted to gain market share, or if there was a surplus of ammonium nitrate (the main raw material in the explosives business), a price war was often a result. Orica had tried to distance itself from the commoditization of its core product by developing some more sophisticated products for its customers, such as electronic firing systems to help set off a sequence of very tightly timed blasts. While these new products promised to make a customer's blasting more effective and efficient, most customers showed little interest in this or other new product offerings.

Orica's clients included the quarries and mines of a number of mining companies. Drilling and blasting was often a significant portion of the quarries' costs. The process of setting up a blast and drilling holes in rock faces took several days. Because it was forbidden by law for quarries to store large amounts of explosives on site, they ordered just enough explosives for the day's operation. The exact mix of explosives used was often not totally predictable since it depended on the weather conditions the day of the blast. On that day, the holes were rapidly filled with explosives and the blast was executed. This process was often a race against the clock because blasting times were also severely restricted by law at many quarries. This whole blasting process caused major forecasting headaches for Orica.[146]

Orica began moving towards providing solutions for its customers

Orica gradually changed from being a product provider, vulnerable to strong pricing pressures, to being more of a blasting solutions provider that was much more insulated from strong price competition. The company first started this transition by providing emulsion explosives in bulk form. After a customer placed an order, Orica sent a mobile manufacturing unit to the site. The chemicals were mixed on site and because there were no restrictions on carrying the materials (which were only combustible once mixed). Orica could then determine, with the client, at the last minute what the best mix was for a particular blast on a particular day. With the mobile unit, it could make more calls than before, not only saving costs for the company but also increasing flexibility for the customer. Orica then moved to drawing profiles of rock faces with lasers to identify the best places for drilling and using its electronic firing systems to control the firing sequence, making blasting a more precise science. The emulsion explosives used were more consistent with its new computer-enabled rock face profiling service – quarries had to drill fewer holes that resulted in cost reductions for the quarries themselves and improving yields. Orica also began to offer drilling services to its clients, accepting liability for the process as well.[147]

As Orica developed this process, it began to move away from just selling explosives to selling a solutions package that it could tailor to each customer's requirements – a real innovation in the explosives industry. By 2005, the company was billing many customers according to the quantities of broken rock it delivered that met the customer's size specifications.

Orica leveraged its global leadership position to stay ahead

Orica provided customers with services ranging from blasting to technical consulting. The move from selling products to providing solutions changed the entire explosives business for the company. The very precise blasting meant that Orica could deliver more rock that met the user's specifications and could significantly improve a customer's operational efficiency. The company benefited from the move to offering solutions in numerous ways.

The price of the service provided was less transparent than the product alone; therefore, it made Orica less vulnerable to price pressure and commoditization. And by selling blasting solutions instead of explosives, the company increased its average transaction value and revenues.

The resulting savings for customers made many of them enthusiastic about the solutions approach. It allowed them to outsource a difficult and costly part of their operation to a sophisticated and reliable supplier. Over time, customers became more dependent on the services Orica provided. Providing their own blasting services became a less viable option as they no longer had the specialized blasting personnel, the equipment or the knowledge (the people responsible for blasting and their equipment at a quarry or mine were often transferred to Orica). Performing the blast on the customer's site gave Orica access to customer data and made it an integral part of the customer's processes. By specializing in blasting services and operating all over the world under a variety of different operating conditions, Orica developed a wealth of technical and applications knowledge. This data enabled Orica to improve its own blasting performance and efficiency as well as offer more value to its customers. All of these factors made it less likely that customers would switch to competitors who were unable to deliver as much value to their businesses.[148]

Orica was successful in transforming its business model from selling commoditized products to selling solutions that met the customer's core need. As a result, it was in much less direct competition with low cost players and transformed itself from being a solid player in the market to being the preeminent global supplier.

There were, however, a couple of major risks from the customer perspective. Clearly, the counterpoint to a point made earlier is that the customer is much more dependent on Orica than it was previously. The barriers to switching away from Orica are high. In addition, given how Orica is often compensated (on the basis of the amount of rock on the ground that meets the customer's specifications), the company could take shortcuts that might benefit it, but which might not be in the customer's best interest. For example, Orica might only exploit the most easily and cheaply accessible parts of the resource available in a quarry or a mine since these are the easiest and most profitable for it to blast. But the customer may be more interested in exploiting the full potential of the resource. This underlines the point that in a relational leadership business, mutual trust between customer and supplier is particularly critical.

In 2006 Orica acquired Dyno Nobel's Global Commercial Explosives interests (except in Australia and New Zealand), making it the leading blasting solutions company in the world. This acquisition was highly complementary to Orica's mining business and afforded considerable possibilities for synergy and future growth. The rapid consolidation taking place in the world's mining industry favored explosives companies that could provide a global service and Orica was well placed to take advantage of this. With the world demand for mined and quarried materials growing, the next decade should see the mining division continue to be the largest and most profitable part of Orica's business.

Tesco built relational value in a mass-market

In the early 1990s, Tesco found itself in the position of being the UK's number two supermarket after Sainsbury's. Tesco had made an enormous effort in the late 1970s to get away from its "pile 'em high, sell 'em cheap" reputation by revamping all its stores and creating a modern and pleasant shopping environment. Despite achieving relative success, and having a market share lead over such competitors as Asda and Safeway, it seemed to be a permanent number two to Sainsbury's lead position.

An emerging challenge for Tesco in the early 1990s was the hard discounters; Aldi Sud entered the market in 1989 and was soon followed by Netto and Lidl. They were capturing a small but growing share of the UK grocery retailing market. As discussed in earlier chapters, the hard discounters, led by Aldi and Lidl, had captured a dominant and growing share of the German grocery market and were expanding internationally. While none of the three hard discounters had a major presence in the UK, by the mid-1990s some grocery retailers, including Tesco, viewed them as a serious future threat. Somewhat later, Tesco faced a new challenge when Wal-Mart, the world's largest retailer, entered the UK market in 1999 by acquiring Asda. Wal-Mart was widely viewed as one of the most effective low cost competitors – in any industry.

Tesco combated the threat of the hard discounters by creating customer value

In 1992, Tesco launched a series of initiatives designed to deal with the two challenges: capturing market leadership over Sainsbury's and dealing with the potential threat of the hard discounters. The first initiative was the launch of the "Value" line of no-frills, low-priced products designed for cost-conscious shoppers who might be attracted by a hard discounter. A second initiative was the introduction of the "one in front" policy in 1994, designed to reduce lines at checkouts and thereby improve customer service. Tesco also launched a new store format that same year. The new stores were smaller than traditional supermarkets (less than 280 m^2) but were conveniently located in city centers, small shopping areas and even petrol forecourts. They carried a narrower range of SKUs than a typical Tesco store but offered a broader selection than the hard discounters offered. The fourth, and arguably most important, initiative was the introduction of a "loyalty" card called Clubcard. It was the result of several years of lobbying by the then marketing director (later CEO and later still Sir) Terry Leahy for a loyalty card. The four initiatives helped to blunt the assault from Aldi and the other hard discounters.

Tesco's core mission was "to create value for customers to earn their lifetime loyalty". One of the values embodying this mission was "no one tries harder for customers". As a self-service format store, Tesco did not have a history of connecting with its customers as individuals. It needed a compelling reason, other than price, for customers to want to shop at its outlets rather than those of its competitors, particularly Sainsbury's. Terry Leahy was convinced that a loyalty scheme was the key to gaining this customer preference. Clubcard was intended, on one hand, to "reward" customers for their loyalty; on the other hand, in light of Tesco's market share ambitions, it was intended to encourage consumers to purchase more (value and frequency) at Tesco. The idea behind the card was to positively influence the shopper's behavior and gain an emotional commitment to the scheme and, by default, to Tesco.

Clubcard trials began in 1993 in three stores. They were gradually expanded and finally rolled out nationally in 1995. Customers who signed up for Clubcard were asked for their names and addresses and some basic information about the size and ages of their families. Tesco could already track all of its sales data with an electronic point-of-sales system. By swiping the customer's Clubcard on every store visit, the sales data could be tied to a particular customer and with the consumer's name and address, Tesco was able to send them quarterly Clubcard mailings. The mailings included the Clubcard cash back vouchers worth 1% of their total purchases at the chain, as well as targeted and relevant coupons, based on shopping habits. By 1999, the mass customization of the mailings had risen to 145 000 different versions. Tesco viewed this as a "thank you" to its customers for their loyalty. At the end of the trial phase, it became apparent that the concept had struck a responsive chord with consumers – of every £10 spent in the trial stores, £6 was spent by Clubcard holders; this soon rose to 80% of all purchases.[149]

The coupons were either for products the customer already bought, or for products that, according to the market research, similar customers bought regularly and, thus, should be of interest to the customer. The sales peaks created by the mailings were equivalent to that created by an event such as Christmas. But, by using Clubcard data, Tesco could anticipate the demand, make sure in-store supplies were adequate and prepare its staff to deal with the extra business.

Within a few years of the Clubcard launch, Tesco had become an extremely sophisticated user of the data it gathered, which allowed the retailer to develop a very deep understanding of its customers. As one of the executives at Dunnhumby, the marketing firm that ran Clubcard for Tesco, stated: "It's just like standing behind somebody in the checkout line and making assumptions about their lifestyle based on what is in their trolley."[150] Dunnhumby had developed some 40 flags such as convenience, cooking from scratch, organic, environmentally aware, high price, low priced family sizes, etc. and attached one or more of these labels to each product. Given the flags on the items in a shopper's shopping cart, the company could then build a picture of each consumer and use this data to cluster them into segments. Customers buying a lot of Tesco value products might be labeled as "price sensitive", whereas customers buying a lot of environmentally friendly products might be labeled as "green".

Over time, Tesco took customer relationship management one step further. Using the data it gathered, it was able to target groups of customers, such as first time mothers (Baby Club), children (Toddlers and Kids Clubs), etc. These focused efforts resulted in a further growth in business, especially in the all important non-food area – a priority for Sir Terry Leahy, as the company's ability to grow in the traditionally grocery business became more limited due to its increasingly high market share.

Nestlé credited the Clubcard and related initiatives with creating loyal shoppers, which in Nestlé's view has been the key to Tesco's success. According to Nestlé the number of loyal Tesco customers doubled between 1996 and 2005, and the average weekly spending of these customers doubled during the same period.[151]

With this deep customer understanding, the company was much more targeted and effective in its overall marketing strategies. Competitor Asda had a strong reputation for low prices and that was expected to accelerate with its acquisition by Wal-Mart in 1999. Tesco was determined to capture price sensitive shoppers from Asda. One option was to cut the prices across the board for those items bought by the price sensitive customer segment. However, this would be very costly since many of the items bought by this segment, such as bananas, were also bought by a broad cross-section of customers. But by using the data it had gathered on its customers, Tesco was able to identify some products that were bought almost exclusively by price sensitive customers. By investing in significant price cuts in these products, Tesco could appeal strongly to price sensitive customers in a highly targeted and cost-effective way.

Tesco also managed its costs very effectively

While Tesco clearly paid a lot of attention to its marketing, it also recognized that to compete effectively with the potential threat from low cost players, like the hard discounters and Wal-Mart's Asda, it had to have a really effective, efficient supply chain and to manage all its other costs very carefully.

Tesco sourced its products from a wide range of suppliers, both branded and unbranded. Many of its unbranded and private label manufacturers were small- and medium-sized companies. Tesco's buyers focused on delivered cost, product quality and delivery reliability. Since Tesco did not want to carry more inventory than it needed, the supplier's flexibility to respond to Tesco's needs was an important factor in supplier selection.

Tesco was reputed to spend £200 to £300 million a year upgrading its logistics network, and industry experts credited Tesco with having one of the best distribution networks in the world.[152] Tesco used point-of-sale data to trigger stock replenishment in stores. The replenishment system polled the stores regularly for the sales of individual products. It also took into account the shelf capacities, sales forecasts and business of the store on different days of the week before sending a reorder right through the supply chain. In the case of fast-moving products, the stores might be replenished twice a day. The system tracked the trucks, equipped with satellite navigation systems, to try to schedule the deliveries just as the stock ran out so that there was room on the shelves for the new consignment. The retailer worked with its suppliers to develop innovative solutions to minimize handling of goods. For goods that needed frequent replenishment, it used mobile merchandising units with wheels; these were filled by companies like Coca-Cola, or a milk supplier at the factory, and could be wheeled into position in the stores, dramatically reducing handling costs. Its distribution centers used "cross-docking" to get the goods from the in-bound trucks bringing goods from suppliers to the waiting store-bound trucks with a minimum of handling and delay.

The net impact of improvements in the supply chain in fiscal 2005 was savings of £270 million. One analyst estimated that Tesco only spent about 10% on distribution versus Sainsbury's 13%.[153]

Tesco's emphasis on tight cost control permeated the whole organization starting at the top. Terry Leahy, who became the CEO of Tesco in 1997, still drove himself to work and around the UK for his unannounced Friday store visits.[154] Store staff members were admonished not to leave taps dripping because a dripping tap could cost the company £350 per year – not a huge amount in a Tesco Extra store (Tesco's hypermarket format) given that it could have annual revenues of £70 million,[155] but still a saving.

Land for stores was expensive and scarce in the UK and the planning laws were strict. Tesco had developed a capability to build profitable stores on unusually shaped pieces of land. It had also managed to drive down the building cost per sq. meter by about 30% over a five-year period. It had also cut the cost of fitting out the stores by having simpler, low cost store specifications and pre-fabricating standardized parts in a factory off-site; this allowed for quick installation, as well as faster store openings and revenue generation.

Tesco is the clear leader in the UK and is expanding aggressively into new markets

Tesco's long-term growth strategy was based on four pillars: growth in the core business in the UK, significant growth in non-food, following customers into new retailing services (as customers' needs change, so must Tesco's offer of products and services) and international expansion.[156]

In time, Tesco had added a wide variety of non-food items to its range, and many of these were sold under Tesco brands. In 1997, Tesco Personal Finance was launched through a joint venture with the Royal Bank of Scotland. By 2007, Tesco was the UK's third largest issuer of credit cards and the country's fastest growing financial service provider. In 1999, Tesco launched Tesco.com, an Internet business that allowed customers to order products over the Internet and have them delivered to their homes during the evening. Rather than do the fulfillment in special warehouses, the orders were fulfilled in regular Tesco stores at non-peak hours. By 2005, the shopping service was available to 96% of UK households and sales were in excess of £700 million per year. It was believed to be the only large, profitable .com grocery retailer in the world; by 2008, a broad range of groceries, non-food products and Tesco services were available on Tesco.com.

While the UK still accounted for almost 80% of profits in 2007, Tesco was also expanding rapidly internationally. It had major efforts underway in Asia, Eastern Europe and Turkey and, starting in 2007, what promised to be a major push into the US.

By 2008, Tesco was by far the largest grocery retailer in the UK, controlling about 30% of the grocery market (about twice as high as Asda and Sainsbury's) and over 12% of the total retail market. Tesco had responded to the threat of hard discounters much more successfully than had the traditional retailers in most other European countries. Part of this success was due to the fact that it responded proactively, long before the hard discounters had posed a real challenge. It recognized that they were meeting real customer needs. Some UK customers were looking for low-priced, good enough products in some product categories. Other UK customers, often some of the same people, wanted the convenience of fast shopping in relatively small, local stores rather than in large supermarkets or hypermarkets. Tesco's moves, with its Value line and its Tesco Express stores, helped it cater to the needs of these segments. But the retailer also used its deep understanding of its customers from its Clubcard and point-of-sales data to target cost-conscious consumers; they were offered very appealing value propositions without impacting significantly profitable business from other segments. So by using data intelligently, Tesco was able to utilize what could have been crude tools to achieve its objectives of controlling the hard discounters.

Importantly, Tesco did not rest on its laurels. Terry Leahy said in 2007 that Aldi was the rival supermarket chain he admired most in the world. And between 2007 and 2008 Aldi grew by almost 40% in the UK.[157] A British newspaper reported that Tesco had built a mock hard discount store in a warehouse in the UK – it wanted to understand better how the Aldi model worked.[158] As Andy Grove, at the time the CEO of Intel, once said: "Only the paranoid survive."[159]

CHALLENGE QUESTIONS

Can you learn any lessons from Electrolux's more than a decade-long struggle to maintain performance leadership?

Are you facing rising innovation costs and shortening windows to capitalize on innovations? Can you make more use of open business models to change the balance?

Are there things you can do to slow down the leakage of your innovations to your competitors?

Orica is an excellent example of a company which transformed a commoditized product business into a service business where there was an opportunity to build deep relational value and substantial barriers to competition. Are there any opportunities in your company to make similar transformations?

Tesco is an example of a company that used information technology to build "relationships" with millions of customers and offer them customized solutions that helped build loyalty. To date, it has managed to keep its low cost competitors in check. Do you have any opportunities to do similar things in your business, even if you are not in a mass business-to-customer situation like Tesco?

CHAPTER 7

The leadership challenge

Initiating an effective response to existing, or prospective, low cost competition often represents a real leadership challenge. The response to low cost competition usually involves some very tough choices – in many cases there will be a certain sacrifice in short-term profitability for a potential long-term improvement in competitive position. Almost always, the tough choices will involve the CEO of the company or, at the very least, the head of the business unit involved.

In the case of Danfoss (as mentioned in Chapter 4), the leading Danish supplier of industrial controls, CEO Joergen Clausen was heavily involved in the decision to move aggressively into the mid-performance tier of several of the markets in which it competed in China.[160] The decision was partly the result of a personal trip he and his wife made through a remote part of Western China. He was surprised to find that even in this remote region expensive and sophisticated electrical products were available for sale. As cited in Chapter 4, Danfoss was growing by about 35% per year in China and making a profit, but Clausen began to wonder whether the company was even beginning to tap the full potential of the Chinese market. After some more in-depth investigation, the company found that it was only scratching the surface in most of the product markets it served. What particularly astonished executives was the size of the good enough markets for many of its products. Danfoss calculated that it could grow its profits dramatically in some product markets – if it could simply offer the market the right products. If Danfoss did not respond to the opportunity – leaving the lower performance segments of the markets to its Chinese competitors – it would not be able to compete with the local players in the long run, either in China or ultimately elsewhere, due to the economies of scale the Chinese competitors would enjoy. Ultimately, this analysis led to the concept of China being Danfoss' "second home market" after Europe. But to achieve this goal required major changes in the way the company operated; for Clausen and his leadership team, it represented a major leadership challenge.

The situation faced by Danfoss is quite common today. For a particular company the threat may not come from China or elsewhere in Asia – instead, it may come from a domestic competitor. A typical company facing this challenge is one that has often been successful in the past by developing market leading products or services. For the reasons discussed in Chapters 2 and 6, a company may have found it increasingly expensive to stay ahead of the competition – its cutting edge products may be matched more quickly by competitors and, even worse, fewer customers may be willing to pay a premium for its latest products and services. For a number of customers, the existing products on the market are good enough for their needs. Much to some firms' consternation, growth in the market may increasingly be in segments seeking good enough products and services at low prices, or in segments that are looking for suppliers to provide them with a complete and integrated "solution" – a solution for which they are willing to pay a higher price.

As a result, many companies and their top management teams face a stark choice: fight it out in the familiar performance value-oriented market segments, even though their share of the overall market is declining, or transition to a new strategy. This strategy might involve creating products and services for customers who want good enough performance at very low prices and/or start to build more intimate relationships with customers who are really looking for "solutions" that meet their particular needs. Moves in either or both of these directions are often very difficult transitions to manage. Many companies do not successfully navigate the path successfully.

We'll begin this chapter with a cautionary story about Compaq Computer Corporation – a company that was very successful in its early years, but failed to make a successful transition away from performance value leadership as its market environment shifted and as it faced increasing competition from low cost competitors.

Then, we will continue by discussing how meeting the challenge of low cost competition often requires a major change management initiative. Unfortunately, getting the management and the company's employees to recognize the need for change in a timely manner is often a major barrier facing companies. Using the appropriate financial analysis can be an important tool in helping the organization recognize the need for change. We will then focus on a couple of the major leadership challenges that management faces in competing successfully in the price value segment of the market, if that is a direction in which the top management team feels the company needs to move. Here, companies typically face challenges concerning engineering or product design, marketing, sales and distribution, as well as the need to create a totally cost- and cost innovation-focused culture. Finally, we will turn to the particular challenges in creating and managing a relational value business. The difficulties here often revolve around designing an appropriate organizational structure and support systems, developing and using deep customer and market knowledge and inculcating a customer-focused culture throughout the organization.

COMPAQ FAILED TO MAKE A SUCCESSFUL TRANSITION

Compaq was founded in 1982 by three engineers who had a vision of building a portable computer that would be fully compatible with the IBM PC, which had been launched the year before. They launched the product successfully and Compaq became the fastest growing company in history for several years.

The company soon became recognized as the performance value leader in the PC industry, often being the first major computer company to bring innovative features and products to market. This image of performance leadership was epitomized in 1986 when Compaq was the first manufacturer to bring a PC to market with Intel's advanced 386 microprocessor – it was the only manufacturer to have such a machine for a few months, which was the result of an effective alliance with both Intel and Microsoft. Many customers viewed the product quality offered by Compaq as being particularly strong. In its early years, the company relied heavily on specialty retailers, such as Computerland and Sears Business Centers, to sell to the business customers who were its initial target.

By 1990, the traditional corporate market began to slow as a result of a recession, while almost simultaneously growth shifted to two other market segments. Home-users and small businesses were beginning to buy computers in large volumes but many of these customers were focused less on performance value and more on price value. At about the same time, in some organizations, particularly medium and large firms, there was increasing emphasis on building local area networks that would link computers, printers, servers and other information technology resources together. Unfortunately, Compaq's retail partners were poorly positioned to serve either segment. They were too expensive relative to the mass-market channels (that some of the more price conscious home-users and small businesses preferred) and most lacked the expertise to build the local area networks that larger organizations were seeking. In addition, Compaq's personal computers were sometimes more than 25% more expensive than the products of some of its competitors. By this time a number of new lower cost competitors, including Dell, had entered the market and some were becoming significant players. Many customers still viewed Compaq's PCs as being very high quality, and they were. Compaq designed and built some of its own components and subsystems. For example, it designed and built the power supplies for its own computers. These power supplies were undoubtedly superior to the industry standard ones most of its competitors used, but few customers either knew or cared – the industry standard components delivered good enough performance and most customers weren't thinking about the power supply when they chose a PC.

In part as a result of market developments and the company's strategic choices, Compaq suffered its first quarterly loss in 1991. The board of directors appointed a new CEO, Eckhard Pfeiffer, who led a major strategy change that resulted in Compaq targeting almost all the major segments of the personal computer market. It added thousands of new retail outlets around the world, selling its PCs to home users and small businesses through computer superstores and mass merchandisers, as well as its traditional outlets. At the same time, it began selling through value-added resellers and systems integrators in order to be able to offer solutions that were more sophisticated to its small business and corporate clients. Compaq also launched a massive cost cutting campaign that resulted in research and development expenses being reduced significantly as a percentage of sales (from 6% of revenues in 1991 to 2% in 1994).[161] Despite the cost-cutting moves, Compaq found itself under increasing pressure from direct sellers like Dell Computer and aggressive competitors like Packard Bell in traditional channels. In addition, Intel was aggressively commoditizing the PC hardware business by providing sophisticated engineering and marketing support for computer manufacturers. It manufactured PC motherboards and developed reference designs for motherboards so that low cost Asian manufacturers could also make them. It developed the Intel Inside campaign, which caused many customers to focus on the brand of the microprocessor, rather than the brand of the PC manufacturer. These moves made it much easier for new entrants and other PC manufacturers to compete with market leaders like IBM, HP and Compaq. Margins on the hardware came under increasing pressure as the battle for customers intensified. Low cost manufacturers benefited a lot from these moves by Intel.

In order to build stronger capabilities in selling and serving enterprise customers – some of whom wanted a closer and more intimate relationship with their IT suppliers – Compaq acquired Tandem Computers in 1995 and Digital Equipment Corporation in 1998. But the acquisition of Digital did not go particularly well, partly as a result of strong cultural differences between the two companies – one having its roots in Texas and the other having its roots in New England. Additionally, Compaq continued to face very tough competition from IBM and HP in the enterprise space and did not seem to gain much traction in this market despite the acquisitions.

Initially, Pfeiffer's strategy of rapid expansion of Compaq's segment coverage combined with the dramatic cost cutting led to rapid growth in net income. By the late 1990s, however, Compaq's financial performance was poor, and in 1999, Pfeiffer was forced to resign. The transition from a company with performance leadership products in the 1980s to competing in both the price value and relationship value segments of the market in the 1990s ended largely in failure. Compaq never really managed to get business units to successfully focus on either of these two broad segments of the market or to successfully implement the necessary strategies and action plans. A lot of its energy was wasted on a fruitless and losing battle with its largest supplier, Intel. In 2002, Compaq merged with HP.

MEETING THE CHALLENGE OF LOW COST COMPETITION OFTEN REQUIRES A CORPORATE TRANSFORMATION

As the Compaq example suggests, a company often has to face a real crisis before it will face up to challenges that threaten its business' position and survival. In Compaq's case, the quarterly loss in 1991 seemed to finally spur the board of directors to take some decisive action and replace the CEO. John Kotter, perhaps the leading expert on transformational change management, has pointed out that creating a sense of urgency is the crucial first step in any management change initiative (see Figure 7.1).[162] It is particularly difficult to do if a company's management, or individual managers, are trying to get the organization to respond proactively to an emerging challenge. And as we have discussed earlier, this is the optimal time to make the tough decisions about how best to respond to emerging, or potential, low cost competition. This is also usually a time when the

1.   How can we create sense of urgency?
2.   Who will help us to make the change happen (guiding coalition)?
3.   What's the appealing vision we are selling?
4.   What is the communication program for the vision and strategies and how can we make it as effective as possible?
5.   What are the likely obstacles and how will we remove them?
6.   Where are the quick wins?
7.   Where will we go next?
8.   How will we make the change part of the culture?

FIGURE 7.1   Implementing major change: the eight questions
Source: Based on John Kotter, "Leading Change: Why Transformation Efforts Fail", *Harvard Business Review*, January 2007.

company has the capacity to be able to invest significant human and financial resources in developing and implementing an effective response.

The performance curve in Figure 7.2 shows the changing strategic performance of a business over time that is perhaps failing to adjust its strategy to changes that are happening in its external environment. Perhaps the company is an industry pioneer with performance leadership products facing increasing competition from low cost competitors with good enough products that meet the needs of a growing proportion of customers. Initially the business does well and in the early period increasingly well. But as the market starts to change, performance gradually starts to flatten out. Then, if nothing is done, performance plateaus and begins to decline, gradually at first and then more rapidly, until it finally plunges.

In the anticipatory stage, the current performance is still good but is not improving as rapidly as before. While some people in the organization may see the need for some change, most will not. Since performance curves are seldom as smooth as the one shown in the diagram, some people will claim that any deterioration in performance is temporary. They will make such arguments as "once our new product line is out things will get better", or "we only need to work a bit faster and harder and we can turn things around". Most people, at least at the early stages, will not see the need for a fundamental change in strategy.

Tetra Pak was the world leader in aseptic and non-aseptic carton packaging for long shelf life products, such as UHT (Ultra Heat Treated) milk and pasteurized products, such as fresh milk and fruit juices.[163] Tetra Pak had pioneered the

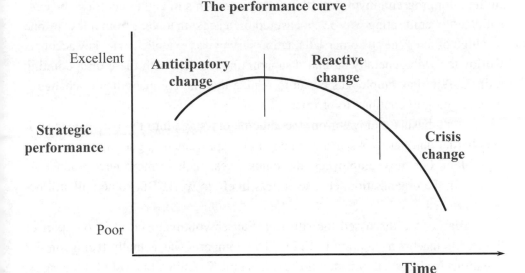

FIGURE 7.2   The strategic performance curve
Source: Mary M. Crossan, Joseph N. Fry and Peter J. Killing, *Strategic Analysis and Action*, Prentice-Hall Canada, 2005.

development of proprietary equipment, materials and supplies for these applications and was the acknowledged performance value leader. Its growth, however, had slowed in the late 1990s as a result of the slowing growth of, or even the decline in, milk consumption in many of its key markets. There was also an increasing impact of large aggressive multinational price competitors like Combibloc and smaller low cost competitors starting to appear in several Asian markets. Despite the slowdown in growth, many Tetra Pak employees were quite complacent. They were sure that they were doing a great job for their customers and were providing both very good products and a high level of relational value. Top management was convinced that the way forward for the company was to develop much deeper, and more intimate relationships with its customers to counter the growing threat of Combibloc and other competitors that developed products that were good enough for many customers and sold them at attractive prices.

In order to increase Tetra Pak's intimacy with its customers, the company launched a customer satisfaction initiative in early 2000. One of the key elements of this initiative was a customer satisfaction survey conducted among key clients.

In the pilot program, involving 18 important accounts in eight countries, the consolidated overall rating was 3.2, measured on a scale that went from a low of one to a high of five. The customer satisfaction survey was extended to all key accounts worldwide with generally similar disappointing results. With these disappointing ratings, Tetra Pak employees began to realize that the company had to change if it were going to continue to prosper.

As a business moves from the anticipatory stage into the reactive stage, it gets harder and harder for management and employees to argue that there is not a problem. For most employees, the quick fixes, such as more new products, a change in the organization, etc., seem less likely to work. But some will still not be convinced.

Earlier we discussed the situation Saurer Volkmann faced in one part of the textile machinery market in China. The company was actually facing similar situations in almost all of its textile business units in China. In most of these cases, low cost competitors were beginning to move from the lower performance tiers of the market into the higher performance tiers that had previously been dominated by Saurer and other European and Japanese equipment suppliers. The initial efforts of Saurer's business units focused on trying to significantly reduce their costs by outsourcing more of the parts production from Western Europe to lower cost sources in Eastern Europe and China. At first, some of the Saurer employees who were involved in facilitating this transition were treated as "traitors" by fellow employees who saw the moves as destroying jobs in countries like Germany and Switzerland.[164] One of the ways that Henry Fischer, Saurer's CEO, and his management team got people to accept the need for this change, both intellectually and emotionally, was to ensure that many key employees, including the leaders of the unions, had a chance to visit China and meet with Chinese customers and Chinese competitors. By bringing these people face-to-face with the competitive reality, more of the Saurer Textiles employees began to realize that the move to Eastern Europe and China was absolutely essential for the company's survival and to preserve the remaining jobs that would be left in Europe.

By the time a company has moved from the anticipatory stage, through the reactive stage, to the crisis stage, almost everyone in the organization will see the need for change; they will recognize that decisive action is needed but the type of action needed may still be a matter of intense debate. The focus here can become very short term, but clearly, the organization has to also consider the long term. While dramatic cost cutting may help with the short-term financial situation, if carried to an extreme, such severe reductions in R&D may jeopardize the survival of the company in the longer term.

As Kotter has pointed out, a third important step in a transformational change process involves creating a compelling vision that will be appealing to all the major stakeholders, particularly customers, employees and the shareholders or other owners. Having a compelling and believable vision is absolutely essential because almost any transformational change required to respond to the threat of low cost competition will involve significant dislocation in the organization and may result in a short-term deterioration in financial results and perhaps loss of jobs. Too often, particularly when a company decides to respond to the threat from low cost competition when it is already in crisis, all the stakeholders see is aggressive cost cutting and employee layoffs. They don't see a compelling vision of where the company is moving to, or how all the actions will lead to it being better positioned in its markets in the future.

Numbers can support the need for change

One of the most important tools for supporting both the creation of a sense of urgency and a compelling vision of the future is the effective use of financial analysis to help develop believable future scenarios. One scenario assumes that the company maintains its current course and fails to respond to low cost competition; the second scenario assumes that the company does respond in an appropriate way to the low cost challenge. This response may be to challenge the low cost competitors in their market segment and/or strengthen the company's position among those customers who are seeking either performance value or relational value. We discussed this at some length in Chapter 4, and Figure 4.4 is a useful summary of the correct and incorrect way to look at the two scenarios. The leadership challenge is to get the whole organization focused on the future scenarios and prevent them from falling back to an unproductive and unrealistic comparison between the present and the future objectives. There can be genuine disagreement about what the best direction might be for the business, and these debates are healthy. The best future scenario in the face of low cost competition may not be viewed as being very attractive relative to where the company has been in the past but when vigorously compared with the other future alternatives, it might be seen as quite attractive.

Too often, however, we see management teams debating the merits of the present versus the future in terms of developing a new product or service. The present was wonderful while it lasted but it is gone forever; the real issue is which of the two "future" scenarios leaves the business unit better positioned for the future.

BUILDING AND MANAGING A SUCCESSFUL PRICE VALUE BUSINESS

Two of the biggest challenges companies face in directly confronting low cost competitors are the engineering challenge and the sales/distribution challenge. Both Danfoss and Saurer faced these challenges once they had made the decision to move into the lower tiers of the Chinese markets with their products. Making a successful entry and sustaining the growth of the lower-end business requires constant cost innovation.

Product and service design challenge

In Danfoss' case, the company was already manufacturing high-end and middle-performance products in China. These products had been designed and developed in Europe by European engineers. The company recognized that if it was to be competitive in China, it had to develop some completely new products that could be manufactured at low cost and sold at very competitive prices. In practice, this meant developing products that utilized a high percentage of local components and that could be manufactured with less capital-intensive manufacturing processes. Danfoss felt that this practice could not be executed by taking European products and then trying to reduce their costs. Most companies that have tried the approach of trying to cost-reduce an existing product or service have found that it simply doesn't work. It might be a quick, short-run fix while a totally new product or service is being designed from the ground up, but it does not work in the long run. Another approach that Danfoss dismissed was giving the design challenge to its European engineers. As the CEO, Joergen Clausen, said, "They [Danfoss' European engineers] don't have the right mentality and would set excessively high standards for even the smallest details, ending up with an over-engineered and too expensive product."[165] As mentioned in Chapter 5, one Danfoss strategy for closing the gap for some of its product lines was to acquire local Chinese companies and leverage their existing products, R&D and distribution. Danfoss would then work with the engineers at the acquired company to improve the product quality, while trying to preserve its low cost structure.

Saurer faced the same type of engineering challenge in its textile machinery business units. Its Volkmann business unit, which manufactured twisting machines for cotton and wool yarn, was the dominant player globally in the high performance segment of the market.[166] Saurer Volkmann had been manufacturing equipment in China for the local and export markets for about five years but the overall machine design and engineering and the manufacturing of some of the key components were still done in Germany. When Saurer decided to move into the mid-performance segment of the market, dominated in China by local players, it lacked the engineering capability to design the machine in China. It assigned the design of the new machine to a group of relatively junior engineers in Germany. These engineers worked closely with the sales force and other Saurer personnel in China to try to design a machine that would meet the needs of Chinese customers and could be competitively priced. The rationale for assigning the project to relatively junior engineers was that they would be less committed to the traditional design philosophy of building performance-leading equipment – machines that would simply be over-engineered and too expensive for the target segment in China. As the CEO of the company Henry Fischer noted, the tremendous pride of many of Saurer's German engineers could sometimes get in the way of developing commercially successful low cost products.[167] Over time, as Saurer (now owned by Oerlikon) builds up its R&D capabilities in China, the design of the lower cost lines of products will probably be increasingly done by Saurer's Chinese engineers in their home country.

Other Saurer business units used different approaches in trying to develop products that would be competitive in the mid-performance and low-performance segments of the market. In the ring-spinning business, Saurer set up a joint venture with a Chinese company, Jinsheng, to accelerate its penetration of these market segments. The joint venture, in which Saurer held a 70% share, developed both components and machines.[168]

Marketing, sales and distribution challenge

Developing the product or service to meet the needs of the customer seeking price value is often the easiest part of the battle. The more difficult challenge is getting the products or services in front of the target customer and making sure that they are effectively positioned and sold.

In the case of companies like Ryanair and ING DIRECT, the emergence and growth of the Internet has greatly simplified the task. The first movers have a particular advantage in this regard, particularly as they gain scale and scope. When many people in Europe think of taking a weekend break and flying somewhere, the first airlines that come to mind are the two leaders – Ryanair and easyJet. For the smaller low cost airlines, the challenge can be much bigger. If they are the dominant low cost carrier in a particular country or region, they may also have good top-of-mind awareness in the local community. But if they don't, then it is really tough. Some potential customers will use the websites of companies that aggregate price and departure data from the websites of all the low cost carriers, although not everyone is aware of, or uses, these sites.

As mentioned briefly in Chapter 1, Nestlé has made a major push in recent years to develop Popularly Positioned Products (PPP) for consumers in the developing world.[169] These are affordable, good quality products that have good nutritional value. They are designed to meet the needs of customers with incomes at purchasing power parity of between $3000 and $13000. There were about 3.4 billion consumers in this segment in 2005, and the number is expected to grow to about 4.5 billion by 2015. The first Nestlé PPP products were introduced in the 1970s, and in 1992, Nestlé put into place its first policy on PPPs. This program, however, really didn't gather significant momentum until after 2000. In many of the countries where these consumers were concentrated, more than 50% of grocery sales were made in traditional trade outlets such as street stalls or tiny shops and by salespeople selling from bicycles or mobile carts. For example, in the Philippines an important distribution outlet for PPP products was sari sari stores. These stores, often part of a person's home, gave people convenient, neighborhood access to basic products in small quantities. For example, a person could buy one cigarette or a single serving of shampoo or breakfast cereal. In order to reach its target consumers for its PPPs, Nestlé had to reach thousands of these types of small buying points through micro-distributors who might service the retailers with tricycles, scooters or other very basic forms of transportation.

Saurer Volkmann faced a somewhat similar challenge in selling and distributing its mid-performance textile machinery to its customers in China, India and other Asian countries. In China, its traditional sales force, which was made up of college-educated, technically trained salespeople who spoke English, earned a good base salary plus commissions based on sales and had contact with perhaps

20–25% of the total customers in the twisting machines market. These customers were clustered in major textile manufacturing areas. However, the customers that were the target market for the mid-performance machines were more widely dispersed across China and were more likely to be found in some of the smaller and more remote towns and villages. The selling job for the mid-performance equipment was less technical and more personal; it required salespeople who had good relationships and local knowledge. To reach this segment of the market, Saurer Volkmann began recruiting "local" salespeople who were not required to speak English and who were based in the local area. These salespeople were paid a much lower base salary and most of their compensation was expected to be from commissions on sales. If they needed technical support to make a sale, or if they saw the opportunity to sell a high performance machine, they could call on their more highly trained colleagues for assistance. The new strategy of selling both mid- and high-performance machines in China and other Asian countries helped to significantly increase Saurer's market share for several of its business units in these countries.

The cost control challenge

While cost control is clearly an important issue in both product and service design and in sales, marketing and distribution, it is such a crucial aspect in the price value businesses that it deserves some further discussion. As we saw in Chapter 3, companies like Ryanair and ING DIRECT are often quite innovative in terms of how they control costs. In almost every cost area, Ryanair focuses relentlessly, and continually, on driving costs out of its business. As we discussed, the carrier has continually redefined what is included in its basic offer, to see if it can be simplified by eliminating "extras" such as a free checked baggage allowance. This ensures that one customer is not cross-subsidizing another. When customers are asked to pay for an additional product or service, such as a soft drink or checking in at the airport (versus using the Internet), they use less of it than they would use if it were "free". If they still want the extra, they will pay for it and Ryanair will make a profit. If they decide they don't need it, then Ryanair's costs are reduced and it gets another opportunity to pass some of this on to its customers through lower "headline" fares.

As we have seen in numerous examples, many businesses focusing on price value outsource many of their non-core activities to best-in-class suppliers who have the scale and expertise to achieve acceptable results at very low cost levels.

In some cases, their compensation is based on both volume and performance in terms of quality, meeting delivery schedules, etc.

To be a truly successful price value player, an organization has to have a culture where all employees are focused on cost control and cost reduction. The various systems and processes in the organization, such as recruiting, training, compensation and evaluation and control systems, should all emphasize cost control. This doesn't necessarily mean that a price value player should have low compensation levels. In fact, some of the very successful low cost players are known for their relatively high average compensation systems. The successful hard discounters are believed to pay their employees well, as does Ryanair. In return, they expect employees to be very productive and very flexible in terms of "getting the job done".

CREATING AND MANAGING A RELATIONAL VALUE BUSINESS

As in Tetra Pak's case, many companies face the difficult leadership challenge of moving from a company or a business unit that focuses on creating high performance products to one that is more focused on building tight and intimate relationships with customers. Building relational value is often a long and difficult journey requiring strong and committed leadership. At Tetra Pak the journey required major coordinated changes in a number of areas related to developing a deep understanding of its customers and their industry dynamics; it needed to align the organization, and its various policies and procedures, to place the necessary focus on its customers and establish a customer-oriented culture throughout the organization.[170]

Over the years, several frameworks have been proposed for thinking about organizational effectiveness. One of the frameworks widely used for a number of years, and by many organizations, is the McKinsey 7-S model.[171] One of the key arguments made in the McKinsey model and several other frameworks is the importance of getting an alignment in the organization that recognizes, supports and encourages the successful implementation of the chosen strategy.[172] Clearly, in an organization where a key element of the strategy is building strong relational value for a select group of customers, all the other elements should support this.

One of the key initiatives Tetra Pak used to improve strategic alignment with customers was to encourage all of the Tetra Pak market companies (typically countries) to form key account teams for Tetra Pak's largest accounts and other smaller, but nevertheless strategic, accounts. It was hoped that these teams would develop an in-depth knowledge of the opportunities and challenges that these accounts faced so that they could work jointly to develop winning strategies that would benefit both the account and Tetra Pak. To encourage and reinforce these and other related efforts, Tetra Pak also established a balanced scorecard where one of the key metrics was customer satisfaction and innovation. An outstanding performance on the scorecard could lead to an annual bonus equal to 75% of a manager's base salary.

A second element of strengthening relational value was focused on developing better information within the Tetra Pak organization that could be used to create relational value for its customers. The annual customer satisfaction survey, which involved personal interviews with key customer executives, was a key element in helping the account teams and more senior management develop a deeper understanding of how each surveyed customer viewed Tetra Pak; this was relative to the customer's best supplier on a variety of different dimensions. Since this information was collected on an annual basis, trends in the data could clearly be seen. One of the benefits of the key account management program was the depth and quality of the data on Tetra Pak's customers and markets. Some of the non-confidential data could be shared among account teams around the world. Tetra Pak also provided training seminars to build the skills and competence of the account teams and management in such areas as value chain analysis, customer-focused marketing, innovation and key account management. All of these elements contributed to the account teams being able to develop deeper, and more meaningful, relationships with their accounts.

A final element was establishing a culture of customer orientation throughout Tetra Pak. Several of the initiatives described above contributed to this: customer satisfaction measurement, training seminars, the balanced scorecard and, of course, the key account program. One of the country organizations even assigned every employee, including the receptionist, to one of its account teams to try to drive the point home that building relational value is everybody's responsibility, not just those in sales and marketing. Tetra Pak also instituted an employee satisfaction program because it believed that satisfied employees were a necessary condition for creating satisfied customers.

Kotter argued that an important step in transforming an organization was planning and creating short-term wins (see Figure 7.1). In the case of Tetra Pak, one thing that became very obvious in the pilot customer satisfaction surveys was that many of Tetra Pak's filling machines were not reliable enough for many customers. Their excessive downtime was seriously damaging the customers' operational efficiency. In order to make a highly visible commitment to improving customer satisfaction, Tetra Pak decided to retrofit thousands of machines around the world, at its expense, to improve machine uptime. The initiative cost €50 million. This was not only highly visible to its customers all over the world but also to its employees. The employees realized that if the company was willing to make this investment in improving its customers' satisfaction, then building relational value was really a serious initiative and not just "the flavor of the month".

Three years after the initiative began, the initial results of Tetra Pak's program looked positive. Customer satisfaction had risen significantly, revenue growth had accelerated, short-term profits were up and the company felt that the percentage of loyal customers had jumped significantly.

Now let's refocus a little and take a closer look at each of the three elements that Tetra Pak worked on: designing an organization that will encourage building relational value, developing deep customer and market knowledge and inculcating a customer-focused culture throughout the organization.[173] All of these elements, of course, must be designed with a clear view of the target segment, the core value proposition and with the appropriate allocation of resources to support the strategy.

Designing an organization that will encourage building relational value

As we saw in the case of Tetra Pak, one of the basic elements of creating strong relational value is having an organizational structure that makes it very clear who has overall responsibility for the customer relationship. At Tetra Pak, all of the major and strategic accounts had a key account manager and an account team. Clearly not all accounts should be treated as key accounts and usually, as with Tetra Pak, the selection of key accounts is not based solely on account sales. Other factors that are frequently taken into account are account profitability, the potential for revenue and profit growth, the willingness to partner and the importance of the company's product and service to the client's business. If the company's product has the potential to really add value to the customer's business or save them cost, then a key account relationship is likely to be valued by the client. If a supplier can help the customer really differentiate their offering, and they are willing to reward the supplier for the value created, then a key account relationship may be warranted. Clearly, some customers are only interested in "using" the supplier and not paying them for the ideas and the value they bring to the relationship. These kinds of customers are not good candidates for a key account relationship that has to be based on a high level of mutual trust.

Generally, an organization will have both a stronger capability to respond effectively to customer needs and will be more responsive to customer needs if it is organized around customer groups and processes, rather than simply functions, product lines and geographies. The capability is enhanced because the deeper the knowledge of the needs of particular customers or segments of customers is, the more likely that the company will develop products and solutions that really meet those needs and deliver them in a timely and effective manner.

Michael Dell attributed much of Dell Computer's success in the 1990s to its use of "ever finer cuts" at customer segmentation.[174] As the business grew, it kept breaking large segments into smaller sub-segments and using them as an important way to manage the rapidly growing business. For example, the large customer segment of 1994 was divided into three groups: large customers, medium customers and governmental and educational organizations. By 1997, the government segment had been further broken down into federal, state, local and education. Michael Dell argued that clear segmentation of the market and assigned teams with clear segment responsibility were the only ways to keep abreast of emerging issues, to forecast demand effectively and to make sure that somebody had clear responsibility for solving a particular group of customers' problems.

Another company that placed increased emphasis on building relational value to fight the inevitable drift to commoditization in its industry was SKF – the world's largest manufacturer of bearings.[175] Bearings are present in virtually all products that involve some rotational movement of mechanical parts, such as washing machines, wind turbines, cars and photocopiers. SKF organized its business around five technology platforms including basic bearing products and lubricants and seals. The sales force was organized around some 20 different business or application segments, such as medical equipment or household appliances. The sales teams worked closely with customers in the application segments to identify needs and to suggest products to meet their needs. If no suitable products were available then the sales team interfaced with the appropriate technology groups to try to design a new "customized" product that would work. About one-third of SKF's sales were coming from these customized products by 2007. The effective functioning of the sales organization with the technology groups was critical to SKF meeting its objectives.

While organization is an important element to support alignment, as the McKinsey model suggests, it is only one factor. Others aspects that have proven to be very important are the performance measurement and reward systems and having the right kind of people and training programs to equip staff with the right skills.

Many top performing companies with relational value core strategies view the reward systems and the metrics to which they are linked as being a key success factor. Siebel, itself a supplier of customer relationship management software, based its salesperson compensation partly on quarterly customer satisfaction ratings with the service and implementation of the products they had purchased.[176] This encouraged the salesperson to not only get the software up and running but also to make sure that the customer felt that he or she was getting real business value from it. Because about 50% of Seibel's business came from new sales to existing customers, this approach to compensation made good sense. And in view of the fact that the responsibility for the customer's business success was not just the responsibility of the salesperson, customer satisfaction scores also impacted the compensation of many others in the Siebel organization, including people in engineering and executive management.

Finding the right metric to base rewards on usually requires a deep understanding of what is important to the customer. GE Plastics (now part of SABIC) found that delivery at the time agreed upon was critical for its customers. If the product was delivered either early or late, customer satisfaction was lower. Therefore, the company started aligning its incentives with meeting delivery promises with both early and late deliveries resulting in lower incentive payments.

In 2006, Jeffrey Immelt, the CEO of GE, told managers throughout the company that customer satisfaction scores would be a factor in their bonuses.[177] Since many of its business units place a heavy emphasis on creating and maintaining strong relationships with their customers, this move probably made good sense.

Developing and using deep customer and market knowledge

One company that prided itself on its deep knowledge of its customers' businesses and the technical and business challenges they faced was Hilti. Based in

Liechtenstein, Hilti designed, manufactured and marketed high-quality power tools for construction, building maintenance and mining. More than half of its 16 000 employees worked in the field and each of them visited 10 to 15 customers per day.[178] Additionally, management, all the way up to the executive board, also spent a significant portion of their time in the field. For example, members of the company's executive board spent about 25% of their time in the field listening to customers.[179] Unlike some companies, most of these visits were not for social or entertainment purposes, but rather to deepen Hilti's understanding of its customers' businesses and their business issues.

It is one thing to have information in the minds of a company's employees but it is another issue to bring this information to bear on solving customer problems. Hilti's value proposition is about offering advice and support to professionals, generally on the job site. So Hilti had to be able to ensure that the "learnings" from helping a customer solve a problem in one part of the world were made available to customers facing similar application challenges in other parts of the world. This was not only about having high-quality and thorough knowledge about customer and application issues, but also about ensuring the availability of this information to the rest of the organization. This included other employees in the field, to the people charged with developing strategy and tactics and to those in the research and development community who were working on the next generation of products. An effective customer relationship management system can help an organization such as Hilti capture and use customer and market knowledge, as well as present internal data in a manner that helps the organization deepen its customer relationships. Hilti seemed to do this effectively.

In some organizations, individuals tend to hoard information and not share it. They feel that control of information is a source of personal power, but this, of course, is not supportive of developing strong relational value. The information, when acquired and shared, can be used to help the company segment its markets, set priorities among segments and customers, develop winning customer solutions, develop targeted marketing programs and support the sales force in making profitable sales.

Inculcating a customer focused culture throughout the organization

To create and sustain strong relational value requires that the whole company be customer focused. This must start with the CEO and other members of the top management team. John Chambers of Cisco Systems, a leading telecommunications equipment company, is reported to spend a large proportion of his time in face-to-face meetings with the CEOs of customers or potential customer companies. However, as befits the CEO of a company that makes networking equipment, he was trying to use Cisco's latest video-conferencing technology – a service called Telepresence – to replace at least some of these face-to-face meetings with virtual meetings that apparently come very close to duplicating the real thing.[180] He also receives almost daily voice mail updates on the status of critical Cisco accounts (major new accounts that it may be on the verge of winning, or important existing accounts from which it may be in danger of losing business). These voice mails are then forwarded to other executives so that key Cisco managers are aware of developments at these accounts and they are expected to help, if they can.

It is important to note that being customer focused does not mean treating all customers the same. Customer focused organizations recognize that some customers are more important than others are and should be treated differently. Some customers are much more valuable to the organization than others are as discussed earlier. The same approach can be seen in many business-to-consumer companies. Most airlines, for example, identify their most valuable customers and try to provide them with a higher level of service than they do a regular passenger.

One company that did this in a very sophisticated way was Capital One, one of the world's largest credit card companies with major operations in North America and Europe. Capital One conducted tens of thousands of sophisticated experiments each year to deepen its understanding of the drivers of customer behavior.[181] One area that it studied extensively over the years was response to direct mail solicitations. Each piece of direct mail was targeted to a specific recipient. Did the recipient respond to the solicitation, did they subsequently use their cards, did they carry balances (which provided interest income to Capital One) and did they default on their loans? Capital One built up a great deal of information on developing the likely optimal offer for, and the likely value of, particular customers. All of this required a very sophisticated IT system. The results of all the testing were, for example, used when a cardholder made an enquiry by telephone. Capital One received tens of millions of such enquiries annually. When a customer call was received, the system attempted to identify the cardholder based on the number he or she had provided or had used on previous calls. If it was successful, then it tried to predict the reason for the call (perhaps the customer was bumping up against the card's credit limit and wanted an increase in the limit) and how Capital One might respond to the customer call or request. The system could identify the reason for the call with more than 70% accuracy. Depending upon the potential value of the customer to the company, and other factors, the system decided whether to route the call to an interactive voice response system or to a customer service representative. If the call was routed to a customer service representative, the computer system selected the best available representative to answer the likely inquiry. This required that Capital One build up a database comprised of the knowledge and skills of each of its thousands of customer service representatives. Each of the representatives was compensated on the basis of an individually tailored incentive plan, based on both objective and subjective measures including sales, service and productivity. With this sophisticated approach and the company's IT system, Capital One was able to tailor its treatment of each specific customer, despite the fact that it had millions of them.

Building relational value is not a quick fix

Building relational value is not a process that happens quickly, as the above discussion suggests. The whole organization process has to go through a transformation and that takes a good deal of time. Designing an organization that will encourage building relational value may be fairly quick but building the skills and competencies of the staff, hiring new staff and developing all the processes and systems to support the new strategy will take considerable time. Often the information systems need to be radically overhauled to develop information that can be used to support building relational value.

Fidelity Investments, a major international provider of financial services and investment resources to individual investors, is another company that embarked on the journey to try to become a relational value leader in its industry.[182] As we have seen in some earlier examples, identifying clearly defined target segments was a key element in helping the firm make a relatively successfully transition from a product leadership focused company to one more focused on relational value. The move was precipitated by the growing competition from its low cost competitors; in Fidelity's case, this meant discount brokers and independent financial advisers. The company identified seven customer segments, such as active traders and high value ($2 million plus) investors, and created dedicated customer facing groups to develop solutions appropriate for each segment, in line with their profit potential. The customer facing groups were supported by product groups

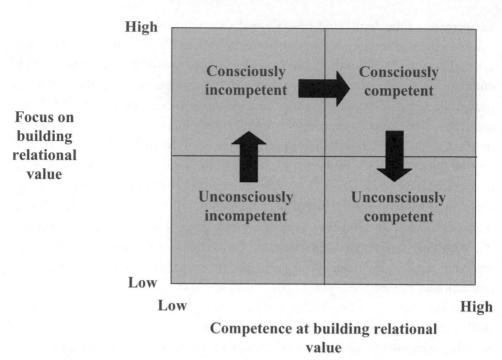

FIGURE 7.3   Building relational value is a journey – often a long one
Source: Based on Esther Cameron and Mike Green. *Making Sense of Change Management: A Complete Guide to the Models, Tools & Techniques of Organizational Change*, London: Kogan Page, 2004, p. 13.

that developed and managed investment funds and other services that could be bundled for the different, targeted segments. Managers at Fidelity estimated that it took more than three years to achieve about 60% of its objective, largely because of the time it took to redesign and implement the necessary systems.

For many organizations, the process of moving towards high relational value is a journey of learning. A useful way to think about the journey is to consider it involving the four stages shown in Figure 7.3.

Most organizations start off in the "unconsciously incompetent" box. As we saw with Tetra Pak, it may take some crises in the business – or some very weak customer satisfaction survey results – to wake the whole organization up to the fact that it faces a serious issue. As the focus shifts – "we need to do something to improve our relationships with our customers" – the competence to do something about it is often lacking, so the organization moves into the "consciously incompetent" quadrant. If the company is successful in implementing initiatives to build relational value, the organization will gradually move across to the "consciously competent" quadrant, where most people in the organization are focused on building satisfied customers and creating relational value. What most business leaders hope for, over time, is that this focus on customer satisfaction and relational value is built into the DNA of the organization so that employees do the "right thing" for the customer without even thinking about it.

One example of doing the right thing instinctively occurred when a couple of a major airline's incoming flights were late and several of the passengers on these flights had very tight connections that made it quite likely that some of their bags might miss the connection. The agent manning the gate was using the airline's customer relationship management system and noticed that an élite traveler on one of these late flights had lost a bag on a tight connection a couple of months earlier. Once she had verified that this passenger's bag had made the connection and was on the plane, she went onto the plane just before the door closed and reassured the passenger that this time his bag had made the connection. Given his previous experience, the passenger was probably quite concerned about this possibility, even though he hadn't voiced his concern to an airline employee. Proactively telling the passenger the good news probably had a very positive impact on the airline's relationship with the customer and may have even generated some positive word-of-mouth to other prospective customers. This is a good example of an employee doing the right thing to enhance the customer relationship, even though there was probably no standard procedure for this circumstance.

This example illustrates the challenge of hiring and developing the thousands of employees that must execute their customer impacting activities flawlessly if true relationship value is to be created. It only takes one employee's inconsiderate or thoughtless action to destroy the good work of dozens of others. In one case, a business traveler stayed multiple times at a particular hotel within a fairly short period of time. The hotel management decided to reward him with a nice gift of wine on his next visit. When he checked in at the hotel, the receptionist announced that he would find a gift in his room and explained that the hotel was appreciative of his frequent visits. The executive expressed his gratitude, finished the expedited check-in and just as he was leaving the reception, the receptionist pointed across the lobby and said, "Enjoy your stay – you will find the elevator down that hall on your left." Suddenly for the executive, the magic of the moment was lost – as a frequent guest, he of course knew where the elevator was located. All the effort that had been taken by the hotel's management team to make its most frequent guests feel noticed and appreciated had, to a large degree, been destroyed by a receptionist thoughtlessly following a rote script.

CHALLENGE QUESTIONS

Where on the performance curve (Figure 7.2) is your company or business unit? Would all members of the top management team agree with that assessment? If you asked a cross-section of people working lower down in the organization, would they agree as well? If there is not strong agreement, why do the assessments differ?

For businesses moving into a price value segment:

- Does your company have the right products or services to be competitive? If not, do you have any innovative ideas about the process the business might use to get them? Could you develop them internally? And if so, how? Might an acquisition work for your particular company given its market situation and its internal culture?
- If your business had the "right" price value product or service, does it have the marketing expertise and the sales and distribution resources to effectively reach the target segments?
- Does the business unit responsible for the price value product or service have the business culture to support the relentless drive to keep reducing costs? Not all employees want to work in that sort of obsessively cost-focused culture.

For a business trying to transform itself into a relational value business:

- Does the company have, or can it develop, an organization that will encourage and support building relational value?
- Is it organized around customer groups or processes, or is it organized around functions, product lines or geographies? Are the metrics and reward systems

aligned appropriately? Are people in the organization truly accountable for the business' performance with particular customers or groups of customers?

- Is the business developing relevant and deep customer and market knowledge and linking it with the appropriate internal data to support developing deep and mutually beneficial customer relationships? Does the company have the systems to make the appropriate customer information available to those that need it?

- Does the business have a strong customer focused culture throughout the organization? Does it start at the top? How do the top managers spend their time? Does the company really set priorities among customers and potential customers so that it gets the customer mix it wants – a mix that will support its long-term ambitions?

- Does the organization have a realistic timetable for achieving its relational value objectives? In which cell in the matrix can your organization currently be found?

CHAPTER 8

An even more challenging future

Meeting the growing challenge of low cost competitors is a tough and exhausting challenge for executives and managers in traditional companies. It would be music to their ears if they could see the threat declining in the years ahead. But, let's face it, the threat is not going to go away; in fact, it will almost certainly accelerate. As the pop song written by Randy Bachman in the 1970s puts it: "You ain't seen nothing yet".

For traditional companies, cost innovation must be on every executive's mind if they want to reduce their vulnerability to low cost competition. And that doesn't just go for those that see themselves playing in the arena of good enough products and services. Firms competing with performance value or relational value strategies must also make sure that they are performing in the most cost-effective manner possible and that unnecessary activities – ones that don't create real customer value – are not done at all.

And, it's important to keep in mind that the future is certainly not plain sailing for all low cost players. While those with strong capabilities in designing and delivering good enough products and services at low prices are often in a strong competitive position, they also face their own challenges – both internal and external. Executives in traditional companies should take these into account as they develop their own strategies. We will discuss this later in the chapter.

Traditional companies will have to improve their ability to anticipate emerging threats from low cost competitors and respond to those that pose a credible threat to their business in a timely manner. For many executives, responding creatively and forcefully to the challenge posed by low cost competition will cause them to rethink some of the core assumptions on which their companies' business strategies have been based. Simple, focused strategies don't seem quite as straightforward and as obvious as they once did, especially when there are competitors playing the game in new, disruptive ways. Assuming that a company with a focused performance leadership strategy can win consistently over the long term seems increasingly questionable in many industries.

This paranoia, however, about unnecessary costs and anticipating long-term competitive threats must be complemented with an intense focus on customers and their emerging needs. A company cannot hope to gain, and sustain, competitive advantage by focusing solely on costs and competitors; it must understand emerging customer needs and respond to them in innovative ways. Only in this way can it hope to successfully meet the challenge from low cost competition.

COST INNOVATION MUST BE PART OF EVERYBODY'S GAME

While cost innovation is at the core of what low cost competitors must do to be successful, it is also an essential part of the success equation for businesses that have either a performance value focus or a relational value focus. But the pursuit of cost beating must often be a bit more nuanced for companies that have performance value or relational value strategies. It's a matter of trying to identify what elements of the value offering can be reduced, or eliminated, without jeopardizing the core value proposition for the target segment. Are there activities a company is performing or product or service specifications that are expensive to achieve that are not creating value commensurate with their costs for the targeted customers?

As we saw in Chapter 7, Cisco is experimenting aggressively with the use of its new video-conferencing service, Telepresence, to try to replace some of its high cost face-to-face interactions with customers and strategic partners. If it can achieve 80–90% of the benefits of some of its face-to-face meetings at a fraction of the cost, then this could be a very effective move. The challenge is to get the balance right.

GlaxoSmithKline (GSK) faced a similar type of issue in the pharmaceutical industry.[183] From the 1970s through the 1990s, the pharmaceutical industry lived in a world of massive R&D expenditures that resulted in a number of very successful "blockbuster" drugs with global sales that could be measured in billions of dollars, with very attractive margins. Over time, this largesse led to bureaucratic organizations that "over-engineered" the R&D process so that experiments were done that created information that was of no value to decision-making. The head of R&D at GSK estimated that perhaps 50–60% of the company's experiments were unnecessary. Finally, the rising costs, fewer breakthrough drugs and shorter windows to capitalize on the few successes put pharmaceutical companies under increasing pressure and forced companies like GSK to act. But deciding to change the situation, acting and seeing the impact on costs takes time. The old risk-avoiding behavior of asking all possible questions and conducting the necessary research to answer them was deeply embedded in the company culture and took time to change.

If not done carefully, the exercise of eliminating activities and features in products or services or doing them in a lower cost way can lead to the value advantage being eroded. Customers then begin to wonder what benefits they are receiving for the premium price they are paying. This has become an issue for some "full-service" airlines. Some have trimmed their free checked baggage allowances or even begun charging some passengers for checking a bag, and reduced their cabin baggage allowances, in-flight services and number of staff members in an attempt to bring their costs under control. These actions were taken so that they can price more competitively with the low cost carriers. But this has caused some of their customers to wonder why they are still paying a fare that may be multiples of the fare that they would pay on a low cost carrier. The same thing has happened in many full-service department stores in North America. In their eagerness to cut costs to be able to compete with Wal-Mart, many have moved to reducing staff and replacing checkout positions distributed throughout the stores with centralized checkouts. In some cases, this means that they now have fewer sales staff on the floor than Wal-Mart. For many customers, higher prices and lower service levels are not part of a winning value proposition!

THE THREAT FROM LOW COST COMPETITION WILL INTENSIFY

Some of the fundamental forces destabilizing traditional companies in many industries, which were discussed in Chapter 2, will continue to support the development and growth of low cost competitors. In particular, the challenge that networks of specialized customer relationship, innovation and infrastructure companies pose to traditional, horizontally integrated companies will increase as more industries "unbundle" and become more modular. This is being driven by dramatic and interrelated improvements in IT systems, the Internet and sophisticated logistics systems.

Some low cost competitors act as the lead player in their network and take advantage of specialized partners to develop and deliver product and services to their customers. For other low cost competitors, this is their entry point into a business. They perhaps start as an outsource manufacturing partner building products or helping deliver services designed and developed by others who have the relationship with the ultimate customer. But over time, these low cost competitors may take on a bigger and bigger role in the network as they learn more about customer needs and enough about some of the neighboring roles in the network to do those roles themselves. Some even graduate to becoming the lead player in their network – usually the one owning the customer relationship.

This is how some of the Taiwan-based electronics companies have developed into branded players. They initially started out as companies providing electronic manufacturing services to OEMs in the West. As they learned more about customer needs, they began offering design services as part of their package, particularly if the customer was just looking for cosmetic changes. It was then a short step to doing evolutionary designs that took advantage of advances in components and sub-systems. The next step, and one that has been challenging for many of these companies, was to become a more traditional brand owner attempting to sell their products in competition with their OEM customers.

Acer followed this route from being a contract manufacturer of personal computers to a branded manufacturer. The transition was not without its difficulties as it faced a real conflict-of-interest issue with its branded line competing with its contract manufacturing customers' own products.[184] It eventually resolved the problem by spinning off the contract manufacturing business and outsourcing its own Acer business to other contract manufacturers. It also acquired a couple of other major PC manufacturers – Gateway and Packard Bell – and by 2008, it was one of the top four PC manufacturers in the world.[185]

As more of the capability to design, develop, make and deliver a product or service becomes accessible to a variety of companies that wish to compete in a market, it becomes increasingly difficult for traditional performance leaders to stay ahead of emerging competitors and still get an adequate return on their investments in new products. When the emerging competitors have access to much of the innovative capacity that is relevant to a particular industry through specialist suppliers, they are able to copy innovative new products or services very quickly. In some cases, they can even beat traditional players. Similarly, with access to a network of infrastructure players that collectively can often match or beat the traditional companies in terms of producing or delivering the products or services, they can bring their products to market very quickly.

Additionally, as we saw in Chapter 6, in some industries, the cost of developing new products and services, as well as making or delivering these products and services, is rising exponentially. With both increasing investment and shortening windows to take advantage of their successful innovations, the challenge for some performance leaders has become insurmountable; they are unable to earn an adequate return on their investments. At one time, some of these companies were able to get an attractive return on their investment by first introducing innovations into segments at the very top of the market with high prices; they would then gradually cascade this technology over time, maximizing the return on their investment. Today some of their low cost competitors introduce the latest advances quickly into the lower and middle reaches of the market, as soon as they can get access to it. This destroys the profitable cascading strategy favored by many high value-added competitors.

TRADITIONAL COMPANIES CAN LEVERAGE NETWORKS TO TRY TO STAY AHEAD

By taking advantage of the opportunities provided by a more collaborative and open business model, companies can both reduce the costs of development and access new sources of revenue. Companies can reduce development costs by partnering with other firms or individuals who are able to provide some aspects of the innovative solution less expensively. As Bill Joy (one of the founders of Sun Microsystems) is reported to have said, "Most of the smart people in the world don't work for you." The company can also offset some of its innovation and development costs by selling or licensing some of the intellectual property it has developed. As we also saw in Chapter 6, numerous traditional companies like IBM and P&G are taking advantage of these opportunities.

Despite the best efforts of traditional companies to take advantage of the opportunities afforded by a more open business environment, it is likely that the pressure on them will only intensify. Many of their low cost competitors will have "grown up" in and will be more at ease in a collaborative, networked environment. The culture, systems and processes will have been developed in this environment, often giving them a significant competitive advantage.

Even companies stressing relational value find that it is a challenge to stay ahead of some of their low cost competitors. Here again, elements of the value proposition are being commoditized. Typically, it is the "hard" parts, rather than the "soft" human parts, that the lower cost players find easiest to match without seriously jeopardizing their business models. Again, to draw on an example we used in Chapter 4, easyJet is trying to build more relational value with business travelers by coming closer to matching the intra-European offerings of flag carriers like BA and Lufthansa. For example, it began offering more flights between major business hubs, matched BA's business class carry-on baggage allowance, offered paid-for lounge access, provided priority boarding for a fee and free transfer to an earlier flight if the traveler arrived at the airport early. Clearly, it still did not offer the "full package" that a BA or Lufthansa provided with respect to on-board services and the types of personal support that these airlines provided to élite travelers in the event of flight cancellations or emergency situations. But easyJet did narrow the gap and made the traditional airlines work harder to justify their price premiums.

Over time, improvements in the Internet and IT systems will make it easier and easier for low cost competitors to come closer to matching certain aspects of the offer from companies adopting a relational value strategy in a variety of industries. Through leveraging technology and systems, they will try to duplicate what the traditional relational value players provide through people and a customer service-oriented culture.

LOW COST COMPETITORS FACE THEIR OWN CHALLENGES

Some of this discussion can leave an executive in a very pessimistic frame of mind. Many of the forces encouraging, and supporting the growth of low cost competitors seem inexorable and clearly there are major opportunities for those low cost competitors who manage to build a culture that supports constant cost reduction.

As we have seen, some of these low cost players move up, or out, of their initial markets to take advantage of more attractive growth opportunities in neighboring market segments or because these segments might be useful stepping-stones to give them access to more attractive market segments in the future. Companies are sometimes forced to move up because they have lost the battle in the price leadership segment of the market to someone else. For these companies that are armed with a relatively low cost structure, the "bottom" of the performance value or relational value segments looks like a relatively "soft" target.

However, the low cost competitors have their own challenges. For those based in countries such as China and India, some of their initial success was based on access to low cost resources, whether it was R&D, engineering or manufacturing. Over time, these advantages tend to diminish as wage costs rise and their competitors in developed countries move some of their operations to take advantage of the same resources and capabilities.

An additional factor that affects all low cost players over time is keeping up the pressure to drive down costs year after year. Leadership is challenged to find ways to keep the momentum up and keep the employees motivated. Expansion, geographically as well as into new product and service categories, can help create new challenges. By expanding, the low cost competitors may take on the "giants" in new markets and be able to re-create the "underdog" mentality that often helped them in their early days.

However, the move into new geographies and new segments invariably complicates the business model making it harder to maintain focus. New resources and capabilities are needed and some may be less easy to acquire or develop. The talent to manage a more complex, sometimes global, organization is not always readily available. Brand building in unfamiliar markets is another difficult challenge that is not always easily mastered, even with access to the best consulting firms and advertising agencies.

At some point, these companies and their management teams start to face new, often less familiar challenges. In the pursuit of low costs, they often cause actual or perceived damage to some stakeholders such as employees, customers or society at large. The pressure exerted by these stakeholders can gradually weigh down the company and impact its performance.

Usually, the industry leader becomes the main target of these stakeholders. Wal-Mart was targeted by the labor unions, consumer groups, other non-governmental organizations and even governments as the symbol of everything that is wrong with discount retailers. In its industry, Ryanair is targeted by the same groups, particularly environmentalists and unions. As the symbol of what is wrong with its industry, more and more management time and company resources are spent on "setting the record straight" or trying to ameliorate the "damage" they may be causing. Ultimately, this loss of focus takes its toll on a company's performance.

ANTICIPATE POSSIBLE FUTURE COMPETITIVE MOVES AND PROACT

As many companies have discovered, much to their chagrin, once a low cost competitor is established in a market it's very difficult to control them or push them back. Often they do not need to be established in the market in a major way – a strong position in a defensible niche can be enough. It became much more difficult to dislodge Haier in the US major appliance market once it had established a presence in some of the major appliance distribution channels with its compact refrigerators and wine coolers. As long as its products were good quality and Haier worked effectively with its distributors, there was a high likelihood that these retailers would be willing to carry Haier's full-size refrigerators, even if it meant giving less floor space to their traditional suppliers.

Once they have become strongly established, many of the low cost competitors discussed in this book have survived, and even prospered, when their more traditional competitors have tried to defeat or contain them. In business-to-consumer markets, they can even use the attack by an incumbent to their advantage. After BA launched its low cost subsidiary Go in May 1998, easyJet accused BA of illegally cross-subsidizing the new airline. To attract publicity, and to try to take advantage of its underdog status, easyJet ran a contest offering free easyJet flights to those people who came closest to guessing Go's losses in their first fiscal year.

The challenge for the traditional players is to anticipate the potential moves of low cost competitors – how smart low cost competitors might make a sequence of moves over time that might dramatically strengthen their competitive position and weaken that of the traditional player. This requires a combination of humility and paranoia. Humility in the sense that incumbents should, if anything, underestimate their own strengths and overestimate their vulnerabilities. Paranoia in the sense that, if anything, we should believe that the worst is going to happen and

that each potential competitor will take the maximum advantage of any vulnerabilities that a company might have.

After anticipating the potential moves, management must decide whether
to move in against the low cost competitor and decide where the best place is to
challenge them. Too often, traditional companies don't move quickly and robustly
enough, allowing the low cost competitors to achieve easy wins and quickly gain
momentum. Usually, it is better to challenge them aggressively in carefully chosen
markets, or market segments, and make them fight hard for every gain. Ideally,
the challenge should be mounted in a very smart way to reduce the risk of cannibalization. In Chapter 6, we saw how Tesco very intelligently challenged the hard
discounters, and Asda, by offering value propositions that were attractive to the
price sensitive customer but which minimized cannibalization of the profitable
business it was generating in other customer segments that were less price sensitive. But these strategies and tactics were based on a deep understanding of its
customers, something not all companies have. In some cases, although this is not
the case in the Tesco situation, the low cost competitors may decide to withdraw
and go after more attractive opportunities where they don't have to fight vigorously against a smart incumbent for every small win!

BE WILLING TO RE-THINK TRADITIONAL BUSINESS WISDOM

Low cost competitors can emerge rapidly, quickly matching the products and
sometimes the services of traditional companies – in some cases, at a significantly
lower price. In responding to this threat, executives must often question some of
the conventional wisdom with which they have grown up. Traditionally, performance leaders could sometimes stay comfortably ahead of low cost competitors
playing a price leadership game. There were often significant barriers to entry
around their segments, and it wasn't easy for new players to enter, particularly
ones that emphasized cost leadership. Yes, these performance leaders competed,
sometimes fiercely, with other players. Typically, though, these competing companies were playing the same performance leadership game – they had similar
resources, capabilities and strategies. Today the performance leaders face not
only their traditional competitors but also the low cost competitors that may be
moving against them with what the traditional players view as disruptive
strategies.

To successfully defend their positions, incumbents must often attack the low cost competitors in their markets before they face them in their own. Moving "down" in a market always seems to be a much bigger challenge than moving "up" in the market. It means competing in segments where costs are critical and sometimes in geographies and markets where the traditional companies have little or no experience. They can no longer assume that peripheral markets in Africa, Latin America and other less developed parts of the world are largely irrelevant. If they do move into these markets, they cannot do it late or slowly with old technology and products. Traditional companies may now face low cost competitors in these markets that aggressively introduce the latest technology and innovative business models. These technologies and business models may allow the competitors to target and access these markets in a profitable way, as they build the volume, experience, resources and references they know that they will need as they move towards key markets in Europe, North America and Japan.

It may mean dropping prices to what would have once been unthinkable levels to attempt to stimulate demand in a market that might be more price elastic than they had ever assumed, even if there were to be significant cannibalization of their high-end products. If they don't do this, they can be sure that a low cost competitor will, and, if successful, will build a huge base of business on which to grow. By looking at other markets, such as air travel, DVD players, industrial projectors, distributed copying, mobile phones, handheld ultrasound machines and mobile phone services, they realize that many markets are much more responsive to low prices than was often assumed.

Even if the traditional companies base these new low cost businesses in separate business units – in an attempt to both leverage the opportunity to the maximum and maintain focus – coordination is needed and the overall management task will be much more complex. But this is a price that might have to be paid if the company is to remain competitive.

PUT THE CUSTOMER ON CENTER STAGE

While being paranoid about the competition undoubtedly has benefits, it is not without its risks. Achieving significant changes in customer value creation rarely comes from observing or copying the competition. The success of businesses that are focusing on creating performance value or relational value depends to a significant degree on identifying new or latent customer needs that they can address with innovative products, services or "solutions". Apple's success is largely based on creating great user experiences, which requires a deep understanding of user needs, often ones the consumer is not even able to articulate.[186] Too great a focus on the competition can detract from this attention to customer needs. A successful performance or relational value leader must be balanced in its attention to both customers and their emerging needs, as well as to the potential moves of competitors – particularly the low cost competitors that can ultimately threaten its business model. Companies need humility, paranoia *and* innovative responsiveness to serve the needs of their customers.

There are almost always customer segments in every market that value the best and are willing to pay for it. Perhaps these customers want products or services that lead the market in some aspect of performance, whether it be innovative features, better functionality, intuitive ease of use or great design. Or perhaps they want to deal with a company who really does try to cater to their needs and provide a truly tailored solution. These segments may not be as proportionately large as they were at an earlier stage of the product category's life cycle, but they will usually be there. The world of good enough products and services is not for all customers on all occasions.

References

1. Gail Edmondson, "China's Brilliance: Back from Disaster", *Business Week*, 14 September 2007.
2. Paul Gao, "A Global Road Map for China's Automakers", *McKinsey Quarterly*, 2008, Number 3, pp. 90–98.
3. "Global Survey of Business Executives", *McKinsey Quarterly*, 2006, Number 3, p. 21.
4. Hervé Cathelin, "European Discount Initiative", presentation at Nestlé Investor Seminar, Vevey, Switzerland, 8–9 June 2005.
5. "Top Environmental Performance of the Low-Cost/Low-Fares Business Model Confirmed by the Latest ELFAA Members Statistics", European Low Fares Airline Association press release, 11 January 2007.
6. Duncan Russell, "Further Broadening the ING DIRECT Model", *Fox-Pitt, Kelton Company Update*, 1 February 2007, p. 1.
7. Telgo website http://www.switel.com/v4/index.php?language=en&page=company.
8. Christopher Lawton, Yukari Iwatani Kane and Jaone Dean, "U.S. Upstart Takes on TV Giants in Price War", *Wall Street Journal*, 15 April 2008.
9. Presentation by Scott McNealy, Chairman and co-founder, Sun Microsystems at AeA-Stanford Executive Institute, 14 August 2008.
10. Antone Gonsalves, "IBM Joins Linux Distributors in Attacking Microsft Windows, Office", *Information Week*, 6 August 2008.
11. John D. Stoll, "Boeing CEO Sees Third Big Player Emerging in Coming Decades", *Wall Street Journal*, 23 May 2007.
12. John Selly Brown and John Hagel III, "Innovation Blowback: Disruptive Management Practices from Asia", *McKinsey Quarterly*, 2005, Number 1, pp. 34–45.
13. Brian Bloch, "Choice that Sends out the Wrong Buying Signals", *Telegraph*, 23 February 2005.
14. James C. Anderson, James A. Narus, and Wouter van Rossum, "Customer Value Propositions in Business Markets", *Harvard Business Review*, March 2006, pp. 91–99.
15. For example, Treacy and Wiersema popularized the terms product leadership, operational excellence and customer intimacy. See Michael E. Treacy and Frederik D.

Wiersema, "Customer Intimacy and Other Value Disciplines", *Harvard Business Review*, January–February 1993, pp. 84–93.

16. Jerry Useem, "Simply Irresistible: Why Apple is the Best Retailer in America", *Fortune*, 19 March 2007, pp. 53–57.

17. Steve McKee, "How Solid Is Your Brand?" *Business Week Online*, 14 September 2007.

18. Carol J. Loomis, "The Bloomberg", *Fortune*, 28 May 2007, pp. 59–67.

19. Or more correctly, it is the cost of the value-added activities to its inputs that should decline over time. For example, in an industry where the cost of energy is a major input and where the cost of energy is rising, costs and prices may appear to be rising. However, if the cost of energy is removed or held constant, costs and prices are likely to fall in a competitive industry.

20. Vijay Vaitheeswaren, "Something New Under the Sun", *The Economist*, 13 October 2007, p. 10.

21. Thomas H. Davenport, "The Coming Commoditization of Processes", *Harvard Business Review*, June 2005, pp. 100–108.

22. John Hagel III and Marc Singer, "Unbundling the Corporation", *Harvard Business Review*, March–April 1999, pp. 133–141.

23. Op. cit.

24. For example, see Justin Scheck, "Dell Plans to Sell Factories in Effort to Cut Costs", *Wall Street Journal*, 5 September 2008.

25. One part-time masseuse at Google, who was hired to provide massages to weary software engineers in 1999, retired a multi-millionaire after five years as a result of the stock options she received (Katie Hafner, "Google Options Make Masseuse a Multimillionaire", *New York Times*, 12 November 2007). Those days are long gone even in most Silicon Valley companies!

26. In the last few years Cisco has been moving to do more of its innovation activity in-house and has had some initial successes. See Kevin Allison, "Cisco Goes Back to the Garage", *Financial Times*, 6 June 2007.

27. Clay Chandler, "Wireless Wonder: India's Sunil Mittal", *Fortune*, 17 January 2007.

28. Bharti Airtel Annual Report 2007–2008.

29. Vijay Vaitheeswaren, "Something New Under the Sun", *The Economist*, 13 October 2007, p. 6.

30. Robin Pagnanenta, "AstraZeneca to Outsource Manufacturing", *The Times*, 17 September 2007.

31. Anita Greil and Cassandra Petrakis Zwahlen, "Novartis Plans to Buy Speedel, Gaining Control Over Key Drug", *Wall Street Journal*, 10 July 2008.

32. Larry Huston and Nabil Sakkab, "Connect and Develop: Inside Procter & Gamble's New Model for Innovation", *Harvard Business Review*, March 2006, pp. 58–66.

33. See http://www.innocentive.com/.

34. "Innovation Networks: Looking for Ideas Outside the Company" Knowledge@ Wharton, 14 November 2007.

35. August Cole, "Boeing Blames Latest Delay in 787 Jet on Supplier Issues", *Wall Street Journal*, 17 January 2008.

36. Nicholas Casey and Mary Ellen Lloyd, "Recalls Hurt Mattel's Profits", *Wall Street Journal*, 16 October 2007.

37. "What Does It Take to Compete in a Flat World?" Knowledge@Wharton, 31 October 2007.

38. F. Warren McFarland and Fred Young, "Li & Fung: Internet Issues (A)", Harvard Business School Case 9-301-009, 2001.

39. Stephen Shankland, "Intel Program to Certify Server Components", *Globe and Mail*, 15 June 2004, p. 65.

40. European Low Fares Airline Association, Liberalization of European Air Transport: The Benefits of Low Fare Airlines to Consumers, Airports, Regions and the Environment, Brussels, 2004.

41. "Fact Sheet: Industry Statistics", IATA Corporate Communications, 12 September 2005, p. 1.

42. "Airline Profitability – 2006", IATA Economics Briefing, 5 June 2007, p. 2.

43. Some of this discussion is based on Atul Pahwa and Adrian Ryans, "Ryanair: Defying Gravity", IMD Case IMD-3-1633, 2005.

44. Both figures are for the Ryanair financial year ending 31 March 2007.

45. Tom Chesshyre, "It's Cheap but Why Not More Cheerful?" *The Times*, 5 January 2002.

46. "Deutscher Regionalflughafen wachsen schneller", *Franfurter Allgememeine Zeitung*, 11 January 2008.

47. Ultimately Ryanair was required by the European Commission to repay €4 million of these payments, because it was viewed by the Commission as constituting illegal state aid. See Mary Watkins, "Ryanair Faces Order to Repay €4 Million in Aid", *Financial Times*, 3 February 2004.

48. "Ryanair Responds to Latest Commission Leaks", Ryanair news release, 13 November 2007.

49. From presentation made at Ryanair Investor Day, 28 September 2007, London, p. 59.

50. "Ryanair's Route to Riches", BBC Money Programme, first broadcast 4 June 2003.

51. For example, see Alan Ruddock, *Michael O'Leary: A Life in Full Flight*, Dublin: Penguin Ireland, 2007, p. 296.

52. "Mobile Charge Ban for Air Staff", BBC News, 22 April 2005. Michael O'Leary has claimed that Ryanair never had such a ban. However, the story was so newsworthy and made Ryanair look so cost conscious that the airline decided not to deny it.

53. *World Air Transport Statistics* 51st Edition, IATA, June 2007.

54. Some of this discussion is based on Stephanie Sequeira, Adrian Ryans, and Terry Deutscher, "ING DIRECT USA: Rebel with a Cause", IMD Case IMD-3-1845, 2007.

55. Dick Harryman, "ING DIRECT: A Growing Success Story", Merrill Lynch European Banking and Insurance Conference, London, 9 October 2003.

56. Barbara Kiviat, "How a Man on a Mission (and a Harley) Reinvented Banking", *Time*, 25 June 2007, pp. 44–46.

57. Personal communications from Arkadi Kuhlmann, 2 May 2008.

58. Melanie Trottman, "As Competition Rebounds, Southwest Faces Squeeze", *Wall Street Journal*, 27 June 2007, p. A1.

59. Based on Robert J. Dolan, "Sealed Air Corporation", Harvard Business School, Case 582–103, 1982.

60. Alan Ruddock, *Michael O'Leary: A Life in Full Flight*, Dublin: Penguin Ireland, 2007, p. 252.

61. One analyst estimated that ING DIRECT spent about €450 million on advertising globally in 2005. See Benjamin Ensor, "Best Practices: The Sources of ING DIRECT's Success", Forrester, 25 April 2007, p. 2.

62. http://www.mind-advertising.com/de/index.html.

63. "Ryanair calls on Regulator to Reject £2.2 billion 'Taj Mahal' at Stansted", Ryanair press release 30 January 2007.

64. Author's calculation based on cost data contained in the presentation accompanying the fiscal 2006 financial results and data on the Ryanair website documenting the number of passengers carried each year. The figures were apparently not adjusted for inflation, so the real rate at which costs were reduced was higher than 20%.

65. William C. Taylor, "Rebels with a Cause, and a Business Plan", *New York Times*, 2 January 2005.

66. ING DIRECT Corporate Brochure Q1 2007, p. 17.

67. Ryanair figure from presentation made at Ryanair Investor Day, 29 September 2006, New York City, p. 38. British Airways figure calculated from information published on the British Airways website in 2007.

68. Barbara Cassani and Kenny Kemp, *Go: An Airline Adventure*, London: Time Warner, 2003, p. 274.

69. Scott McCartney, "United Pushes to Upgrade Service", *Wall Street Journal*, 21 March 2006.

70. George Stalk Jr., "Curveball: Strategies to Fool the Competition", *Harvard Business Review*, September 2006.

71. Lex, "Telecoms Equipment", *Financial Times*, 14 February 2008.

72. Jonathan R. Woetzel, "Reassessing China's State-Owned Enterprises", *McKinsey Quarterly*, 2008, Number 3, pp. 59–65.

73. Clayton M. Christensen, *The Innovator's Dilemma: When New Technologies Cause Great Firms to Fail*, Boston, Mass: Harvard Business School Press, 1997.

74. Daniel Fisher, "Open-Sourcing the Law", *Forbes*, 30 June 2008, pp. 70–73.

75. Adrian Ryans, "*Saurer: Meeting the China Challenge (A)*", IMD Case IMD-5-0688, 2005.

76. William E. Hoover Jr., "Making China Your Second Home Market: An Interview with the CEO of Danfoss", *McKinsey Quarterly*, 2006, Number 1, pp. 84–93.

77. George C. Strachan, "The State of the Discount Store Industry", Goldman Sachs, 6 April 1994.

78. See Figure 3.1 and the accompanying discussion in Chapter 3.

79. Kevin Done, "Lufthansa: German Carrier Aims High with Own Fleet", *Financial Times*, 19 May 2008.

80. Trond Riiber Knudsen, Andreas Randel, and Jorgen Rugholm, "The Vanishing Middle Market", *McKinsey Quarterly*, 2005, Number 4, pp. 6–9.

81. Trond Riiber Knudsen, "Escaping the Middle-market Trap: An Interview with the CEO of Electrolux", *McKinsey Quarterly*, 2006, Number 4, pp. 73–79.

82. "Competition from China: Two McKinsey Surveys", *McKinsey Quarterly*, 2008, Number 3, pp. 18–21.

83. Bernard Condon, "Don't Worry, Be Happy", *Forbes*, 26 March 2007.

84. "Nanjing Auto Buys Collapsed British MG Rover", *China Daily*, 23 July 2005.

85. Neil Winton, "Tata for Now", *Wall Street Journal*, 27 March 2008.

86. Chris Noon, "Whirlpool's Fettig Looks to Sew up Maytag Deal", *Forbes*, 15 August 2005.

87. Tomas Koch and Oliver Ramsbottom, "A Growth Strategy for a Chinese State-Owned Enterprise: An Interview with ChemChina's President", *McKinsey Quarterly*, 2008, Number 3, pp. 51–58.

88. Ming Zeng and Peter J. Williamson, *Dragons at Your Door: How Chinese Cost Innovation Is Disrupting Global Competition*, Boston, Mass: Harvard Business School Press, 2007, pp. 66–67.

89. Op. cit., pp. 106–116.
90. Alexandra Harney, "Huawei Wins 3G Contract from Telfort", *Financial Times*, 9 December 2004.
91. Yibing Wu, "China's Refrigerator Magnate", *McKinsey Quarterly*, 2003, Number 3, pp. 106–115.
92. Zeng and Williamson, op. cit., p. 60.
93. Rod Stone, "Silverjet Grounds Flights after Financing Collapses", *Wall Street Journal*, 31 May 2008.
94. Orit Gadiesh and Till Vestring, "China's 'Good Enough' Market", *Wall Street Journal Asia*, 5 September 2006.
95. Barbara Cassani and Kenny Kemp, *Go: An Airline Adventure*, London: Time Warner, 2003.
96. For example, see Ingo Beyer von Morgenstern and Xiaoyu Xia, "China's High-tech Market: A Race to the Middle", *McKinsey Quarterly*, September 2006.
97. Ellen Byron, "P&G's Global Target: Shelves of Tiny Stores", *Wall Street Journal*, 16 July 2007, p. A1.
98. Term life insurance covers the insured person for a particular term, such as five years, and only pays a death benefit if the insured dies during this period. Permanent life insurance on the other hand is for the life of the insured and provides a payment at the end of the insured's life. It also has a cash value that accrues over time.
99. See Carl Shapiro and Hal R. Varian, *Information Rules*, Boston, Mass: Harvard Business School Press, 1999.
100. Soren Petersen, "Solidifying Leadership in Emerging Markets", Nokia Capital Markets Day, 4 December 2007.
101. Based on a personal communication from Jacques Horovitz, former Director General of Grand Optical and now professor at IMD, Lausanne, Switzerland.
102. Clive Humby and Terry Hunt (with Tim Phillips). *Scoring Points: How Tesco is Winning Customer Loyalty*, London and Philadelphia: Kogan Press, 2003.
103. Clayton M. Christensen, *The Innovator's Dilemma: When New Technologies Cause Great Firms to Fail*, Boston, Mass: Harvard Business School Press, 1997.
104. John Williamson, "MVNOs: Adapt or Die", *Telecom Redux*, 31 May, 2005.
105. Barbara Cassani and Kenny Kemp, *Go: An Airline Adventure*, London: Time Warner, 2003, p. 75.
106. "Danfoss Aquires Chinese Frequency Converter Company", Danfoss Group press release, 3 November 2005.
107. Ingo Beyer von Morgenstern and Xiaoyu Xia, "China's High-tech Market: A Race to the Middle", *McKinsey Quarterly*, September 2006.

108. Sundeep Tucker and Jeff Dyer, "Carlyle's Xugong Contract Lapses", *Financial Times*, 4 July 2008.

109. "Europe: The Netherlands: Bank Acquisition", *New York Times*, 6 February 2003.

110. Shige Makino, Christine M. Chan, Takehiko Isobe, and Paul W. Beamish, "Intended and Unintended Termination of International Joint Ventures", *Strategic Management Journal*, Volume 28, 2007, pp. 1113–1132.

111. See James T. Areddy, "Partners Fight over Wahaha in China", *Wall Street Journal*, Geoff Dyer, "How Danone's China Venture Turned Sour", *Financial Times*, 11 April 2007 and Stewart Hamilton and Jinxuan Zhang, "Danone and Wahaha: A Bitter-Sweet Partnership", IMD Case IMD-3-1949, 2008.

112. See Jeffrey F. Rayport and Dickson L. Louis, "First Direct (A)", Harvard Business School Case 9-897-079, 1997.

113. Barbara Martinez and Jacob Goldstein, "Big Pharma Faces Grim Prognosis", *Wall Street Journal*, 6 December 2007.

114. John Selly Brown and John Hagel III, "Innovation Blowback: Disruptive Management Practices from Asia", *McKinsey Quarterly*, 2005, Number 1, pp. 34–45.

115. Ellen Byron, "P&G's Global Target: Shelves of Tiny Stores", *Wall Street Journal*, 16 July 2007, p. A1.

116. David Rocks, "A Firm Grip on Handset Design", *Business Week*, 24 October 2005, p. 28.

117. Frank Rose, "Hello, Ningbo", *Wired*, Issue 12.04, April, 2004.

118. Bruce Upbin, "The Next Billion", *Forbes*, 12 November 2007, pp. 48–56.

119. Op. cit.

120. Soren Petersen, "Solidifying Leadership in Emerging Markets", Nokia Capital Markets Day, 4 December 2007.

121. Rick Simonson, CFO Presentation Nokia Capital Markets Day, 4 December 2007.

122. Soren Petersen, "Solidifying Leadership in Emerging Markets", Nokia Capital Markets Day, 4 December 2007.

123. Much of this discussion is based on Kamran Kashani and Inna Francis, "Xiameter: The Past and Future of a 'Disruptive Innovation'", IMD Case IMD-5-0702, 2006.

124. To be more precise, there were three sub-segments in the non-price seeking segments, but for our purposes this adds little to the discussion. See the case for more details.

125. Trond Riiber Knudsen, Andreas Randel, and Jorgen Rugholm, "The Vanishing Middle Market", *McKinsey Quarterly*, 2005, Number 4, pp. 6–9.

126. Michelle Conlin, "Champions of Innovation", *Business Week*, 19 June 2006, p. 18.

127. Trond Riiber Knudsen, "Escaping the Middle-market Trap: An Interview with the CEO of Electrolux", *McKinsey Quarterly*, 2006, Number 4, pp. 73–79.

128. Aeppel, Timothy, "Home of the Range", *Wall Street Journal*, 25 October 2006, p. B1.

129. DataMonitor/Marketline report on AB Electrolux, 26 June 2006.

130. Deborah Steinborn, "Talking about Design", *Wall Street Journal*, 23 June 2008.

131. Jay Greene, "Where Designers Rule", *Business Week*, 5 November 2007.

132. Barbara Martinez and Jacob Goldstein, "Big Pharma Faces Grim Prognosis", *Wall Street Journal*, 6 December 2007.

133. Christopher P. Adams and Van V. Brantner, "Estimating the Cost of New Drug Development: Is it Really $802 Million?" *Health Affairs*, Vol. 25, No. 2, 2006, pp. 420–428.

134. Henry W. Chesbrough, "Why Companies Should Have Open Business Models", *MIT Sloan Management Review*, Vol. 48 No. 2, Winter 2007, pp. 22–28.

135. For one example see "Protecting the Family Jewels", *The Economist*, 24 June 2004.

136. Larry Huston and Nabil Sakkab, "Connect and Develop: Inside Procter & Gamble's New Model for Innovation", *Harvard Business Review*, March 2006, pp. 58–66 and Chesbrough, op. cit. p. 26.

137. Vijay Vaitheeswaren, "Something New Under the Sun", *The Economist*, 13 October 2007, p. 8.

138. Henry W. Chesbrough, "Why Companies Should Have Open Business Models", *Sloan Management Review*, Winter 2007, Vol. 48, No. 2, pp. 22–28.

139. See Leander Kahney, "Inside Look at Birth of the iPod", *Wired*, 21 July 2004, and Leander Kahney, *Inside Steve's Brain*, New York: Penguin Books, 2008, p. 229.

140. This example is based on Dennis H. Gensch, Nicolas Aversa, and Steven P. Moore, "A Choice-modeling Market Information System that Enables ABB Electric to Expand Its Market Share", *Interfaces*, January–February 1990, pp. 6–25.

141. Peter Marsh, "The Masters of Good Service", *Financial Times*, 29 June 2006.

142. Alan Mitchell, "P&G Takes Shoppers to Another World in War of the Brands", *Financial Times*, 18 October 2006.

143. NASCAR (National Association for Stock Car Auto Racing) is a type of car racing that developed in the United States; it uses racing cars loosely based on stock (or regular production) cars. It is an extremely popular spectator sport in the United States with millions of avid fans and is now spreading to some other countries.

144. Nextel Annual Report 2003.

145. Nextel Communications Inc., United States Securities and Exchange Commission Form 10-K, Annual Report for the Year Ending 31 December 2004.

146. Robert S. Collins, Michael L. Gibbs, and Henning von Spreckelsen, "ICI-Nobel's Explosives Company", IMD Case IMD-6-1070, 1995.

147. Nirmalya Kumar, "Strategies to Fight Low-cost Rivals", *Harvard Business Review*, December 2006, pp. 104–112.

148. Niraj Dawar and Mark Vandenbosch, "Mastering Innovation 3: Deriving Value from Customer Relations", *Financial Times*, 1 October 2004.

149. Clive Humby and Terry Hunt (with Tim Phillips), *Scoring Points: How Tesco is Winning Customer Loyalty*, London and Philadelphia: Kogan Press, 2003.

150. Richard Fletcher, "Tesco's Success Puts Clubcard Firm on the Map", *Sunday Times*, 19 December 2004.

151. Hervé Cathelin, "European Discount Initiative", Nestlé Investor Seminar, Vevey, Switzerland, 8–9 June 2005.

152. David E. Bell, "Tesco PLC", Harvard Business School, Case 503-036, 2006.

153. "Every Little Helps in the Battle of the Supermarkets", *Finance Week*, 23 February 2005.

154. Damian Reece, "Sir Terry Leahy, Chief Executive of Tesco: Surviving Success, by Tesco's Finest", *Independent*, 23 January 2004.

155. Juliette Jowit, "Supermarket Superpower", *Sunday Observer*, 26 December 2004.

156. Tesco Plc Website. See http://www.tescoplc.com/plc/about_us/strategy/.

157. Steve Hawkes, "Aldi Throws Down a Gauntlet to Tesco", *The Times*, 29 August 2008.

158. James Hall, "Tesco Moves to Counter Aldi and Lidl", *Daily Telegraph*, 7 January 2008.

159. Andrew S. Grove, *Only the Paranoid Survive: How to Exploit the Crisis Points that Challenge Every Company*, New York: Doubleday Publishing, 1996.

160. William E. Hoover Jr., "Making China Our Second Home Market: An Interview with the CEO of Danfoss", *McKinsey Quarterly*, 2006, Number 1, pp. 85–93.

161. Adrian Ryans and Mark Vandenbosch, "*Compaq Computer Corporation 1995 (Abridged)*", Richard Ivey School of Business, Case 9B00A003, 2000.

162. John P. Kotter, "Leading Change: Why Transformation Efforts Fail", *Harvard Business Review*, January 2007, pp. 96–103.

163. Janet Shaner and Kamran Kashani, "Tetra Pak (A) and (B)", IMD Cases IMD-5-0604 and 0605, 2002.

164. Adrian Ryans, "Saurer: The China Challenge Video", IMD-5-0688-V, 2005.

165. William E. Hoover Jr., "Making China Our Second Home Market: An Interview with the CEO of Danfoss", *McKinsey Quarterly*, 2006, Number 1, pp. 85–93.

166. Adrian Ryans, "Saurer: The China Challenge (A) and (B)", IMD Cases IMD-5-0688 and 0689, 2005.

167. Adrian Ryans, "Saurer: The China Challenge Video", IMD-5-0688-V, 2005.

168. "Saurer Founds Joint Venture with Jinsheng: Extension of Mid-Range and Low-End Offer for Spinning Components and Equipment for Cotton Spinning", Saurer press release, Winterthur, Switzerland, 31 December 2005.

169. Thomas Schelling, "Nutrition and Affordability in Emerging Markets: An Opportunity for Profitable Growth", Nestlé Investor Seminar, Vevey, Switzerland: 7–8 June 2007.

170. The following discussion is based on Janet Shaner and Kamran Kashani, "Tetra Pak (C): Implementing New Initiatives", IMD Case IMD-5-0606, 2003.

171. R.H. Waterman, T.J. Peters, and J.R. Phillips, "Structure is Not Organization", *Business Horizons*, June 1980, pp. 14–26.

172. In the case of McKinsey's 7-S model the authors argued that building an effective organization depends on having a high degree of fit between strategy, structure, systems, staff, skills, style and shared values (see previous reference for a full discussion).

173. This builds partly on the work of George Day. See for example, George S. Day, *The Market Driven Organization: Understanding, Attracting and Keeping Valuable Customers*, New York: The Free Press, 1999, pp. 127–33 and George S. Day, "Creating a Superior Customer-Relating Capability", *Sloan Management Review*, Spring 2003, pp. 77–82.

174. Joan Magretta, "The Power of Virtual Integration: An Interview with Dell Computer's Michael Dell", *Harvard Business Review*, March–April 1998, pp. 72–84.

175. Peter Marsh, "Back on a Roll in the Bearings Business", *Financial Times*, 6 February 2007.

176. Eilene Zimmerman, "Quota Busters", *Sales and Marketing Management*, Vol. 153, No. 1, January 2001, pp. 58–63.

177. Katherine Kranhold, "GE Embraces Measurement of Customers' Experience: Winning Back 'Detractors'", *Wall Street Journal*, 10 July 2006.

178. Andreas Schiendorfer, "Interview with Hilti CEO Pius Baschera", *Credit Suisse e-Magazine*, 19 January 2006.

179. Sean Meehan and Pius Baschera, "Lessons from Hilti: How Customer and Employee Contact Improves Strategy Implementation", *Business Strategy Review*, Vol. 13, No. 2, 2002, pp. 31–39.

180. Kevin Allison, "Cisco's Chief Places His Next Online Bet", *Financial Times*, 14 July 2007.

181. The following discussion is based on Victoria Chang and Garth Saloner, "*Capital One Financial Corporation: Setting and Shaping Strategy*", Stanford Graduate School of Business Case SM-135, 2005 and Christopher H. Paige, Bharat Anand, and Michael G. Rukstad, "*Capital One Financial Corporation*", Harvard Business School Case 9-700-124, 2000.

182. George S. Day, "Aligning the Organization with the Market", *Sloan Management Review*, Vol. 49, No. 1, 2006, pp. 41–49.
183. This paragraph is based on comments in Andrew Jack, "GSK Shake-up Aims to Speed Medicines", *Financial Times*, 11 December 2007.
184. "Acer: Riding a Hot Streak", *Business Week*, 17 May 2004.
185. "A Racer called Acer", *Business Week*, 2 January 2007.
186. There are numerous examples of this in Leander Kahney, *Inside Steve's Brain*, New York: Penguin Books, 2008.

Index